THE WORKS

OF

ROBERT LOUIS STEVENSON

SKERRYVORE

EDITION

ROBERT LOUIS STEVENSON

ESSAYS LITERARY
AND CRITICAL

VOL. XXIV

THE SKERRYVORE EDITION

LONDON

WILLIAM HEINEMANN LTD

in association with CHATTO & WINDUS : CASSELL & CO. LIMITED
and LONGMANS, GREEN & COMPANY

Essays in the Art of Writing.

The seven essays were first collected under this title in the *Tusitala Edition* of Stevenson's works, 1923. The individual essays were first published as follows :

(1) *Letter to a Young Gentleman* in *Across the Plains*, 1892, having previously appeared in *Scribner's Magazine*, 1888.

(2) *On the Choice of a Profession* in 1916, having previously appeared in *Scribner's Magazine*, 1915.

(3) *Popular Authors* in the *Vailima Edition* of Stevenson's works, 1922, having previously appeared in *Scribner's Magazine*, 1888.

(4) *On Some Technical Elements of Style in Literature* in the *Edinburgh Edition* of Stevenson's works, 1895, having previously appeared in *The Contemporary Review*, 1885.

(5) *The Morality of the Profession of Letters* in the *Edinburgh Edition*, 1895, having previously appeared in *The Fortnightly Review*, 1881.

(6) *Books Which Have Influenced Me* in *British Weekly Extras*, 1887, having previously appeared in *The British Weekly*, May, 1887.

(7) *A Note on Realism* in the *Edinburgh Edition*, 1895, having previously appeared in *The Magazine of Art*, 1883.

Earlier Works.

History of Moses and *The Book of Joseph* were first published in the *Vailima Edition* of Stevenson's works, 1923.

The Pentland Rising was first published in the *Edinburgh Edition* of Stevenson's works, 1896. Originally printed as a pamphlet in 1866.

College Papers were first published in the *Edinburgh Edition* of Stevenson's works, 1895, having previously appeared in the *Edinburgh University Magazine*, January–April, 1871. A sixth paper contributed to the same publication, *An Old Scots Gardener*, is omitted in this place, having been reprinted with corrections by the author himself in *Memories and Portraits* (Vol. XXV).

The two essays under the headings *Scientific Papers* were first published in the *Appendix* of the *Edinburgh Edition* of Stevenson's works, 1899. The first had previously appeared in *Transactions of the Royal Scottish Society of Arts*, 1873, and the second in *Proceedings of the Royal Society of Edinburgh*, 1875.

Wellington and *The late Sam Bough, R.S.A.*, were first published in the *Vailima Edition* of Stevenson's works, 1923, the latter having appeared in *The Academy*, 1878.

The essays in *Criticisms* were first published as follows :

Nos. I–III, in the *Edinburgh Edition* of Stevenson's works, 1896, having previously appeared as follows :

I in *The Fortnightly Review*, 1874.
II in *The Academy*, 1876.
III in *The Magazine of Art*, 1882.

Nos. IV–XIV, in the *Vailima Edition* of Stevenson's works, 1923, having previously appeared as follows :

IV in *The Academy*, 1874.
V in *The Academy*, 1874.
VI in *The Encyclopædia Britannica*, 9th Edition, 1875.
VII in *The Academy*, 1875.
VIII in *The Academy*, 1876.
IX in *The Academy*, 1876.
X in *The Academy*, 1876.
XI in *The Magazine of Art*, 1882.
XII in *The Academy*, 1874.
XIII in *The Academy*, 1877.
XIV in *The Academy*, 1874.

Protest on Behalf of Boer Independence was first published in the *Vailima Edition* of Stevenson's works, 1923.

First published, SKERRYVORE EDITION, 1925

PRINTED IN GREAT BRITAIN

CONTENTS

ESSAYS IN THE ART OF WRITING

EARLIER WORKS

v

Contents

ESSAYS IN THE ART OF WRITING

ESSAYS IN THE ART OF WRITING

LETTER TO A YOUNG GENTLEMAN WHO PROPOSES TO EMBRACE THE CAREER OF ART

WITH the agreeable frankness of youth, you address me on a point of some practical importance to yourself and (it is even conceivable) of some gravity to the world: Should you or should you not become an artist? It is one which you must decide entirely for yourself; all that I can do is to bring under your notice some of the materials of that decision; and I will begin, as I shall probably conclude also, by assuring you that all depends on the vocation.

To know what you like is the beginning of wisdom and of old age. Youth is wholly experimental. The essence and charm of that unquiet and delightful epoch is ignorance of self as well as ignorance of life. These two unknowns the young man brings together again and again, now in the airiest touch, now with a bitter hug; now with exquisite pleasure, now with cutting pain; but never with indifference, to which he is a total stranger, and never with that near kinsman of indifference, contentment. If he be a youth of dainty senses or a brain easily heated, the interest of this series of experiments grows upon him out of all proportion to the pleasure he receives. It is not beauty that he loves, nor pleasure that he seeks, though he may think so; his design and his sufficient reward is to verify his own existence and taste the variety of human fate. To him, before the razor-edge of curiosity is dulled, all that is not actual living and the hot chase of experience wears a face of a disgusting dryness difficult to recall in later

3

days; or if there be any exception—and here destiny steps in—it is in those moments when, wearied or surfeited of the primary activity of the senses, he calls up before memory the image of transacted pains and pleasures. Thus it is that such an one shies from all cut-and-dry professions, and inclines insensibly toward that career of art which consists only in the tasting and recording of experience.

This, which is not so much a vocation for art as an impatience of all other honest trades, frequently exists alone; and so existing, it will pass gently away in the course of years. Emphatically, it is not to be regarded, it is not a vocation, but a temptation; and when your father the other day so fiercely and (in my view) so properly discouraged your ambition, he was recalling not improbably some similar passage in his own experience. For the temptation is perhaps nearly as common as the vocation is rare. But again we have vocations which are imperfect; we have men whose minds are bound up, not so much in any art, as in the general *ars artium* and common base of all creative work; who will now dip into painting, and now study counterpoint, and anon will be inditing a sonnet: all these with equal interest, all often with genuine knowledge. And of this temper, when it stands alone, I find it difficult to speak; but I should counsel such an one to take to letters, for in literature (which drags with so wide a net) all his information may be found some day useful, and if he should go on as he has begun, and turn at last into the critic, he will have learned to use the necessary tools. Lastly we come to those vocations which are at once decisive and precise; to the men who are born with the love of pigments, the passion of drawing, the gift of music, or the impulse to create with words, just as other and perhaps the same men are born with the love of hunting, or the sea, or horses, or the

4

turning-lathe. These are predestined; if a man love the labour of any trade apart from any question of success or fame, the gods have called him. He may have the general vocation too: he may have a taste for all the arts, and I think he often has; but the mark of his calling is this laborious partiality for one, this inextinguishable zest in its technical successes, and (perhaps above all) a certain candour of mind, to take his very trifling enterprise with a gravity that would befit the cares of empire, and to think the smallest improvement worth accomplishing at any expense of time and industry. The book, the statue, the sonata, must be gone upon with the unreasoning good faith and the unflagging spirit of children at their play. *Is it worth doing ?* —when it shall have occurred to any artist to ask himself that question, it is implicitly answered in the negative. It does not occur to the child as he plays at being a pirate on the dining-room sofa, nor to the hunter as he pursues his quarry; and the candour of the one and the ardour of the other should be united in the bosom of the artist.

If you recognise in yourself some such decisive taste, there is no room for hesitation: follow your bent. And observe (lest I should too much discourage you) that the disposition does not usually burn so brightly at the first, or rather not so constantly. Habit and practice sharpen gifts; the necessity of toil grows less disgusting, grows even welcome in the course of years; a small taste (if it be only genuine) waxes with indulgence into an exclusive passion. Enough, just now, if you can look back over a fair interval, and see that your chosen art has a little more than held its own among the thronging interests of youth. Time will do the rest, if devotion help it; and soon your every thought will be engrossed in that beloved occupation.

But even with devotion, you may remind me, even

5

with unfaltering and delighted industry, many thousand artists spend their lives, if the result be regarded, utterly in vain: a thousand artists, and never one work of art. But the vast mass of mankind are incapable of doing anything reasonably well, art among the rest. The worthless artist would not improbably have been a quite incompetent baker. And the artist, even if he does not amuse the public, amuses himself; so that there will always be one man the happier for his vigils. This is the practical side of art: its inexpugnable fortress for the true practitioner. The direct returns—the wages of the trade—are small, but the indirect—the wages of the life—are incalculably great. No other business offers a man his daily bread upon such joyful terms. The soldier and the explorer have moments of a worthier excitement, but they are purchased by cruel hardships and periods of tedium that beggar language. In the life of the artist there need be no hour without its pleasure. I take the author, with whose career I am best acquainted; and it is true he works in a rebellious material, and that the act of writing is cramped and trying both to the eyes and the temper; but remark him in his study, when matter crowds upon him and words are not wanting—in what a continual series of small successes time flows by; with what a sense of power as of one moving mountains, he marshals his petty characters; with what pleasures, both of the ear and eye, he sees his airy structure growing on the page; and how he labours in a craft to which the whole material of his life is tributary, and which opens a door to all his tastes, his loves, his hatreds, and his convictions, so that what he writes is only what he longed to utter. He may have enjoyed many things in this big, tragic playground of the world; but what shall he have enjoyed more fully than a morning of successful work? Suppose it ill paid: the wonder is it should be paid at all.

Letter to a Young Gentleman

Other men pay, and pay dearly, for pleasures less desirable.

Nor will the practice of art afford you pleasure only; it affords besides an admirable training. For the artist works entirely upon honour. The public knows little or nothing of those merits in the quest of which you are condemned to spend the bulk of your endeavours. Merits of design, the merit of first-hand energy, the merit of a certain cheap accomplishment which a man of the artistic temper easily acquires—these they can recognise, and these they value. But to those more exquisite refinements of proficiency and finish, which the artist so ardently desires and so keenly feels, for which (in the vigorous words of Balzac) he must toil " like a miner buried in a landslip," for which, day after day, he recasts and revises and rejects—the gross mass of the public must be ever blind. To those lost pains, suppose you attain the highest pitch of merit, posterity may possibly do justice; suppose, as is so probable, you fail by even a hair's breadth of the highest, rest certain they shall never be observed. Under the shadow of this cold thought, alone in his studio, the artist must preserve from day to day his constancy to the ideal. It is this which makes his life noble; it is by this that the practice of his craft strengthens and matures his character; it is for this that even the serious countenance of the great emperor was turned approvingly (if only for a moment) on the followers of Apollo, and that sternly gentle voice bade the artist cherish his art.

And here there fall two warnings to be made. First, if you are to continue to be a law to yourself, you must beware of the first signs of laziness. This idealism in honesty can only be supported by perpetual effort; the standard is easily lowered, the artist who says "*It will do*," is on the downward path; three or four pot-boilers are enough at times (above all at wrong times) to falsify a talent, and by the practice of journalism a man runs the risk of becoming wedded to cheap finish. This is the danger on the one side; there is not less upon the other. The consciousness of how much the artist is (and must be) a law to himself, debauches the small heads. Perceiving recondite merits very hard to attain, making or swallowing artistic formulæ, or perhaps falling in love with some particular proficiency of his own, many artists forget the end of all art: to please. It is doubtless tempting to exclaim against the ignorant bourgeois; yet it should not be forgotten, it is he who is to pay us, and that (surely on the face of it) for services that he shall desire to have performed. Here also, if properly considered, there is a question of transcendental honesty. To give the public what they do not want, and yet expect to be supported: we have there a strange pretension, and yet not uncommon, above all with painters. The first duty in this world is for a man to pay his way; when that is quite accomplished, he may plunge into what eccentricity he likes; but emphatically not till then. Till then, he must pay assiduous court to the bourgeois who carries the purse. And if in the course of these capitulations he shall falsify his talent, it can never have been a strong one, and he will have preserved a better thing than talent—character. Or if he be of a mind so independent that he cannot stoop to this necessity, one course is yet open: he can desist from art, and follow some more manly way of life.

I speak of a more manly way of life, it is a point on which I must be frank. To live by a pleasure is not a high calling; it involves patronage, however veiled; it numbers the artist, however ambitious, along with dancing-girls and billiard-markers. The French have a romantic evasion for one employment, and call its practitioners the Daughters of Joy. The artist is of the same family, he is of the Sons of Joy, chose his trade

8

to please himself, gains his livelihood by pleasing others, and has parted with something of the sterner dignity of man. Journals but a little while ago declaimed against the Tennyson peerage; and this Son of Joy was blamed for condescension when he followed the example of Lord Lawrence and Lord Cairns and Lord Clyde. The poet was more happily inspired; with a better modesty he accepted the honour; and anonymous journalists have not yet (if I am to believe them) recovered the vicarious disgrace to their profession. When it comes to their turn, these gentlemen can do themselves more justice; and I shall be glad to think of it; for to my barbarian eyesight, even Lord Tennyson looks somewhat out of place in that assembly. There should be no honours for the artist; he has already, in the practice of his art, more than his share of the rewards of life; the honours are pre-empted for other trades, less agreeable and perhaps more useful.

But the devil in these trades of pleasing is to fail to please. In ordinary occupations, a man offers to do a certain thing or to produce a certain article with a merely conventional accomplishment, a design in which (we may almost say) it is difficult to fail. But the artist steps forth out of the crowd and proposes to delight: an impudent design, in which it is impossible to fail without odious circumstances. The poor Daughter of Joy, carrying her smiles and finery quite unregarded through the crowd, makes a figure which it is impossible to recall without a wounding pity. She is the type of the unsuccessful artist. The actor, the dancer, and the singer must appear like her in person, and drain publicly the cup of failure. But though the rest of us escape this crowning bitterness of the pillory, we all court in essence the same humiliation. We all profess to be able to delight. And how few of us are! We all pledge ourselves to be able to continue to delight. And the day

9

will come to each, and even to the most admired, when
the ardour shall have declined and the cunning shall be
lost, and he shall sit by his deserted booth ashamed.
Then shall he see himself condemned to do work for
which he blushes to take payment. Then (as if his lot
were not already cruel) he must lie exposed to the gibes
of the wreckers of the press, who earn a little bitter
bread by the condemnation of trash which they have
not read, and the praise of excellence which they cannot
understand.

And observe that this seems almost the necessary end
at least of writers. *Les Blancs et les Bleus* (for instance)
is of an order of merit very different from *Le Vicomte
de Bragelonne* ; and if any gentleman can bear to spy
upon the nakedness of *Castle Dangerous*, his name I
think is Ham: let it be enough for the rest of us to
read of it (not without tears) in the pages of Lockhart.
Thus in old age, when occupation and comfort are most
needful, the writer must lay aside at once his pastime
and his breadwinner. The painter indeed, if he succeed
at all in engaging the attention of the public, gains
great sums and can stand to his easel until a great age
without dishonourable failure. The writer has the
double misfortune to be ill-paid while he can work, and
to be incapable of working when he is old. It is thus a
way of life which conducts directly to a false position.

For the writer (in spite of notorious examples to the
contrary) must look to be ill-paid. Tennyson and Montépin make handsome livelihoods; but we cannot all
hope to be Tennyson, and we do not all perhaps desire
to be Montépin. If you adopt an art to be your trade,
weed your mind at the outset of all desire of money.
What you may decently expect, if you have some talent
and much industry, is such an income as a clerk will
earn with a tenth or perhaps a twentieth of your nervous
output. Nor have you the right to look for more; in

the wages of the life, not in the wages of the trade, lies your reward; the work is here the wages. It will be seen I have little sympathy with the common lamentations of the artist class. Perhaps they do not remember the hire of the field labourer; or do they think no parallel will lie? Perhaps they have never observed what is the retiring allowance of a field officer; or do they suppose their contributions to the arts of pleasing more important than the services of a colonel? Perhaps they forget on how little Millet was content to live; or do they think, because they have less genius, they stand excused from the display of equal virtues? But upon one point there should be no dubiety: if a man be not frugal, he has no business in the arts. If he be not frugal, he steers directly for that last tragic scene of *le vieux saltimbanque ;* if he be not frugal, he will find it hard to continue to be honest. Some day, when the butcher is knocking at the door, he may be tempted, he may be obliged, to turn out and sell a slovenly piece of work. If the obligation shall have arisen through no wantonness of his own, he is even to be commended; for words cannot describe how far more necessary it is that a man should support his family, than that he should attain to—or preserve—distinction in the arts. But if the pressure comes through his own fault, he has stolen, and stolen under trust, and stolen (which is the worst of all) in such a way that no law can reach him.

And now you may perhaps ask me, if the débutant artist is to have no thought of money, and if (as is implied) he is to expect no honours from the State, he may not at least look forward to the delights of popularity? Praise, you will tell me, is a savoury dish. And in so far as you may mean the countenance of other artists, you would put your finger on one of the most essential and enduring pleasures of the career of art. But in so far as you should have an eye to the commendations of the public or the notice of the newspapers, be sure you would but be cherishing a dream. It is true that in certain esoteric journals the author (for instance) is duly criticised, and that he is often praised a great deal more than he deserves, sometimes for qualities which he prided himself on eschewing, and sometimes by ladies and gentlemen who have denied themselves the privilege of reading his work. But if a man be sensitive to this wild praise, we must suppose him equally alive to that which often accompanies and always follows it—wild ridicule. A man may have done well for years, and then he may fail; he will hear of his failure. Or he may have done well for years, and still do well, but the critics may have tired of praising him, or there may have sprung up some new idol of the instant, some "dust a little gilt," to whom they now prefer to offer sacrifice. Here is the obverse and the reverse of that empty and ugly thing called popularity. Will any man suppose it worth the gaining?

ON THE CHOICE OF A PROFESSION*

You write to me, my dear sir, requesting advice at one of the most momentous epochs in a young man's life. You are about to choose a profession; and with a diffidence highly pleasing at your age, you would be glad, you say, of some guidance in the choice. There is nothing more becoming than for youth to seek counsel; nothing more becoming to age than to be able to give it; and in a civilisation old and complicated like ours, where practical persons boast a kind of practical philosophy superior to all others, you would very naturally expect to find all such questions systematically answered. For the dicta of the Practical Philosophy, you come to me. What, you ask, are the principles usually followed by the wise in the like critical junctures? There, I confess, you pose me on the threshold. I have

* The original manuscript of this essay lay for years in a bundle of old papers, and was always assumed to be the "Letter to a Young Gentleman Who Proposes to Embrace the Career of Art." Recently, however, a closer examination revealed it to be a hitherto unpublished piece of work, and for a while I was greatly mystified as to its origin and the reason for its suppression. Its general character, the peculiar quality of the paper, even the handwriting itself—all went to show it was composed in Saranac in the winter of 1887–88. But why had it been suppressed?

Then in the dim, halting way things recur to one, I began to recall its history. It had been adjudged too cynical, too sombre in tone, too out of keeping with the helpful philosophy always associated with R. L. S. Instead of assisting the Young Gentleman it was thought to be only too likely to discourage and depress him. Thus it was laid aside in favour of the other essay on the Career of Art. Whether we are right in publishing it now is for the public to decide. We seem to be going against the wishes of the author, who had evidently been content to leave it in oblivion ; yet on the other hand it appears wrong to keep so fine an effort, and one so brilliant and grimly humorous, from the many who would find pleasure in it. After all, there are others to be considered besides Young Gentlemen ; and perhaps with these warned away we shall incur no reproach from the general lovers of literature, but on the contrary gain their support and commendation in the course we have taken. [Lloyd Osbourne.]

examined my own recollections; I have interrogated others; and with all the will in the world to serve you better, I fear I can only tell you that the wise, in these circumstances, act upon no principles whatever. This is disappointing to you; it was painful to myself; but if I am to declare the truth as I see it, I must repeat that wisdom has nothing to do with the choice of a profession.

We all know what people say, and very foolish it usually is. The question is to get inside of these flourishes, and discover what it is they think and ought to say: to perform, in short, the Socratic Operation.— The more ready-made answers there are to any question, the more abstruse it becomes; for those of whom we make the inquiry have the less need of consideration before they reply. The world being more or less beset with Anxious Enquirers of the Socratic persuasion, it is the object of a Liberal Education to equip people with a proper number of these answers by way of passport; so they can pass swimmingly to and fro on their affairs without the trouble of thinking. How should a banker know his own mind? It takes him all his time to manage his bank. If you saw a company of pilgrims, walking as if for a wager, each with his teeth set; and if you happened to ask them one after another: Whither they were going? and from each you were to receive the same answer: that positively they were all in such a hurry, they had never found leisure to enquire into the nature of their errand:—confess, my dear sir, you would be startled at the indifference they exhibited. Am I going too far, if I say, that this is the condition of the large majority of our fellow-men and almost all our fellow-women?

I stop a banker.

" My good fellow," I say, " give me a moment."

" I have not a moment to spare," says he.

On the Choice of a Profession

" Why ? " I enquire.

" I must be banking," he replies. " I am so busily engaged in banking all day long that I have hardly leisure for my meals."

" And what," I continue my interrogatory, " is banking?"

" Sir," says he, " it is my business."

" Your business? " I repeat. "And what is a man's business?"

" Why," cries the banker, " a man's business is his duty." And with that he breaks away from me, and I see him skimming to his avocations.

But this is a sort of answer that provokes reflection. Is a man's business his duty? Or perhaps should not his duty be his business? If it is not my duty to conduct a bank (and I contend that it is not) is it the duty of my friend the banker? Who told him it was? Is it in the Bible? Is he sure that banks are a good thing? Might it not have been his duty to stand aside, and let some one else conduct the bank? Or perhaps ought he not to have been a ship-captain instead? All these perplexing queries may be summed up under one head: the grave problem which my friend offers to the world: Why is he a Banker?

Well, why is it? There is one principal reason, I conceive: that the man was trapped. Education, as practised, is a form of harnessing with the friendliest intentions. The fellow was hardly in trousers before they whipped him into school; hardly done with school before they smuggled him into an office; it is ten to one they have had him married into the bargain; and all this before he has had time so much as to imagine that there may be any other practicable course. Drum, drum, drum; you must be in time for school; you must do your Cornelius Nepos; you must keep your hands clean; you must go to parties—a young man should

15

make friends; and, finally—you must take this opening
in a bank. He has been used to caper to this sort of
piping from the first; and he joins the regiment of bank
clerks for precisely the same reason as he used to go to
the nursery at the stroke of eight. Then at last, rubbing
his hands with a complacent smile, the parent lays his
conjuring pipe aside. The trick is performed, ladies and
gentlemen; the wild ass's colt is broken in; and now
sits diligently scribing. Thus it is, that, out of men, we
make bankers.

You have doubtless been present at the washing of
sheep, which is a brisk, high-handed piece of manœuv-
ring, in its way; but what is it, as a subject of contemplation, to the case of the poor young animal, Man,
turned loose into this roaring world, herded by robus-
tious guardians, taken with the panic before he has wit
enough to apprehend its cause, and soon flying with all
his heels in the van of the general stampede? It may
be that in after years, he shall fall upon a train of reflection, and begin narrowly to scrutinise the reasons
that decided his path and his continued mad activity in
that direction. And perhaps he may be very well pleased
at the retrospect, and see fifty things that might have
been worse, for one that would have been better; and
even supposing him to take the other cue, bitterly to
deplore the circumstances in which he is placed and
bitterly to reprobate the jockeying that got him into
them, the fact is, it is too late to indulge such whims.
It is too late, after the train has started, to debate the
needfulness of this particular journey: the door is
locked, the express goes tearing overland at sixty miles
an hour; he had better betake himself to sleep or
the daily paper, and discourage unavailing thought.
He sees many pleasant places out of the window:
cottages in a garden, angles by the riverside, balloons
voyaging the sky; but as for him, he is booked for

all his natural days, and must remain a banker to the end.

If the juggling only began with school-time, if even the domineering friends and counsellors had made a choice of their own, there might still be some pretension to philosophy in the affair. But no. They too were trapped; they are but tame elephants unwittingly ensnaring others, and were themselves ensnared by tame elephants of an older domestication. We have all learned our tricks in captivity, to the spiriting of Mrs. Grundy and a system of rewards and punishments. The crack of the whip and the trough of fodder: the cut direct and an invitation to dinner: the gallows and the Shorter Catechism: a pat upon the head and a stinging lash on the reverse: these are the elements of education and the principles of the Practical Philosophy. Sir Thomas Browne, in the earlier part of the Seventeenth Century, had already apprehended the staggering fact that geography is a considerable part of orthodoxy; and that a man who, when born in London, makes a conscientious Protestant, would have made an equally conscientious Hindu if he had first seen daylight in Benares. This is but a small part, however important, of the things that are settled for us by our place of birth. An Englishman drinks beer and tastes his liquor in the throat; a Frenchman drinks wine and tastes it in the front of the mouth. Hence, a single beverage lasts the Frenchman all afternoon; and the Englishman cannot spend above a very short time in a café, but he must swallow half a bucket. The Englishman takes a cold tub every morning in his bedroom; the Frenchman has an occasional hot bath. The Englishman has an unlimited family and will die in harness; the Frenchman retires upon a competency with three children at the outside. So this imperative national tendency follows us through all the privacies of life, dictates our thoughts,

17

and attends us to the grave. We do nothing, we say nothing, we wear nothing, but it is stamped with the Queen's Arms. We are English down to our boots and into our digestions. There is not a dogma of all those by which we lead young men, but we get it ourselves, between sleep and waking, between death and life, in a complete abeyance of the reasoning part.

" But how, sir," (you will ask) " is there then no wisdom in the world? And when my admirable father was this day urging me, with the most affecting expressions, to decide on an industrious, honest and lucrative employment——? " Enough, sir; I follow your thoughts, and will answer them to the utmost of my ability. Your father, for whom I entertain a singular esteem, is, I am proud to believe, a professing Christian: the Gospel, therefore, is or ought to be his rule of conduct. Now, I am of course ignorant of the terms employed by your father; but I quote here from a very urgent letter, written by another parent, who was a man of sense, integrity, great energy, and a Christian persuasion, and who has perhaps set forth the common view with a certain innocent openness of his own:

" You are now come to that time of life," he writes to his son, " and have reason within yourself to consider the absolute necessity of making provision for the time when it will be asked, Who is this man? Is he doing any good in the world? Has he the means of being ' One of us '? I beseech you," he goes on, rising in emotion, and appealing to his son by name, " I beseech you do not trifle with this till it actually comes upon you. Bethink yourself and bestir yourself as a man. This is the time——" and so forth. This gentleman has candour; he is perspicacious, and has to deal apparently with a perspicacious pick-logic of a son; and hence the startling perspicacity of the document. But, my dear sir, what a principle of life! To " do good in the world " is to be received into a society, apart from personal affection. I could name many forms of evil vastly more exhilarating whether in prospect or enjoyment. If I scraped money, believe me, it should be for some more cordial purpose. And then, scraping money? It seems to me as if he had forgotten the Gospel. This is a view of life not quite the same as the Christian, which the old gentleman professed and sincerely studied to practise. But upon this point, I dare dilate no further. Suffice it to say, that looking round me on the manifestations of this Christian Society of ours, I have been often tempted to exclaim: What, then, is Antichrist?

A wisdom, at least, which professes one set of propositions and yet acts upon another, can be no very entire or rational ground of conduct. Doubtless, there is much in this question of money; and for my part, I believe no young man ought to be at peace till he is self-supporting, and has an open, clear life of it on his own foundation. But here a consideration occurs to me of, as I must consider, startling originality. It is this: That there are two sides to this question as well as to so many others. Make more?—Aye, or spend less? There is no absolute call upon a man to make any specific income, unless, indeed, he has set his immortal soul on being " One of us."

A thoroughly respectable income is as much as a man spends. A luxurious income, or true opulence, is something more than a man spends. Raise the income, lower the expenditure, and, my dear sir, surprising as it seems, we have the same result. But I hear you remind me, with pursed lips, of privations—of hardships. Alas! sir, there are privations upon either side; the banker has to sit all day in his bank, a serious privation; can you not conceive that the landscape painter, whom I take to be the meanest and most lost among contemporary men, truly and deliberately *prefers* the privations upon his side—to wear no gloves, to drink beer, to live on chops or even on potatoes, and lastly, not to be " One of us "—truly and deliberately prefers his privations to those of the banker? I can. Yes, sir, I repeat the words; I can. Believe me, there are Rivers in Bohemia!—but there is nothing so hard to get people to understand as this: That they *pay for their money*; and nothing so difficult to make them remember as this: That money, when they have it, is for most of them, at least, only a cheque to purchase pleasure with. How then if a man gets pleasure in following an art? He might gain more cheques by following another; but then, although there is a difference in cheques, the amount of pleasure is the same. He gets some of his directly; unlike the bank clerk, he is having his fortnight's holiday, and doing what delights him, all the year.

All these patent truisms have a very strange air, when written down. But that, my dear sir, is no fault of mine or of the truisms. There they are. I beseech you, do not trifle with them. Bethink yourself like a man. This is the time.

But, you say, all this is very well; it does not help me to a choice. Once more, sir, you have me; it does not. What shall I say? A choice, let us remember, is almost more of a negative than a positive. You embrace one thing; but you refuse a thousand. The most liberal profession imprisons many energies and starves many affections. If you are in a bank, you cannot be much upon the sea. You cannot be both a first-rate violinist and a first-rate painter: you must lose in the one art if you persist in following both. If you are sure of your preference, follow it. If not—nay, my dear sir, it is not for me or any man to go beyond this point. God made you; not I. I cannot even make you over again. I have heard of a schoolmaster, whose speciality it was to elicit the bent of each pupil: poor schoolmaster, poor pupils! As for me, if you have nothing indigenous in your own heart, no living preference, no fine, human scorn, I leave you to the tide; it will sweep you somewhere. Have you but a grain of inclination, I will help you. If you wish to be a costermonger, be it, shame the devil; and I will stand the donkey. If you wish to be nothing, once more I leave you to the tide.

I regret profoundly, my dear young sir, not only for you in whom I see such a lively promise of the future, but for the sake of your admirable and truly worthy father and your no less excellent mamma, that my remarks should seem no more conclusive. I can give myself this praise, that I have kept back nothing; but this, alas! is a subject on which there is little to put forward. It will probably not much matter what you decide upon doing; for most men seem to sink at length to the degree of stupor necessary for contentment in their different estates. Yes, sir, this is what I have observed. Most men are happy, and most men dishonest. Their mind sinks to the proper level; their honour easily accepts the custom of the trade. I wish you may find degeneration no more painful than your neighbours, soon sink into apathy, and be long spared in a state of respectable somnambulism, from the grave to which we haste.

R. L. S.

The scene is the deck of an Atlantic liner, close by the doors of the ashpit, where it is warm: the time, night: the persons, an emigrant of an inquiring turn of mind and a deck hand. " Now," says the emigrant, " is there not any book that gives a true picture of a sailor's life ? " —" Well," returns the other, with great deliberation and emphasis, " there is *one* ; that is *just* a sailor's life. You know all about it, if you know that."—" What do you call it ? " asks the emigrant.—" They call it *Tom Holt's Log*," says the sailor. The emigrant entered the fact in his note-book: with a wondering query as to what sort of stuff this *Tom Holt* would prove to be: and a double-headed prophecy that it would prove one of two things: either a solid, dull, admirable piece of truth, or mere ink and banditti. Well, the emigrant was wrong: it was something more curious than either, for it was a work by STEPHENS HAYWARD.

I

In this paper I propose to put the authors' names in capital letters; the most of them have not much hope of durable renown; their day is past, the poor dogs— they begin swiftly to be forgotten; and HAYWARD is of the number. Yet he was a popular writer; and what is really odd, he had a vein of hare-brained merit. There never was a man of less pretension; the intoxicating presence of an ink-bottle, which was too much for the strong head of Napoleon, left him sober and light-hearted; he had no shade of literary vanity; he was never at the trouble to be dull. His works fell out of date in the days of printing. They were the unhatched eggs of Arab tales; made for word-of-mouth recitation, certain (if thus told) to captivate an audience of boys or any simple people—certain, on the lips of a generation or two of public story-tellers, to take on new merit and become cherished lore. Such tales as a man, such rather as a boy, tells himself at night, not without smiling, as he drops asleep; such, with the same exhilarating range of incident and the same trifling ingenuities, with no more truth to experience and scarcely more cohesion, HAYWARD told. If we so consider *The Diamond Necklace, or the Twenty Captains*, which is what I remember best of HAYWARD, you will find that staggering narrative grow quite conceivable.

A gentleman (his name forgotten—HAYWARD had no taste in names) puts an advertisement in the papers, inviting nineteen other gentlemen to join him in a likely enterprise. The nineteen appear promptly, nineteen, no more, no less: see the ease of the recumbent story-teller, half-asleep, hanging on the verge of that country of dreams, where candles come alight and journeys are accomplished at the wishing! These twenty, all total strangers, are to put their money together and form an association of strict equality: hence its name—*The Twenty Captains*. And it is no doubt very pleasant to be equal to anybody, even in name; and mighty desirable (at least in the eyes of young gentlemen hearing this tale in the school dormitory) to be called captain, even in private. But the deuce of it is, the founder has no enterprise in view, and here, you would think, the least wary capitalist would leave his chair, and buy a broom and a crossing with his money, rather than place it in the hands of this total stranger, whose mind by his own confession was a blank, and whose real name was probably Macaire. No such matter in the book. With the ease of dreaming, the association is founded; and again with the ease of dreaming (HAYWARD being now three parts asleep) the enterprise, in the shape of a persecuted heiress and a truly damnable and idiotic aristocrat, appears upon the scene. For some time, our drowsy story-teller dodges along upon the frontiers of incoherence, hardly at the trouble to invent, never at the trouble to write literature; but suddenly his interest brightens up, he sees something in front of him, turns on the pillow, shakes off the tentacles of slumber, and puts his back into his tale. Injured innocence takes a special train to Dover; damnable idiot takes another and pursues; the twenty captains reach the station five minutes after, and demand a third. It is against the rules, they are told; not more than two specials (here is good news for the railway traveller) are allowed at the same time upon the line. Is injured innocence, with her diamond necklace, to lie at the mercy of an aristocrat? Forbid it, Heaven and the Cheap Press! The twenty captains slip unobserved into the engine-house, steal an engine, and forth upon the Dover line! As well as I can gather, there were no stations and no pointsmen on this route to Dover, which must in consequence be quick and safe. One thing it had in common with other and less simple railways, it had a line of telegraph wires; and these the twenty captains decided to destroy. One of them, you will not be surprised to learn, had a coil of rope—in his pocket, I suppose; another—again I shall not surprise you—was an Irishman and given to blundering. One end of the line was made fast to a telegraph post; one (by the Irishman) to the engine: all aboard—full steam ahead—a double crash, and there was the telegraph post upon the ground, and here—mark my HAYWARD! was something carried away upon the engine. All eyes turn to see what it is: an integral part of the machinery! There is now no means of reducing speed; on thunders the engine, full steam ahead, down this remarkable route to Dover; on speed the twenty captains, not very easy in their minds. Presently, the driver of the second special (the aristocrat's) looks behind him, sees an engine on his track, signals, signals in vain, finds himself being overhauled, pokes

24

up his fire and—full steam ahead in flight. Presently
after, the driver of the first special (injured innocence's)
looks behind, sees a special on his track and an engine
on the track of the special, signals, signals in vain, and
he too—full steam ahead in flight. Such a day on the
Dover line! But at last the second special smashes into
the first, and the engine into both; and for my part, I
think there was an end of that romance. But HAYWARD
was by this time fast asleep: not a life was lost; not
only that, but the various parties recovered consciousness and resumed their wild career (only now, of course,
on foot and across country) in the precise original
order: injured innocence leading by a length, damnable
aristocrat with still more damnable valet (like one man)
a good second, and the twenty captains (again like one
man) a bad third; so that here was the story going on
again just as before, and this appalling catastrophe on
the Dover line reduced to the proportions of a morning
call. The feelings of the company (it is true) are not
dwelt upon.

Now, I do not mean that *Tom Holt* is quite such
high-flying folly as *The Twenty Captains ;* for it is no
such thing, nor half so entertaining. Still it flowed
from the same irresponsible brain; still it was the mere
drowsy divagation of a man in bed, now tedious, now
extravagant—always acutely untrue to life as it is, often
pleasantly coincident with childish hopes of what life
ought to be—as (for instance) in the matter of that
little pleasure-boat, rigged, to every block and rope, as
a full-rigged ship, in which Tom goes sailing—happy
child! And this was the work that an actual tarry seaman recommended for a picture of his own existence!

II

It was once my fortune to have an interview with
Mr. HAYWARD's publisher: a very affable gentleman

in a very small office in a shady court off Fleet Street.
We had some talk together of the works he issued and
the authors who supplied them; and it was strange to
hear him talk for all the world as one of our publishers
might have talked of one of us, only with a more
obliging frankness, so that the private life of these
great men was more or less unveiled to me. So and so
(he told me, among other things) had demanded an
advance upon a novel, had laid out the sum (apparently
on spirituous drinks) and refused to finish the work.
" We had to put it in the hands of BRACEBRIDGE
HEMMING," said the publisher with a chuckle: " he
finished it." And then with conviction: "A most reliable author, BRACEBRIDGE HEMMING." I have no
doubt the name is new to the reader; it was not so to
me. Among these great men of the dust there is a
touching ambition which punishes itself; not content
with such glory as comes to them, they long for the
glory of being bound—long to invade, between six
boards, the homes of that aristocracy whose manners
they so often find occasion to expose; and sometimes
(once in a long lifetime) the gods give them this also,
and they appear in the orthodox three volumes and are
fleered at in the critical press, and lie quite unread in
circulating libraries. One such work came in my mind:
The Bondage of Brandon, by BRACEBRIDGE HEMMING.
I had not found much pleasure in the volumes; but I
was the more glad to think that Mr. Hemming's name
was quite a household word, and himself quoted for
" a reliable author," in his own literary circles.

On my way westward from this interview, I was
aware of a first floor in Fleet Street rigged up with wire
window-blinds, brass straps, and gilt lettering: Office
for the sale of the works of PIERCE EGAN. "Ay, Mr.
EGAN," thought I, " and have you an office all to yourself! " And then remembered that he too had once

revelled in three volumes: *The Flower of the Flock* the book was called, not without pathos for the considerate mind; but even the flower of Egan's flock was not good enough for the critics or the circulating libraries, so that I purchased my own copy, quite unread, for three shillings at a railway bookstall. Poor dogs, I thought, what ails you, that you should have the desire of this fictitious upper popularity, made by hack journalists and countersigned by yawning girls? Yours is the more true. Your butcher, the landlady at your seaside lodgings—if you can afford that indulgence, the bar-maid whom you doubtless court, even the Rates and Taxes that besiege your door, have actually read your tales and actually know your names. There was a waiter once (or so the story goes) who knew not the name of Tennyson: that of HEMMING perhaps had brought the light into his eyes, or VILES perhaps, or ERRYM, or the great J. F. SMITH, or the unutterable Reynolds, to whom even here I must deny his capitals.—Fancy, if you can (thought I), that I languish under the reverse of your complaint; and being an upper-class author, bound and criticised, long for the penny number and the weekly woodcut!

Well, I know that glory now. I have tried and on the whole I have failed: just as EGAN and HEMMING failed in the circulating libraries. It is my consolation that Charles Reade nearly wrecked that valuable property, the *London Journal*, which must instantly fall back on Mr. Egan; and the king of us all, George Meredith, once staggered the circulation of a weekly newspaper. A servant-maid used to come and boast when she had read another chapter of *Treasure Island* : that any pleasure should attend the exercise never crossed her thoughts. The same tale, in a penny paper of a high class, was mighty coldly looked upon; by the delicate test of the correspondence column, I could see

I was far to leeward; and there was one giant on the staff (a man with some talent, when he chose to use it) with whom I very early perceived it was in vain to rival. Yet I was thought well of on my penny paper for two reasons: one that the publisher was bent on raising the standard—a difficult enterprise in which he has to a great extent succeeded; the other, because (like Bracebridge Hemming) I was "a reliable author." For our great men of the dust are apt to be behind with copy.

III

How I came to be such a student of our penny press demands perhaps some explanation. I was brought up on *Cassell's Family Paper*; but the lady who was kind enough to read the tales aloud to me was subject to sharp attacks of conscience. She took the *Family Paper* on confidence; the tales it contained being Family Tales, not novels. But every now and then, something would occur to alarm her finer senses; she would express a well-grounded fear that the current fiction was " going to turn out a Regular Novel "; and the family paper, with my pious approval, would be dropped. Yet neither she nor I were wholly stoical; and when Saturday came round, we would study the windows of the stationer and try to fish out of subsequent woodcuts and their legends the further adventures of our favourites. Many points are here suggested for the casuist; definitions of the Regular Novel and the Family Tale are to be desired; and quite a paper might be written on the relative merit of reading a fiction outright and lusting after it at the stationer's window. The experience at least had a great effect upon my childhood. This inexpensive pleasure mastered me. Each new Saturday I would go from one newsvendor's window to another's, till I was master of the weekly gallery and had

thoroughly digested " The Baronet Unmasked," " So
and so approaching the Mysterious House," " The
Discovery of the Dead Body in the Blue Marl Pit,"
" Dr. Vargas Removing the Senseless Body of Fair
Lilias," and whatever other snatch of unknown story
and glimpse of unknown characters that gallery
afforded. I do not know that I ever enjoyed fiction
more; those books that we have (in such a way) avoided
reading, are all so excellently written! And in early
years, we take a book for its material, and act as our
own artists, keenly realising that which pleases us,
leaving the rest aside. I never supposed that a book
was to command me until, one disastrous day of storm,
the heaven full of turbulent vapours, the streets full of
the squalling of the gale, the windows resounding
under bucketfuls of rain, my mother read aloud to me
Macbeth. I cannot say I thought the experience agreeable; I far preferred the ditch-water stories that a child
could dip and skip and doze over, stealing at times
materials for play; it was something new and shocking
to be thus ravished by a giant, and I shrank under the
brutal grasp. But the spot in memory is still sensitive;
nor do I ever read that tragedy but I hear the gale
howling up the valley of the Leith.

All this while I would never buy upon my own
account; pence were scarce, conscience busy; and I
would study the pictures and dip into the exposed
columns, but not buy. My fall was brought about by
a truly romantic incident. Perhaps the reader knows
Neidpath Castle, where it stands, bosomed in hills, on
a green promontory; Tweed at its base running
through all the gamut of a busy river, from the pouring shallow to the brown pool. In the days when I was
thereabout, and that part of the earth was made a
heaven to me by many things now lost, by boats, and
bathing, and the fascination of streams, and the delights

of comradeship, and those (surely the prettiest and simplest) of a boy and girl romance—in those days of Arcady there dwelt in the upper story of the castle one whom I believe to have been the gamekeeper on the estate. The rest of the place stood open to incursive urchins; and there, in a deserted chamber, we found some half-a-dozen numbers of *Black Bess, or the Knight of the Road*, a work by EDWARD VILES. So far as we are aware, no one had visited that chamber (which was in a turret) since Lambert blew in the doors of the fortress with contumelious English cannon. Yet it could hardly have been Lambert (in whatever hurry of military operations) who had left these samples of romance; and the idea that the gamekeeper had anything to do with them was one that we discouraged. Well, the offence is now covered by prescription; we took them away; and in the shade of a contiguous fir-wood, lying on blaeberries, I made my first acquaintance with the art of Mr. Viles. From this author, I passed on to MALCOLM J. ERRYM (the name to my present scrutiny suggesting an anagram on Merry), author of *Edith the Captive, The Treasures of St. Mark, A Mystery in Scarlet, George Barington, Sea-drift, Townsend the Runner*, and a variety of other well-named romances. Memory may play me false, but I believe there was a kind of merit about Errym. The *Mystery in Scarlet* runs in my mind to this day; and if any hunter after autographs (and I think the world is full of such) can lay his hands on a copy even imperfect, and will send it to me in the care of Messrs. Scribner, my gratitude (the muse consenting) will even drop into poetry. For I have a curiosity to know what the Mystery in Scarlet was, and to renew acquaintance with King George and his valet Norris, who were the chief figures in the work and may be said to have risen in every page superior to history and the ten commandments. Hence I passed on to Mr. EGAN,

whom I trust the reader does not confuse with the
author of *Tom and Jerry* ; the two are quite distinct,
though I have sometimes suspected they were father
and son. I never enjoyed EGAN as I did ERRYM; but
this was possibly a want of taste, and EGAN would do.
Thence again I was suddenly brought face to face with
Mr. Reynolds. A school-fellow, acquainted with my
debasing tastes, supplied me with *The Mysteries of
London*, and I fell back revolted. The same school-
fellow (who seems to have been a devil of a fellow)
supplied me about the same time with one of those
contributions to literature (and even to art) from which
the name of the publisher is modestly withheld. It was
a far more respectable work than *The Mysteries of
London*. J. F. SMITH when I was a child, ERRYM
when I was a boy, HAYWARD when I had attained to
man's estate, these I read for pleasure; the others,
down to SYLVANUS COBB, I have made it my business
to know (as far as my endurance would support
me) from a sincere interest in human nature and
the art of letters.

IV

What kind of talent is required to please this
mighty public? that was my first question, and was
soon amended with the words, " if any." J. F. SMITH
was a man of undeniable talent, ERRYM and HAYWARD
have a certain spirit, and even in EGAN the very tender
might recognise the rudiments of a sort of literary gift;
but the cases on the other side are quite conclusive.
Take Hemming, or the dull ruffian Reynolds, or
Sylvanus Cobb, of whom perhaps I have only seen unfortunate examples—they seem not to have the talents
of a rabbit, and why anyone should read them is a
thing that passes wonder. A plain-spoken and possibly
high-thinking critic might here perhaps return upon

me with my own expressions. And he would have missed the point. For I and my fellows have no such popularity to be accounted for. The reputation of an upper-class author is made for him at dinner-tables and nursed in newspaper paragraphs, and, when all is done, amounts to no great matter. We call it popularity, surely in a pleasant error. A flippant writer in the *Saturday Review* expressed a doubt if I had ever cherished a " genteel " illusion; in truth I never had many, but this was one—and I have lost it. Once I took the literary author at his own esteem; I behold him now like one of those gentlemen who read their own MS. descriptive poetry aloud to wife and babes around the evening hearth; addressing a mere parlour coterie and quite unknown to the great world outside the villa windows. At such pigmy reputation, Reynolds or COBB, or Mrs. SOUTHWORTH can afford to smile. By spontaneous public vote, at a cry from the un-organic masses, these great ones of the dust were laurelled. And for what?

Ay, there is the question: For what? How is this great honour gained? Many things have been suggested. The people (it has been said) like rapid narrative. If so, the taste is recent, for both Smith and Egan were leisurely writers. It has been said they like incident, not character. I am not so sure. G. P. R. James was an upper-class author, J. F. Smith a penny pressman; the two are in some ways not unlike; but—here is the curiosity—James made far the better story, Smith was far the more successful with his characters. Each (to bring the parallel home) wrote a novel called *The Stepmother* ; each introduced a pair of old maids; and let anyone study the result! James's *Stepmother* is a capital tale, but Smith's old maids are like Trollope at his best. It is said again that the people like crime. Certainly they do. But the great ones of the dust have no monopoly of that, and their less fortunate rivals hammer away at murder and abduction unapplauded.

I return to linger about my seaman on the Atlantic liner. I shall be told he is exceptional. I am tempted to think, on the other hand, that he may be normal. The critical attitude, whether to books or life—how if that were the true exception? How if *Tom Holt's Log*, surreptitiously perused by a harbour-side, had been the means of sending my mariner to sea? How if he were still unconsciously expecting the Tom Holt part of the business to begin—perhaps to-morrow? How, even, if he had never yet awakened to the discrepancy between that singular picture and the facts? Let us take another instance. *The Young Ladies' Journal* is an elegant miscellany which I have frequently observed in the possession of the barmaid. In a lone house on a moorland, I was once supplied with quite a considerable file of this production and (the weather being violent) devoutly read it. The tales were not ill done; they were well abreast of the average tale in a circulating library; there was only one difference, only one thing to remind me I was in the land of penny numbers instead of the parish of three volumes: Disguise it as the authors pleased (and they showed ingenuity in doing so) it was always the same tale they must relate: the tale of a poor girl ultimately married to a peer of the realm or (at the worst) a baronet. The circumstance is not common in life; but how familiar to the musings of the barmaid! The tales were not true to what men see; they were true to what the readers dreamed.

Let us try to remember how fancy works in children; with what selective partiality it reads, leaving often the bulk of the book unrealised, but fixing on the rest and living it; and what a passionate impotence it shows—

33

what power of adoption, what weakness to create. It seems to be not much otherwise with uneducated readers. They long, not to enter into the lives of others, but to behold themselves in changed situations, ardently but impotently preconceived. The imagination (save the mark!) of the popular author here comes to the rescue, supplies some body of circumstance to these phantom aspirations, and conducts the readers where they will. Where they will: that's the point; elsewhere they will not follow. When I was a child, if I came on a book in which the characters wore armour, it fell from my hand; I had no criterion of merit, simply that one decisive taste, that my fancy refused to linger in the middle ages. And the mind of the uneducated reader is mailed with similar restrictions. So it is that we must account for a thing otherwise unaccountable: the popularity of some of these great ones of the dust. In defect of any other gift, they have instinctive sympathy with the popular mind. They can thus supply to the shop-girl and the shoe-black vesture cut to the pattern of their naked fancies, and furnish them with welcome scenery and properties for autobiographical romancing.

Even in readers of an upper class, we may perceive the traces of a similar hesitation; even for them a writer may be too exotic. The villain, even the heroine, may be a Feejee islander, but only on condition the hero is one of ourselves. It is pretty to see the thing reversed in the Arabian tale (Torrens or Burton—the tale is omitted in popular editions) where the Moslem hero carries off the Christian amazon; and in the exogamous romance, there lies interred a good deal of human history and human nature. But the question of exogamy is foreign to the purpose. Enough that we are not readily pleased without a character of our own race and language; so that, when the scene of a romance is laid on any distant soil, we look with eagerness and confidence for the coming of the English traveller. With the readers of the penny-press the thing goes further. Burning as they are to penetrate into the homes of the peerage, they must still be conducted there by some character of their own class, into whose person they cheerfully migrate for the time of reading. Hence the poor governesses supplied in the *Young Ladies' Journal.* Hence these dreary virtuous *ouvriers* and *ouvrières* of Xavier de Montépin. He can do nothing with them; and he is far too clever not to be aware of that. When he writes for the *Figaro*, he discards these venerable puppets and doubtless glories in their absence; but so soon as he must address the great audience of the halfpenny journal, out come the puppets and are furbished up, and take to drink again, and are once more reclaimed, and once more falsely accused. See them for what they are—Montépin's decoys; without these he could not make his public feel at home in the houses of the fraudulent bankers and the wicked dukes.

The reader, it has been said, migrates into such characters for the time of reading: under their name escapes the narrow prison of the individual career, and sates his avidity for other lives. To what extent he ever emigrates again, and how far the fancied careers react upon the true one, it would fill another paper to debate. But the case of my sailor shows their grave importance. " Tom Holt does not apply to me," thinks our dully-imaginative boy by the harbour-side, " for I am not a sailor. But if I go to sea it will apply completely." And he does go to sea. He lives surrounded by the fact, and does not observe it. He cannot realise, he cannot make a tale of his own life; which crumbles in discrete impressions even as he lives it, and slips between the fingers of his memory like sand. It is not this that he considers in his rare hours of rumination, but that other life, which was all lit up for him by the humble talent of a Hayward—that other life which, God knows, perhaps he still believes that he is leading—the life of Tom Holt.

ON SOME TECHNICAL ELEMENTS
OF STYLE IN LITERATURE

There is nothing more disenchanting to man than to be shown the springs and mechanism of any art. All our arts and occupations lie wholly on the surface; it is on the surface that we perceive their beauty, fitness, and significance; and to pry below is to be appalled by their emptiness and shocked by the coarseness of the strings and pulleys. In a similar way, psychology itself, when pushed to any nicety, discovers an abhorrent baldness, but rather from the fault of our analysis than from any poverty native to the mind. And perhaps in æsthetics the reason is the same: those disclosures which seem fatal to the dignity of art seem so perhaps only in the proportion of our ignorance; and those conscious and unconscious artifices which it seems unworthy of the serious artist to employ were yet, if we had the power to trace them to their springs, indications of a delicacy of the sense finer than we conceive, and hints of ancient harmonies in nature. This ignorance at least is largely irremediable. We shall never learn the affinities of beauty, for they lie too deep in nature and too far back in the mysterious history of man. The amateur, in consequence, will always grudgingly receive details of method, which can be stated but never can wholly be explained; nay, on the principle laid down in *Hudibras*, that

> " Still the less they understand,
> The more they admire the sleight-of-hand,"

many are conscious at each new disclosure of a diminution in the ardour of their pleasure. I must therefore warn that well-known character, the general reader, that I am here embarked upon a most distasteful business: taking down the picture from the wall and looking on the back; and, like the inquiring child, pulling the musical cart to pieces.

Essays in the Art of Writing

1. *Choice of Words.*—The art of literature stands apart from among its sisters, because the material in which the literary artist works is the dialect of life; hence, on the one hand, strange freshness and immediacy of address to the public mind, which is ready prepared to understand it; but hence, on the other, a singular limitation. The sister arts enjoy the use of a plastic and ductile material, like the modeller's clay; literature alone is condemned to work in mosaic with finite and quite rigid words. You have seen these blocks dear to the nursery: this one a pillar, that a pediment, a third a window or a vase. It is with blocks of just such arbitrary size and figure that the literary architect is condemned to design the palace of his art. Nor is this all; for since these blocks, or words, are the acknowledged currency of our daily affairs, there are here possible none of those suppressions by which other arts obtain relief, continuity, and vigour: no hieroglyphic touch, no smoothed impasto, no inscrutable shadow, as in painting; no blank wall, as in architecture; but every word, phrase, sentence, and paragraph must move in a logical progression, and convey a definite conventional import.

Now the first merit which attracts in the pages of a good writer, or the talk of a brilliant conversationalist, is the apt choice and contrast of the words employed. It is, indeed, a strange art to take these blocks, rudely conceived for the purpose of the market or the bar, and by tact of application touch them to the finest meanings and distinctions; restore to them their primal energy, wittily shift them to another issue, or make of them a drum to rouse the passions. But though this form of merit is without doubt the most sensible and seizing, it is far from being equally present in all writers. The effect of words in Shakespeare, their singular justice, significance, and poetic charm, is

38

On Some Technical Elements

different, indeed, from the effect of words in Addison or Fielding. Or, to take an example nearer home, the words in Carlyle seem electrified into an energy of lineament, like the faces of men furiously moved; whilst the words in Macaulay, apt enough to convey his meaning, harmonious enough in sound, yet glide from the memory like undistinguished elements in a general effect. But the first class of writers have no monopoly of literary merit. There is a sense in which Addison is superior to Carlyle; a sense in which Cicero is better than Tacitus, in which Voltaire excels Montaigne: it certainly lies not in the choice of words; it lies not in the interest or value of the matter; it lies not in force of intellect, of poetry, or of humour. The three first are but infants to the three second; and yet each, in a particular point of literary art, excels his superior in the whole. What is that point?

2. *The Web.*—Literature, although it stands apart by reason of the great destiny and general use of its medium in the affairs of men, is yet an art like other arts. Of these we may distinguish two great classes: those arts, like sculpture, painting, acting, which are representative, or as used to be said very clumsily, imitative; and those, like architecture, music, and the dance, which are self-sufficient, and merely presentative. Each class, in right of this distinction, obeys principles apart; yet both may claim a common ground of existence, and it may be said with sufficient justice that the motive and end of any art whatever, is to make a pattern; a pattern, it may be, of colours, of sounds, of changing attitudes, geometrical figures, or imitative lines; but still a pattern. That is the plane on which these sisters meet; it is by this that they are arts; and if it be well they should at times forget their childish origin, addressing their intelligence to virile tasks, and performing unconsciously that necessary function of

39

their life, to make a pattern, it is still imperative that the pattern shall be made.

Music and literature, the two temporal arts, contrive their pattern of sounds in time; or, in other words, of sounds and pauses. Communication may be made in broken words, the business of life be carried on with substantives alone; but that is not what we call literature; and the true business of the literary artist is to plait or weave his meaning, involving it around itself so that each sentence, by successive phrases, shall first come into a kind of knot, and then, after a moment of suspended meaning, solve and clear itself. In every properly constructed sentence there should be observed this knot or hitch; so that (however delicately) we are led to foresee, to expect, and then to welcome the successive phrases. The pleasure may be heightened by an element of surprise, as, very grossly, in the common figure of the antithesis, or, with much greater subtlety, where an antithesis is first suggested and then deftly evaded. Each phrase, besides, is to be comely in itself; and between the implication and the evolution of the sentence there should be a satisfying equipoise of sound; for nothing more often disappoints the ear than a sentence solemnly and sonorously prepared, and hastily and weakly finished. Nor should the balance be too striking and exact, for the one rule is to be infinitely various; to interest, to disappoint, to surprise, and yet still to gratify; to be ever changing, as it were, the stitch, and yet still to give the effect of an ingenious neatness.

The conjurer juggles with two oranges, and our pleasure in beholding him springs from this, that neither is for an instant overlooked or sacrificed. So with the writer. His pattern, which is to please the supersensual ear, is yet addressed, throughout and first of all, to the demands of logic. Whatever be the obscurities, whatever the intricacies of the argument, the neatness of the fabric must not suffer, or the artist has been proved unequal to his design. And, on the other hand, no form of words must be selected, no knot must be tied among the phrases, unless knot and word be precisely what is wanted to forward and illuminate the argument; for to fail in this is to swindle in the game. The genius of prose rejects the *cheville* no less emphatically than the laws of verse; and the *cheville*, I should perhaps explain to some of my readers, is any meaningless or very watered phrase employed to strike a balance in the sound. Pattern and argument live in each other; and it is by the brevity, clearness, charm, or emphasis of the second, that we judge the strength and fitness of the first.

Style is synthetic; and the artist, seeking, so to speak, a peg to plait about, takes up at once two or more elements or two or more views of the subject in hand; combines, implicates, and contrasts them; and while, in one sense, he was merely seeking an occasion for the necessary knot, he will be found, in the other, to have greatly enriched the meaning, or to have transacted the work of two sentences in the space of one. In the change from the successive shallow statements of the old chronicler to the dense and luminous flow of highly synthetic narrative, there is implied a vast amount of both philosophy and wit. The philosophy we clearly see, recognising in the synthetic writer a far more deep and stimulating view of life, and a far keener sense of the generation and affinity of events. The wit we might imagine to be lost, but it is not so, for it is just that wit, these perpetual nice contrivances, these difficulties overcome, this double purpose attained, these two oranges kept simultaneously dancing in the air, that, consciously or not, afford the reader his delight. Nay, and this wit, so little recognised, is the necessary organ of that philosophy which we so much admire. That style is therefore the most perfect, not, as fools say, which is the most natural, for the most natural is the disjointed babble of the chronicler; but which attains the highest degree of elegant and pregnant implication unobtrusively; or if obtrusively, then with the greatest gain to sense and vigour. Even the derangement of the phrases from their (so-called) natural order is luminous for the mind; and it is by the means of such designed reversal that the elements of a judgment may be most pertinently marshalled, or the stages of a complicated action most perspicuously bound into one.

The web, then, or the pattern: a web at once sensuous and logical, an elegant and pregnant texture: that is style, that is the foundation of the art of literature. Books indeed continue to be read, for the interest of the fact or fable, in which this quality is poorly represented, but still it will be there. And, on the other hand, how many do we continue to peruse and re-peruse with pleasure whose only merit is the elegance of texture? I am tempted to mention Cicero, and since Mr. Anthony Trollope is dead, I will. It is a poor diet for the mind, a very colourless and toothless " criticism of life "; but we enjoy the pleasure of a most intricate and dexterous pattern, every stitch a model at once of elegance and of good sense; and the two oranges, even if one of them be rotten, kept dancing with inimitable grace.

Up to this moment I have had my eye mainly upon prose; for though in verse also the implication of the logical texture is a crowning beauty, yet in verse it may be dispensed with. You would think that here was a death-blow to all I have been saying; and, far from that, it is but a new illustration of the principle involved. For if the versifier is not bound to weave a pattern of his own, it is because another pattern has been formally imposed upon him by the laws of verse.

For that is the essence of a prosody. Verse may be rhythmical; it may be merely alliterative; it may, like the French, depend wholly on the (quasi) regular recurrence of the rhyme; or, like the Hebrew, it may consist in the strangely fanciful device of repeating the same idea. It does not matter on what principle the law is based, so it be a law. It may be pure convention; it may have no inherent beauty; all that we have a right to ask of any prosody is, that it shall lay down a pattern for the writer, and that what it lays down shall be neither too easy nor too hard. Hence it comes that it is much easier for men of equal facility to write fairly pleasing verse than reasonably interesting prose; for in prose the pattern itself has to be invented, and the difficulties first created before they can be solved. Hence, again, there follows the peculiar greatness of the true versifier: such as Shakespeare, Milton, and Victor Hugo, whom I place beside them as versifier merely, not as poet. These not only knit and knot the logical texture of the style with all the dexterity and strength of prose; they not only fill up the pattern of the verse with infinite variety and sober wit; but they give us, besides, a rare and special pleasure, by the art, comparable to that of counterpoint, with which they follow at the same time, and now contrast, and now combine, the double pattern of the texture and the verse. Here the sounding line concludes; a little further on, the well-knit sentence; and yet a little further, and both will reach their solution on the same ringing syllable. The best that can be offered by the best writer of prose is to show us the development of the idea and the stylistic pattern proceed hand in hand, sometimes by an obvious and triumphant effort, sometimes with a great air of ease and nature. The writer of verse, by virtue of conquering another difficulty, delights us with a new series of triumphs. He follows

D

three purposes where his rival followed only two; and the change is of precisely the same nature as that from melody to harmony. Or if you prefer to return to the juggler, behold him now, to the vastly increased enthusiasm of the spectators, juggling with three oranges instead of two. Thus it is: added difficulty, added beauty; and the pattern, with every fresh element, becoming more interesting in itself.

Yet it must not be thought that verse is simply an addition; something is lost as well as something gained; and there remains plainly traceable, in comparing the best prose with the best verse, a certain broad distinction of method in the web. Tight as the versifier may draw the knot of logic, yet for the ear he still leaves the tissue of the sentence floating somewhat loose. In prose, the sentence turns upon a pivot, nicely balanced, and fits into itself with an obtrusive neatness like a puzzle. The ear remarks and is singly gratified by this return and balance; while in verse it is all diverted to the measure. To find comparable passages is hard; for either the versifier is hugely the superior of the rival, or, if he be not, and still persist in his more delicate enterprise, he fails to be as widely his inferior. But let us select them from the pages of the same writer, one who was ambidexter; let us take, for instance, Rumour's Prologue to the Second Part of *Henry IV.*, a fine flourish of eloquence in Shakespeare's second manner, and set it side by side with Falstaff's praise of sherris, act iv. scene i.; or let us compare the beautiful prose spoken throughout by Rosalind and Orlando; compare, for example, the first speech of all, Orlando's speech to Adam, with what passage it shall please you to select —the Seven Ages from the same play, or even such a stave of nobility as Othello's farewell to war; and still you will be able to perceive, if you have an ear for that class of music, a certain superior degree of organisa-

tion in the prose; a compacter fitting of the parts; a
balance in the swing and the return as of a throbbing
pendulum. We must not, in things temporal, take from
those who have little, the little that they have; the
merits of prose are inferior, but they are not the same;
it is a little kingdom, but an independent.

3. *Rhythm of the Phrase.*—Some way back, I used a
word which still awaits an application. Each phrase,
I said, was to be comely; but what is a comely phrase?
In all ideal and material points, literature, being a representative art, must look for analogies to painting and
the like; but in what is technical and executive, being
a temporal art, it must seek for them in music. Each
phrase of each sentence, like an air or a recitative in
music, should be so artfully compounded out of long
and short, out of accented and unaccented, as to gratify
the sensual ear. And of this the ear is the sole judge. It
is impossible to lay down laws. Even in our accentual
and rhythmic language no analysis can find the secret
of the beauty of a verse; how much less then, of those
phrases, such as prose is built of, which obey no law
but to be lawless and yet to please? The little that we
know of verse (and for my part I owe it all to my friend
Professor Fleeming Jenkin) is, however, particularly
interesting in the present connection. We have been
accustomed to describe the heroic line as five iambic
feet, and to be filled with pain and confusion whenever,
as by the conscientious schoolboy, we have heard our
own description put in practice.

" All nìght | the dreàd | less àn | gel ùn | pursùed,"*

goes the schoolboy; but though we close our ears, we
cling to our definition, in spite of its proved and naked
insufficiency. Mr. Jenkin was not so easily pleased,
and readily discovered that the heroic line consisted of

* Milton.

45

four groups, or, if you prefer the phrase, contains four pauses: "All night | the dreadless | angel | unpursued."

Four groups, each practically uttered as one word: the first, in this case, an iamb; the second, an amphibrachys; the third, a trochee; and the fourth, an amphimacer; and yet our schoolboy, with no other liberty but that of inflicting pain, had triumphantly scanned it as five iambs. Perceive, now, this fresh richness of intricacy in the web; this fourth orange, hitherto unremarked, but still kept flying with the others. What had seemed to be one thing it now appears is two; and, like some puzzle in arithmetic, the verse is made at the same time to read in fives and to read in fours.

But again, four is not necessary. We do not, indeed, find verses in six groups, because there is not room for six in the ten syllables; and we do not find verses of two, because one of the main distinctions of verse from prose resides in the comparative shortness of the group; but it is even common to find verses of three. Five is the one forbidden number; because five is the number of the feet; and if five were chosen, the two patterns would coincide, and that opposition which is the life of verse would instantly be lost. We have here a clue to the effect of polysyllables, above all in Latin, where they are so common and make so brave an architecture in the verse; for the polysyllable is a group of Nature's making. If but some Roman would return from Hades (Martial, for choice), and tell me by what conduct of the voice these thundering verses should be uttered—
"*Aut Lacedæmonium Tarentum,*" for a case in point—I feel as if I should enter at last into the full enjoyment of the best of human verses.

But, again, the five feet are all iambic, or supposed to be; by the mere count of syllables the four groups cannot be all iambic; as a question of elegance, I doubt if any one of them requires to be so; and I am certain that for choice no two of them should scan the same. The singular beauty of the verse analysed above is due, so far as analysis can carry us, part, indeed, to the clever repetition of L, D, and N, but part to this variety of scansion in the groups. The groups which, like the bar in music, break up the verse for utterance, fall un-iambically; and in declaiming a so-called iambic verse, it may so happen that we never utter one iambic foot. And yet to this neglect of the original beat there is a limit.

"Athens, the eye of Greece, mother of arts,"*

is, with all its eccentricities, a good heroic line; for though it scarcely can be said to indicate the beat of the iamb, it certainly suggests no other measure to the ear. But begin

" Mother Athens, eye of Greece,"

or merely " Mother Athens," and the game is up, for the trochaic beat has been suggested. The eccentric scansion of the groups is an adornment; but as soon as the original beat has been forgotten, they cease implicitly to be eccentric. Variety is what is sought; but if we destroy the original mould, one of the terms of this variety is lost, and we fall back on sameness. Thus, both as to the arithmetical measure of the verse, and the degree of regularity in scansion, we see the laws of prosody to have one common purpose: to keep alive the opposition of two schemes simultaneously followed; to keep them notably apart, though still coincident; and to balance them with such judicial nicety before the reader, that neither shall be unperceived and neither signally prevail.

The rule of rhythm in prose is not so intricate. Here, too, we write in groups, or phrases, as I prefer to call

* Milton.

them, for the prose phrase is greatly longer and is much more nonchalantly uttered than the group in verse; so that not only is there a greater interval of continuous sound between the pauses, but, for that very reason, word is linked more readily to word by a more summary enunciation. Still, the phrase is the strict analogue of the group, and successive phrases, like successive groups, must differ openly in length and rhythm. The rule of scansion in verse is to suggest no measure but the one in hand; in prose, to suggest no measure at all. Prose must be rhythmical, and it may be as much so as you will; but it must not be metrical. It may be anything, but it must not be verse. A single heroic line may very well pass and not disturb the somewhat larger stride of the prose style; but one following another will produce an instant impression of poverty, flatness, and disenchantment. The same lines delivered with the measured utterance of verse would perhaps seem rich in variety. By the more summary enunciation proper to prose, as to a more distant vision, these niceties of difference are lost. A whole verse is uttered as one phrase; and the ear is soon wearied by a succession of groups identical in length. The prose writer, in fact, since he is allowed to be so much less harmonious, is condemned to a perpetually fresh variety of movement on a larger scale, and must never disappoint the ear by the trot of an accepted metre. And this obligation is the third orange with which he has to juggle, the third quality which the prose writer must work into his pattern of words. It may be thought perhaps that this is a quality of ease rather than a fresh difficulty; but such is the inherently rhythmical strain of the English language, that the bad writer—and must I take for example that admired friend of my boyhood, Captain Reid?—the inexperienced writer, as Dickens in his earlier attempts to be impressive, and the jaded writer, as anyone may see for himself, all tend to fall at once into the production of bad blank verse. And here it may be pertinently asked, Why bad? And I suppose it might be enough to answer that no man ever made good verse by accident, and that no verse can ever sound otherwise than trivial when uttered with the delivery of prose. But we can go beyond such answers. The weak side of verse is the regularity of the beat, which in itself is decidedly less impressive than the movement of the nobler prose; and it is just into this weak side, and this alone, that our careless writer falls. A peculiar density and mass consequent on the nearness of the pauses is one of the chief good qualities of verse; but this our accidental versifier, still following after the swift gait and large gestures of prose, does not so much as aspire to imitate. Lastly, since he remains unconscious that he is making verse at all, it can never occur to him to extract those effects of counterpoint and opposition which I have referred to as the final grace and justification of verse, and, I may add, of blank verse in particular.

4. *Contents of the Phrase.*—Here is a great deal of talk about rhythm—and naturally; for in our canorous language, rhythm is always at the door. But it must not be forgotten that in some languages this element is almost, if not quite, extinct, and that in our own it is probably decaying. The even speech of many educated Americans sounds the note of danger. I should see it go with something as bitter as despair, but I should not be desperate. As in verse no element, not even rhythm, is necessary, so, in prose also, other sorts of beauty will arise and take the place and play the part of those that we outlive. The beauty of the expected beat in verse, the beauty in prose of its larger and more lawless melody, patent as they are to English hearing, are already silent in the ears of our next neighbours;

49

Essays in the Art of Writing

for France the oratorical accent and the pattern of the web have almost or altogether succeeded to their places; and the French prose writer would be astounded at the labours of his brother across the Channel, and how a good quarter of his toil, above all *invita Minerva*, is to avoid writing verse. So wonderfully far apart have races wandered in spirit, and so hard it is to understand the literature next door!

Yet French prose is distinctly better than English; and French verse, above all while Hugo lives, it will not do to place upon one side. What is more to our purpose, a phrase or a verse in French is easily distinguishable as comely or uncomely. There is then another element of comeliness hitherto overlooked in this analysis: the contents of the phrase. Each phrase in literature is built of sounds, as each phrase in music consists of notes. One sound suggests, echoes, demands, and harmonises with another; and the art of rightly using these concordances is the final art in literature. It used to be a piece of good advice to all young writers to avoid alliteration; and the advice was sound, in so far as it prevented daubing. None the less for that was it abominable nonsense, and the mere raving of those blindest of the blind who will not see. The beauty of the contents of a phrase, or of a sentence, depends implicitly upon alliteration and upon assonance. The vowel demands to be repeated; the consonant demands to be repeated; and both cry aloud to be perpetually varied. You may follow the adventures of a letter through any passage that has particularly pleased you; find it, perhaps, denied awhile, to tantalise the ear; find it fired again at you in a whole broadside; or find it pass into congenerous sounds, one liquid or labial melting away into another. And you will find another and much stranger circumstance. Literature is written by and for two senses: a sort of internal ear, quick to perceive "unheard melodies"; and the eye, which directs the pen and deciphers the printed phrase. Well, even as there are rhymes for the eye, so you will find that there are assonances and alliterations; that where an author is running the open A, deceived by the eye and our strange English spelling, he will often show a tenderness for the flat A, and that where he is running a particular consonant, he will not improbably rejoice to write it down even when it is mute or bears a different value.

Here, then, we have a fresh pattern—a pattern, to speak grossly, of letters—which makes the fourth preoccupation of the prose writer, and the fifth of the versifier. At times it is very delicate and hard to perceive, and then perhaps most excellent and winning (I say perhaps); but at times again the elements of this literal melody stand more boldly forward and usurp the ear. It becomes, therefore, somewhat a matter of conscience to select examples; and as I cannot very well ask the reader to help me, I shall do the next best by giving him the reason or the history of each selection. The two first, one in prose, one in verse, I chose without previous analysis, simply as engaging passages that had long re-echoed in my ear.

" I cannot praise a fugitive and cloistered virtue, unexercised and unbreathed, that never sallies out and sees her adversary, but slinks out of the race where that immortal garland is to be run for, not without dust and heat."* Down to " virtue," the current S and R are both announced and repeated unobtrusively, and by way of a grace-note that almost inseparable group PVF is given entire.† The next phrase is a period of

* Milton.
† As PVF will continue to haunt us through our English examples, take, by way of comparison, this Latin verse, of which it forms a chief adornment, and do not hold me answerable for the all-too-Roman freedom of the sense : "Hanc volo, quæ facilis, quæ palliolata vagatur."

repose, almost ugly in itself, both S and R still audible, and B given as the last fulfilment of PVF. In the next four phrases, from " that never " down to " run for," the mask is thrown off, and, but for a slight repetition of the F and V, the whole matter turns, almost too obtrusively, on S and R; first S coming to the front, and then R. In the concluding phrase all these favourite letters, and even the flat A, a timid preference for which is just perceptible, are discarded at a blow and in a bundle; and to make the break more obvious, every word ends with a dental, and all but one with T, for which we have been cautiously prepared since the beginning. The singular dignity of the first clause, and this hammer-stroke of the last, go far to make the charm of this exquisite sentence. But it is fair to own that S and R are used a little coarsely.

" In Xanadv did Kubla Khan	(KĂNDL)
A stately pleasure dome decree,	(KDLSR)
Where Alph the sacred river ran,	(KĂNDLSR)
Through caverns measureless to man,	(KĂNLSR)
Down to a sunless sea."*	(NDLS)

Here I have put the analysis of the main group alongside the lines; and the more it is looked at, the more interesting it will seem. But there are further niceties. In lines two and four, the current S is most delicately varied with Z. In line three, the current flat A is twice varied with the open A, already suggested in line two, and both times ("where" and "sacred") in conjunction with the current R. In the same line F and V (a harmony in themselves, even when shorn of their comrade P) are admirably contrasted. And in line four there is a marked subsidiary M, which again was announced in line two. I stop from weariness, for more might yet be said.

* Coleridge.

On Some Technical Elements

My next example was recently quoted from Shakespeare as an example of the poet's colour sense. Now, I do not think literature has anything to do with colour, or poets anyway the better of such a sense; and I instantly attacked this passage, since " purple " was the word that had so pleased the writer of the article, to see if there might not be some literary reason for its use. It will be seen that I succeeded amply; and I am bound to say I think the passage exceptional in Shakespeare—exceptional, indeed, in literature; but it was not I who chose it.

> " The BaRge she sat iN, like a BURNished throNe
> BURNt oN the water : the POOP was BeateN gold, *per
> PURPle the sails and so PUR* Fumèd that
> The wiNds were love-sick with them."*

It may be asked why I have put the F of " perfumed " in capitals; and I reply, because this change from P to F is the completion of that from B to P, already so adroitly carried out. Indeed, the whole passage is a monument of curious ingenuity; and it seems scarce worth while to indicate the subsidiary S, L, and W. In the same article, a second passage from Shakespeare was quoted, once again as an example of his colour sense:

> "A mole cinque-spotted like the crimson drops
> I' the bottom of a cowslip."†

It is very curious, very artificial, and not worth while to analyse at length: I leave it to the reader. But before I turn my back on Shakespeare, I should like to quote a passage, for my own pleasure, and for a very model of every technical art:

" But in the wind and tempest of her frown,	W.P.V.‡F. (st) (ow)
Distinction with a loud and powerful fan,	W.P.F. (st) (ow) L
Puffing at all, winnows the light away ;	W.P.F.L.
And what hath mass and matter by itself	W.F.L.M.Å.
Lies rich in virtue and unmingled."‖	V.L.M.

* *Antony and Cleopatra.*   † *Cymbeline.*
‡ The V is in " of."   ‖ *Troilus and Cressida.*

From these delicate and choice writers I turned with some curiosity to a player of the big drum—Macaulay. I had in hand the two-volume edition, and I opened at the beginning of the second volume. Here was what I read:

" The violence of revolutions is generally proportioned to the degree of the maladministration which has produced them. It is therefore not strange that the government of Scotland, having been during many years greatly more corrupt than the government of England, should have fallen with a far heavier ruin. The movement against the last king of the house of Stuart was in England conservative, in Scotland destructive. The English complained not of the law, but of the violation of the law."

This was plain-sailing enough; it was our old friend PVF, floated by the liquids in a body; but as I read on, and turned the page, and still found PVF with his attendant liquids, I confess my mind misgave me utterly. This could be no trick of Macaulay's; it must be the nature of the English tongue. In a kind of despair, I turned half-way through the volume; and coming upon his lordship dealing with General Cannon, and fresh from Claverhouse and Killiecrankie, here, with elucidative spelling, was my reward:

" Meanwhile the disorders of Kannon's Kamp went on inKreasing. He Kalled a Kouncil of war to Konsider what Kourse it would be advisable to taKe. But as soon as the Kouncil had met, a preliminary Kuestion was raised. The army was almost eKsKlusively a Highland army. The recent viKtory had been won eKsKlusively by Highland warriors. Great chie*f*s who had brought si*K*s or Seven hundred *f*ighting men into the *f*ield did not think it fair that they should be out*v*oted

54

by gentlemen *from* Ireland, and *from* the Low Koun-
tries, who bore indeed King James's Kommission, and
were Kalled Kolonels and Kaptains, but who were
Kolonels without regiments and Kaptains without
Kompanies."

A moment of FV in all this world of K's! It was
not the English language, then, that was an instrument
of one string, but Macaulay that was an incomparable
dauber.

It was probably from this barbaric love of repeating
the same sound, rather than from any design of clearness, that he acquired his irritating habit of repeating
words; I say the one rather than the other, because such
a trick of the ear is deeper-seated and more original in
man than any logical consideration. Few writers, indeed, are probably conscious of the length to which
they push this melody of letters. One, writing very
diligently, and only concerned about the meaning of
his words and the rhythm of his phrases, was struck
into amazement by the eager triumph with which he
cancelled one expression to substitute another. Neither
changed the sense; both being monosyllables, neither
could affect the scansion; and it was only by looking
back on what he had already written that the mystery
was solved: the second word contained an open A, and
for nearly half a page he had been riding that vowel to
the death.

In practice, I should add, the ear is not always so exacting; and ordinary writers, in ordinary moments,
content themselves with avoiding what is harsh, and
here and there, upon a rare occasion, buttressing a
phrase, or linking two together, with a patch of assonance or a momentary jingle of alliteration. To understand how constant is this preoccupation of good
writers, even where its results are least obtrusive, it is

only necessary to turn to the bad. There, indeed, you will find cacophony supreme, the rattle of incongruous consonants only relieved by the jaw-breaking hiatus, and whole phrases not to be articulated by the powers of man.

Conclusion.—We may now briefly enumerate the elements of style. We have, peculiar to the prose writer, the task of keeping his phrases large, rhythmical, and pleasing to the ear, without ever allowing them to fall into the strictly metrical: peculiar to the versifier, the task of combining and contrasting his double, treble, and quadruple pattern, feet and groups, logic and metre —harmonious in diversity: common to both, the task of artfully combining the prime elements of language into phrases that shall be musical in the mouth; the task of weaving their argument into a texture of committed phrases and of rounded periods—but this particularly binding in the case of prose: and, again common to both, the task of choosing apt, explicit, and communicative words. We begin to see now what an intricate affair is any perfect passage; how many faculties, whether of taste or pure reason, must be held upon the stretch to make it; and why, when it is made, it should afford us so complete a pleasure. From the arrangement of according letters, which is altogether arabesque and sensual, up to the architecture of the elegant and pregnant sentence, which is a vigorous act of the pure intellect, there is scarce a faculty in man but has been exercised. We need not wonder, then, if perfect sentences are rare, and perfect pages rarer.

THE MORALITY OF THE PROFESSION
OF LETTERS

The profession of letters has been lately debated in the public prints; and it has been debated, to put the matter mildly, from a point of view that was calculated to surprise high-minded men, and bring a general contempt on books and reading. Some time ago, in particular, a lively, pleasant, popular writer* devoted an essay, lively and pleasant like himself, to a very encouraging view of the profession. We may be glad that his experience is so cheering, and we may hope that all others, who deserve it, shall be as handsomely rewarded; but I do not think we need be at all glad to have this question, so important to the public and ourselves, debated solely on the ground of money. The salary in any business under heaven is not the only, nor indeed the first, question. That you should continue to exist is a matter for your own consideration; but that your business should be first honest, and second useful, are points in which honour and morality are concerned. If the writer to whom I refer succeeds in persuading a number of young persons to adopt this way of life with an eye set singly on the livelihood, we must expect them in their works to follow profit only, and we must expect in consequence, if he will pardon me the epithets, a slovenly, base, untrue, and empty literature. Of that writer himself I am not speaking: he is diligent, clean and pleasing; we all owe him periods of entertainment, and he has achieved an amiable popularity which he has adequately deserved. But the truth is, he does not, or did not when he first embraced it, regard his profession from this purely mercenary side. He went into it, I shall venture to say, if not with any noble design, at least in the ardour of a first love; and he enjoyed its practice long before he paused to calculate the wage.

* Mr. James Payn.

Essays in the Art of Writing

The other day an author was complimented on a piece
of work, good in itself and exceptionally good for him,
and replied, in terms unworthy of a commercial traveller, that as the book was not briskly selling he did
not give a copper farthing for its merit. It must not
be supposed that the person to whom this answer was
addressed received it as a profession of faith; he knew,
on the other hand, that it was only a whiff of irritation; just as we know, when a respectable writer talks
of literature as a way of life, like shoemaking, but not
so useful, that he is only debating one aspect of a question, and is still clearly conscious of a dozen others more
important in themselves and more central to the matter
in hand. But while those who treat literature in this
penny-wise and virtue-foolish spirit are themselves
truly in possession of a better light, it does not follow
that the treatment is decent or improving, whether for
themselves or others. To treat all subjects in the highest,
the most honourable, and the pluckiest spirit, con-
sistent with the fact, is the first duty of a writer. If he
be well paid, as I am glad to hear he is, this duty
becomes the more urgent, the neglect of it the more
disgraceful. And perhaps there is no subject on which
a man should speak so gravely as that industry, whatever it may be, which is the occupation or delight of
his life; which is his tool to earn or serve with; and
which, if it be unworthy, stamps himself as a mere incubus of dumb and greedy bowels on the shoulders of
labouring humanity. On that subject alone even to
force the note might lean to virtue's side. It is to be
hoped that a numerous and enterprising generation of
writers will follow and surpass the present one; but it
would be better if the stream were stayed, and the roll
of our old honest English books were closed, than that
esurient book-makers should continue and debase a
brave tradition, and lower, in their own eyes, a famous

race. Better that our serene temples were deserted than filled with trafficking and juggling priests.

There are two just reasons for the choice of any way of life: the first is inbred taste in the chooser; the second some high utility in the industry selected. Literature, like any other art, is singularly interesting to the artist; and, in a degree peculiar to itself among the arts, it is useful to mankind. These are sufficient justifications for any young man or woman who adopts it as the business of his life. I shall not say much about the wages. A writer can live by his writing. If not so luxuriously as by other trades, then less luxuriously. The nature of the work he does all day will more affect his happiness than the quality of his dinner at night. Whatever be your calling and however much it brings you in the year, you could still, you know, get more by cheating. We all suffer ourselves to be too much concerned about a little poverty; but such considerations should not move us in the choice of that which is to be the business and justification of so great a portion of our lives; and like the missionary, the patriot, or the philosopher, we should all choose that poor and brave career in which we can do the most and best for mankind. Now Nature, faithfully followed, proves herself a careful mother. A lad, for some liking to the jingle of words, betakes himself to letters for his life; by-and-by, when he learns more gravity, he finds that he has chosen better than he knew; that if he earns little, he is earning it amply; that if he receives a small wage, he is in a position to do considerable services; that it is in his power, in some small measure to protect the oppressed and to defend the truth. So kindly is the world arranged, such great profit may arise from a small degree of human reliance on oneself, and such, in particular, is the happy star of this trade of writing, that it should combine pleasure and profit to both parties, and be at once agreeable, like fiddling, and useful, like good preaching.

This is to speak of literature at its highest; and with the four great elders who are still spared to our respect and admiration, with Carlyle, Ruskin, Browning, and Tennyson before us, it would be cowardly to consider it at first in any lesser aspect. But while we cannot follow these athletes, while we may none of us, perhaps, be very vigorous, very original, or very wise, I still contend that, in the humblest sort of literary work, we have it in our power either to do great harm or great good. We may seek merely to please; we may seek, having no higher gift, merely to gratify the idle nine days' curiosity of our contemporaries; or we may essay, however feebly, to instruct. In each of these we shall have to deal with that remarkable art of words which, because it is the dialect of life, comes home so easily and powerfully to the minds of men; and since that is so, we contribute, in each of these branches, to build up the sum of sentiments and appreciations which goes by the name of Public Opinion or Public Feeling. The total of a nation's reading, in these days of daily papers, greatly modifies the total of the nation's speech; and the speech and reading, taken together, form the efficient educational medium of youth. A good man or woman may keep a youth some little while in clearer air; but the contemporary atmosphere is all-powerful in the end on the average of mediocre characters. The copious Corinthian baseness of the American reporter or the Parisian *chroniquer*, both so lightly readable, must exercise an incalculable influence for ill; they touch upon all subjects, and on all with the same ungenerous hand; they begin the consideration of all, in young and unprepared minds, in an unworthy spirit; on all, they supply some pungency for dull people to quote. The mere body of this ugly matter overwhelms the rare utterances of good men; the sneering, the selfish, and the cowardly are scattered in broad sheets on every table, while the antidote, in small volumes, lies unread upon the shelf. I have spoken of the American and the French, not because they are so much baser, but so much more readable, than the English; their evil is done more effectively, in America for the masses, in French for the few that care to read; but with us as with them, the duties of literature are daily neglected, truth daily perverted and suppressed, and grave subjects daily degraded in the treatment. The journalist is not reckoned an important officer; yet judge of the good he might do, the harm he does; judge of it by one instance only: that when we find two journals on the reverse sides of politics each, on the same day, openly garbling a piece of news for the interest of its own party, we smile at the discovery (no discovery now!) as over a good joke and pardonable stratagem. Lying so open is scarce lying, it is true, but one of the things that we profess to teach our young is a respect for truth; and I cannot think this piece of education will be crowned with any great success, so long as some of us practise and the rest openly approve of public falsehood.

There are two duties incumbent upon any man who enters on the business of writing: truth to the fact and a good spirit in the treatment. In every department of literature, though so low as hardly to deserve the name, truth to the fact is of importance to the education and comfort of mankind, and so hard to preserve, that the faithful trying to do so will lend some dignity to the man who tries it. Our judgments are based upon two things: first, upon the original preferences of our soul; but, second, upon the mass of testimony to the nature of God, man, and the universe which reaches us, in divers manners, from without. For the most part these

divers manners are reducible to one, all that we learn
of past times and much that we learn of our own reach-
ing us through the medium of books or papers, and
even he who cannot read learning from the same
source at second-hand and by the report of him who
can. Thus the sum of the contemporary knowledge or
ignorance of good and evil is, in large measure, the
handiwork of those who write. Those who write have
to see that each man's knowledge is, as near as they can
make it, answerable to the facts of life; that he shall
not suppose himself an angel or a monster; nor take
this world for a hell; nor be suffered to imagine that
all rights are concentred in his own caste or country, or
all veracities in his own parochial creed. Each man
should learn what is within him, that he may strive to
mend; he must be taught what is without him, that he
may be kind to others. It can never be wrong to tell
him the truth; for, in his disputable state, weaving as
he goes his theory of life, steering himself, cheering or
reproving others, all facts are of the first importance to
his conduct; and even if a fact shall discourage or corrupt him, it is still best that he should know it; for it
is in this world as it is, and not in a world made easy
by educational suppressions, that he must win his way
to shame or glory. In one word, it must always be foul
to tell what is false; and it can never be safe to suppress
what is true. The very fact that you omit may be the
fact which somebody was wanting, for one man's meat
is another man's poison, and I have known a person
who was cheered by the perusal of *Candide*. Every fact
is a part of that great puzzle we must set together; and
none that comes directly in a writer's path but has some
nice relations, unperceivable by him, to the totality and
bearing of the subject under hand. Yet there are certain
classes of fact eternally more necessary than others, and
it is with these that literature must first bestir itself.

They are not hard to distinguish, nature once more easily leading us; for the necessary, because the efficacious, facts are those which are most interesting to the natural mind of man. Those which are coloured, picturesque, human, and rooted in morality, and those, on the other hand, which are clear, indisputable, and a part of science, are alone vital in importance, seizing by their interest, or useful to communicate. So far as the writer merely narrates, he should principally tell of these. He should tell of the kind and wholesome and beautiful elements of our life; he should tell unsparingly of the evil and sorrow of the present, to move us with instances; he should tell of wise and good people in the past, to excite us by example; and of these he should tell soberly and truthfully, not glossing faults, that we may neither grow discouraged with ourselves nor exacting to our neighbours. So the body of contemporary literature, ephemeral and feeble in itself, touches in the minds of men the springs of thought and kindness, and supports them (for those who will go at all are easily supported) on their way to what is true and right. And if, in any degree, it does so now, how much more might it do so if the writers chose! There is not a life in all the records of the past but, properly studied, might lend a hint and a help to some contemporary. There is not a juncture in to-day's affairs but some useful word may yet be said of it. Even the reporter has an office, and, with clear eyes and honest language, may unveil injustices and point the way to progress. And for a last word: in all narration there is only one way to be clever, and that is to be exact. To be vivid is a secondary quality which must presuppose the first; for vividly to convey a wrong impression is only to make failure conspicuous.

But a fact may be viewed on many sides; it may be chronicled with rage, tears, laughter, indifference, or admiration, and by each of these the story will be transformed to something else. The newspapers that told of the return of our representatives from Berlin, even if they had not differed as to the facts, would have sufficiently differed by their spirits; so that the one description would have been a second ovation, and the other a prolonged insult. The subject makes but a trifling part of any piece of literature, and the view of the writer is itself a fact more important because less disputable than the others. Now this spirit in which a subject is regarded, important in all kinds of literary work, becomes all-important in works of fiction, meditation, or rhapsody; for there it not only colours but itself chooses the facts; not only modifies but shapes the work. And hence, over the far larger proportion of the field of literature, the health or disease of the writer's mind or momentary humour forms not only the leading feature of his work, but is, at bottom, the only thing he can communicate to others. In all works of art, widely speaking, it is first of all the author's attitude that is narrated, though in the attitude there be implied a whole experience and a theory of life. An author who has begged the question and reposes in some narrow faith cannot, if he would, express the whole or even many of the sides of this various existence; for, his own life being maim, some of them are not admitted in his theory, and were only dimly and unwillingly recognised in his experience. Hence the smallness, the triteness, and the inhumanity in works of merely sectarian religion; and hence we find equal although unsimilar limitation in works inspired by the spirit of the flesh or the despicable taste for high society. So that the first duty of any man who is to write is intellectual. Designedly or not, he has so far set himself up for a leader of the minds of men; and he must see that his own mind is kept supple, charitable, and bright. Everything but prejudice should find a voice through him; he should see the good in all things; where he has even a fear that he does not wholly understand, there he should be wholly silent; and he should recognise from the first that he has only one tool in his workshop, and that tool is sympathy.*

The second duty, far harder to define, is moral. There are a thousand different humours in the mind, and about each of them, when it is uppermost, some literature tends to be deposited. Is this to be allowed? Not certainly in every case, and yet perhaps in more than rigourists would fancy. It were to be desired that all literary work, and chiefly works of art, issued from sound, human, healthy, and potent impulses, whether grave or laughing, humorous, romantic or religious. Yet it cannot be denied that some valuable books are partially insane; some, mostly religious, partially inhuman; and very many tainted with morbidity and impotence. We do not loathe a masterpiece although we gird against its blemishes. We are not, above all, to look for faults, but merits. There is no book perfect, even in design; but there are many that will delight, improve, or encourage the reader. On the one hand, the Hebrew psalms are the only religious poetry on earth; yet they contain sallies that savour rankly of the man of blood. On the other hand, Alfred de Musset had a poisoned and a contorted nature; I am only quoting that generous and frivolous giant, old Dumas, when I accuse him of a bad heart; yet when the impulse under which he wrote was purely creative, he could

* A footnote, at least, is due to the admirable example set before all young writers in the width of literary sympathy displayed by Mr. Swinburne. He runs forth to welcome merit, whether in Dickens or Trollope, whether in Villon, Milton, or Pope. This is, in criticism, the attitude we should all seek to preserve, not only in that, but in every branch of literary work.

give us works like *Carmosine* or *Fantasio*, in which the last note of the romantic comedy seems to have been found again to touch and please us. When Flaubert wrote *Madame Bovary*, I believe he thought chiefly of a somewhat morbid realism; and behold! the book turned in his hands into a masterpiece of appalling morality. But the truth is, when books are conceived under a great stress, with a soul of ninefold power, nine times heated and electrified by effort, the conditions of our being are seized with such an ample grasp, that, even should the main design be trivial or base, some truth and beauty cannot fail to be expressed. Out of the strong comes forth sweetness; but an ill thing poorly done is an ill thing top and bottom. And so this can be no encouragement to knock-kneed, feeble-wristed scribes, who must take their business conscientiously or be ashamed to practise it.

Man is imperfect; yet, in his literature, he must express himself and his own views and preferences; for to do anything else is to do a far more perilous thing than to risk being immoral; it is to be sure of being untrue. To ape a sentiment, even a good one, is to travesty a sentiment; that will not be helpful. To conceal a sentiment, if you are sure you hold it, is to take a liberty with truth. There is probably no point of view possible to a sane man but contains some truth and, in the true connection, might be profitable to the race. I am not afraid of the truth, if anyone could tell it me, but I am afraid of parts of it impertinently uttered. There is a time to dance and a time to mourn; to be harsh as well as to be sentimental; to be ascetic as well as to glorify the appetites; and if a man were to combine all these extremes into his work, each in its place and proportion, that work would be the world's masterpiece of morality, as well as of art. Partiality is immorality; for any book is wrong that gives a misleading

picture of the world and life. The trouble is that the
weakling must be partial; the work of one proving dank
and depressing; of another, cheap and vulgar; of a
third, epileptically sensual; of a fourth, sourly ascetic.
In literature as in conduct, you can never hope to do
exactly right. All you can do is to make as sure as possible; and for that there is but one rule. Nothing should
be done in a hurry that can be done slowly. It is no use
to write a book and put it by for nine or even ninety
years; for in the writing you will have partly convinced
yourself; the delay must precede any beginning; and
if you meditate a work of art, you should first long roll
the subject under the tongue to make sure you like the
flavour, before you brew a volume that shall taste of it
from end to end; or if you propose to enter on the field
of controversy, you should first have thought upon the
question under all conditions, in health as well as in
sickness, in sorrow as well as in joy. It is this nearness
of examination necessary for any true and kind writing,
that makes practice of the art a prolonged and noble
education for the writer.

There is plenty to do, plenty to say, or to say over
again, in the meantime. Any literary work which con-
veys faithful facts or pleasing impressions is a service to
the public. It is even a service to be thankfully proud
of having rendered. The slightest novels are a blessing
to those in distress, not chloroform itself a greater. Our
fine old sea-captain's life was justified when Carlyle
soothed his mind with *The King's Own* or *Newton
Forster*. To please is to serve; and so far from its being
difficult to instruct while you amuse, it is difficult to
do the one thoroughly without the other. Some part of
the writer or his life will crop out in even a vapid book;
and to read a novel that was conceived with any force
is to multiply experience and to exercise the sympathies.
Every article, every piece of verse, every essay, every

entre-filet, is destined to pass, however swiftly, through the minds of some portion of the public, and to colour, however transiently, their thoughts. When any subject falls to be discussed, some scribbler on a paper has the invaluable opportunity of beginning its discussion in a dignified and human spirit; and if there were enough who did so in our public press, neither the public nor the Parliament would find it in their minds to drop to meaner thoughts. The writer has the chance to stumble, by the way, on something pleasing, something interesting, something encouraging, were it only to a single reader. He will be unfortunate, indeed, if he suit no one. He has the chance, besides, to stumble on something that a dull person shall be able to comprehend; and for a dull person to have read anything and, for that once, comprehended it, makes a marking epoch in his education.

Here, then, is work worth doing and worth trying to do well. And so, if I were minded to welcome any great accession to our trade, it should not be from any reason of a higher wage, but because it was a trade which was useful in a very great and in a very high degree; which every honest tradesman could make more serviceable to mankind in his single strength; which was difficult to do well and possible to do better every year; which called for scrupulous thought on the part of all who practised it, and hence became a perpetual education to their nobler natures; and which, pay it as you please, in the large majority of the best cases will still be underpaid. For surely at this time of the day in the nineteenth century, there is nothing that an honest man should fear more timorously than getting and spending more than he deserves.

BOOKS WHICH HAVE
INFLUENCED ME

The Editor* has somewhat insidiously laid a trap for his correspondents, the question put appearing at first so innocent, truly cutting so deep. It is not, indeed, until after some reconnaissance and review that the writer awakes to find himself engaged upon something in the nature of autobiography, or, perhaps worse, upon a chapter in the life of that little, beautiful brother whom we once all had, and whom we have all lost and mourned, the man we ought to have been, the man we hoped to be. But when word has been passed (even to an editor), it should, if possible, be kept; and if sometimes I am wise and say too little, and sometimes weak and say too much, the blame must lie at the door of the person who entrapped me.

The most influential books, and the truest in their influence, are works of fiction. They do not pin the reader to a dogma which he must afterwards discover to be inexact; they do not teach him a lesson which he must afterwards unlearn. They repeat, they rearrange, they clarify the lessons of life; they disengage us from ourselves, they constrain us to the acquaintance of others; and they show us the web of experience, not as we can see it for ourselves, but with a singular change —that monstrous, consuming *ego* of ours being, for the nonce, struck out. To be so, they must be reasonably true to the human comedy; and any work that is so serves the turn of instruction. But the course of our education is answered best by those poems and romances where we breathe a magnanimous atmosphere of thought and meet generous and pious characters. Shakespeare has served me best. Few living friends have had upon me an influence so strong for good as Hamlet or Rosalind. The last character, already well

* Of the *British Weekly*.

beloved in the reading, I had the good fortune to see, I must think, in an impressionable hour, played by Mrs. Scott Siddons. Nothing has ever more moved, more delighted, more refreshed me; nor has the influence quite passed away. Kent's brief speech over the dying Lear had a great effect upon my mind, and was the burthen of my reflections for long, so profoundly, so touchingly generous did it appear in sense, so overpowering in expression. Perhaps my dearest and best friend outside of Shakespeare is D'Artagnan—the elderly D'Artagnan of the *Vicomte de Bragelonne*. I know not a more human soul, nor, in his way, a finer; I shall be very sorry for the man who is so much of a pedant in morals that he cannot learn from the Captain of Musketeers. Lastly, I must name the *Pilgrim's Progress*, a book that breathes of every beautiful and valuable emotion.

But of works of art little can be said; their influence is profound and silent, like the influence of nature; they mould by contact; we drink them up like water, and are bettered, yet know not how. It is in books more specifically didactic that we can follow out the effect, and distinguish and weigh and compare. A book which has been very influential upon me fell early into my hands, and so may stand first, though I think its influence was only sensible later on, and perhaps still keeps growing, for it is a book not easily outlived: the *Essais* of Montaigne. That temperate and genial picture of life is a great gift to place in the hands of persons of to-day; they will find in these smiling pages a magazine of heroism and wisdom, all of an antique strain; they will have their " linen decencies " and excited orthodoxies fluttered, and will (if they have any gift of reading) perceive that these have not been fluttered without some excuse and ground of reason; and (again if they have any gift of reading) they will end by seeing that this old gentleman was in a dozen ways a finer fellow, and held in a dozen ways a nobler view of life than they or their contemporaries.

The next book, in order of time, to influence me, was the New Testament, and in particular the Gospel according to St. Matthew. I believe it would startle and move anyone if they could make a certain effort of imagination and read it freshly like a book, not droningly and dully like a portion of the Bible. Anyone would then be able to see in it those truths which we are all courteously supposed to know and all modestly refrain from applying. But upon this subject it is perhaps better to be silent.

I come next to Whitman's *Leaves of Grass*, a book of singular service, a book which tumbled the world upside down for me, blew into space a thousand cobwebs of genteel and ethical illusion, and, having thus shaken my tabernacle of lies, set me back again upon a strong foundation of all the original and manly virtues. But it is, once more, only a book for those who have the gift of reading. I will be very frank—I believe it is so with all good books except, perhaps, fiction. The average man lives, and must live, so wholly in convention, that gunpowder charges of the truth are more apt to discompose than to invigorate his creed. Either he cries out upon blasphemy and indecency, and crouches the closer round that little idol of part-truths and part-conveniences which is the contemporary deity, or he is convinced by what is new, forgets what is old, and becomes truly blasphemous and indecent himself. New truth is only useful to supplement the old; rough truth is only wanted to expand, not to destroy, our civil and often elegant conventions. He who cannot judge had better stick to fiction and the daily papers. There he will get little harm, and, in the first at least, some good.

Close upon the back of my discovery of Whitman, I

came under the influence of Herbert Spencer. No more persuasive rabbi exists, and few better. How much of his vast structure will bear the touch of time, how much is clay and how much brass, it were too curious to inquire. But his words, if dry, are always manly and honest; there dwells in his pages a spirit of highly abstract joy, plucked naked like an algebraic symbol but still joyful; and the reader will find there a *caput-mortuum* of piety, with little indeed of its loveliness, but with most of its essentials; and these two qualities make him a wholesome, as his intellectual vigour makes him a bracing, writer. I should be much of a hound if I lost my gratitude to Herbert Spencer.

Goethe's Life, by Lewes, had a great importance for me when it first fell into my hands—a strange instance of the partiality of man's good and man's evil. I know no one whom I less admire than Goethe; he seems a very epitome of the sins of genius, breaking open the doors of private life and wantonly wounding friends, in that crowning offence of *Werther*, and in his own character a mere pen-and-ink Napoleon, conscious of the rights and duties of superior talents as a Spanish inquisitor was conscious of the rights and duties of his office. And yet in his fine devotion to his art, in his honest and serviceable friendship for Schiller, what lessons are contained! Biography, usually so false to its office, does here for once perform for us some of the work of fiction, reminding us, that is, of the truly mingled tissue of man's nature, and how huge faults and shining virtues cohabit and persevere in the same character. History serves us well to this effect, but in the originals not in the pages of the popular epitomiser, who is bound, by the very nature of his task, to make us feel the difference of epochs instead of the essential identity of man, and even in the originals only to those who can recognise their own human virtues and defects in strange forms often inverted, and under strange names often interchanged. Martial is a poet of no good repute, and it gives a man new thoughts to read his works dispassionately, and find in this unseemly jester's serious passages the image of a kind, wise, and self-respecting gentleman. It is customary, I suppose, in reading Martial, to leave out these pleasant verses; I never heard of them, at least, until I found them for myself; and this partiality is one among a thousand things that help to build up our distorted and hysterical conception of the great Roman Empire.

This brings us by a natural transition to a very noble book—the *Meditations* of Marcus Aurelius. The dispassionate gravity, the noble forgetfulness of self, the tenderness of others, that are there expressed and were practised on so great a scale in the life of its writer, make this book a book quite by itself. No one can read it and not be moved. Yet it scarcely or rarely appeals to the feelings—those very mobile, those not very trusty parts of man. Its address lies further back: its lesson comes more deeply home; when you have read, you carry away with you a memory of the man himself; it is as though you had touched a loyal hand, looked into brave eyes, and made a noble friend; there is another bond on you thenceforward, binding you to life and to the love of virtue.

Wordsworth should perhaps come next. Everyone has been influenced by Wordsworth, and it is hard to tell precisely how. A certain innocence, a rugged austerity of joy, a sight of the stars, " the silence that is in the lonely hills," something of the cold thrill of dawn, cling to his work and give it a particular address to what is best in us. I do not know that you learn a lesson; you need not—Mill did not—agree with any one of his beliefs; and yet the spell is cast. Such are the best teachers: a dogma learned is only a new error

—the old one was perhaps as good; but a spirit communicated is a perpetual possession. These best teachers climb beyond teaching to the plane of art; it is themselves, and what is best in themselves, that they communicate.

I should never forgive myself if I forgot *The Egoist*. It is art, if you like, but it belongs purely to didactic art, and from all the novels I have read (and I have read thousands) stands in a place by itself. Here is a Nathan for the modern David; here is a book to send the blood into men's faces. Satire, the angry picture of human faults, is not great art; we can all be angry with our neighbour; what we want is to be shown, not his defects, of which we are too conscious, but his merits, to which we are too blind. And *The Egoist* is a satire; so much must be allowed; but it is a satire of a singular quality, which tells you nothing of that obvious mote, which is engaged from first to last with that invisible beam. It is yourself that is hunted down; these are your own faults that are dragged into the day and numbered, with lingering relish, with cruel cunning and precision. A young friend of Mr. Meredith's (as I have the story) came to him in an agony. " This is too bad of you," he cried. " Willoughby is me!" " No, my dear fellow," said the author; " he is all of us." I have read *The Egoist* five or six times myself, and I mean to read it again; for I am like the young friend of the anecdote—I think Willoughby an unmanly but a very serviceable exposure of myself.

I suppose, when I am done, I shall find that I have forgotten much that was most influential, as I see already I have forgotten Thoreau, and Hazlitt whose paper " On the Spirit of Obligations " was a turning-point in my life, and Pen whose little book of aphorisms had a brief but strong effect on me, and Mitford's *Tales of Old Japan*, wherein I learned for the first time the proper attitude of any rational man to his country's laws—a secret found, and kept, in the Asiatic islands. That I should commemorate all is more than I can hope or the Editor could ask. It will be more to the point, after having said so much upon improving books, to say a word or two about the improvable reader. The gift of reading, as I have called it, is not very common, nor very generally understood. It consists, first of all, in a vast intellectual endowment—a free grace, I find I must call it—by which a man rises to understand that he is not punctually right, nor those from whom he differs absolutely wrong. He may hold dogmas; he may hold them passionately; and he may know that others hold them but coldly, or hold them differently, or hold them not at all. Well, if he has the gift of reading, these others will be full of meat for him. They will see the other side of propositions and the other side of virtues. He need not change his dogma for that, but he may change his reading of that dogma, and he must supplement and correct his deductions from it. A human truth, which is always very much a lie, hides as much of life as it displays. It is men who hold another truth, or, as it seems to us, perhaps, a dangerous lie, who can extend our restricted field of knowledge, and rouse our drowsy consciences. Something that seems quite new, or that seems insolently false or very dangerous, is the test of a reader. If he tries to see what it means, what truth excuses it, he has the gift, and let him read. If he is merely hurt, or offended, or exclaims upon his author's folly, he had better take to the daily papers; he will never be a reader.

And here, with the aptest illustrative force, after I have laid down my part-truth, I must step in with its opposite. For, after all, we are vessels of a very limited content. Not all men can read all books; it is only in a chosen few that any man will find his appointed food;

and the fittest lessons are the most palatable, and make themselves welcome to the mind. A writer learns this early, and it is his chief support; he goes on unafraid, laying down the law; and he is sure at heart that most of what he says is demonstrably false, and much of a mingled strain, and some hurtful, and very little good for service; but he is sure besides that when his words fall into the hands of any genuine reader, they will be weighed and winnowed, and only that which suits will be assimilated; and when they fall into the hands of one who cannot intelligently read, they come there quite silent and inarticulate, falling upon deaf ears, and his secret is kept as if he had not written.

A NOTE ON REALISM

Style is the invariable mark of any master; and for the student who does not aspire so high as to be numbered with the giants, it is still the one quality in which he may improve himself at will. Passion, wisdom, creative force, the power of mystery or colour, are allotted in the hour of birth, and can be neither learned nor simulated. But the just and dexterous use of what qualities we have, the proportion of one part to another and to the whole, the elision of the useless, the accentuation of the important, and the preservation of a uniform character from end to end—these, which taken together constitute technical perfection, are to some degree within the reach of industry and intellectual courage. What to put in and what to leave out; whether some particular fact be organically necessary or purely ornamental; whether, if it be purely ornamental, it may not weaken or obscure the general design; and finally, whether, if we decide to use it, we should do so grossly and notably or in some conventional disguise: are questions of plastic style continually re-arising. And the sphinx that patrols the highways of executive art has no more unanswerable riddle to propound.

In literature (from which I must draw my instances) the great change of the past century has been effected by the admission of detail. It was inaugurated by the romantic Scott; and at length, by the semi-romantic Balzac and his more or less wholly unromantic followers, bound like a duty on the novelist. For some time it signified and expressed a more ample contemplation of the conditions of man's life; but it has recently (at least in France) fallen into a merely technical and decorative stage, which it is, perhaps, still too harsh to call survival. With a movement of alarm, the wiser or more timid begin to fall a little back from these extremities; they begin to aspire after a more naked, narrative articulation; after the succinct, the dignified, and the poetic; and as a means to this, after a general lightening of this baggage of detail. After Scott we beheld the starveling story—once, in the hands of Voltaire, as abstract as a parable—begin to be pampered upon facts. The introduction of these details developed a particular ability of hand; and that ability, childishly indulged, has led to the works that now amaze us on a railway journey. A man of the unquestionable force of M. Zola spends himself on technical successes. To afford a popular flavour and attract the mob, he adds a steady current of what I may be allowed to call the rancid. That is exciting to the moralist; but what more particularly interests the artist is this tendency of the extreme of detail, when followed as a principle, to degenerate into mere *feux-de-joie* of literary tricking. The other day even M. Daudet was to be heard babbling of audible colours and visible sounds.

This odd suicide of one branch of the realists may serve to remind us of the fact which underlies a very dusty conflict of the critics. All representative art, which can be said to live, is both realistic and ideal; and the realism about which we quarrel is a matter purely of externals. It is no especial cultus of nature and veracity, but a mere whim of veering fashion, that has made us turn our back upon the larger, more various, and more romantic art of yore. A photographic exactitude in dialogue is now the exclusive fashion; but even in the ablest hands it tells us no more—I think it even tells us less—than Molière, wielding his artificial medium, has told to us and to all time of Alceste or Orgon, Dorine or Chrysale. The historical novel is forgotten. Yet truth to the conditions of man's nature and the conditions of man's life, the truth of literary art, is free of the ages. It may be told us in a carpet comedy, in a novel of adventure, or a fairy tale. The scene may

78

be pitched in London, on the sea-coast of Bohemia, or away on the mountains of Beulah. And by an odd and luminous accident, if there is any page of literature calculated to awake the envy of M. Zola, it must be that *Troilus and Cressida* which Shakespeare, in a spasm of unmanly anger with the world, grafted on the heroic story of the siege of Troy.

This question of realism, let it be then clearly understood, regards not in the least degree the fundamental truth, but only the technical method, of a work of art. Be as ideal or as abstract as you please, you will be none the less veracious; but if you be weak, you run the risk of being tedious and inexpressive; and if you be very strong and honest, you may chance upon a masterpiece.

A work of art is first cloudily conceived in the mind; during the period of gestation it stands more clearly forward from these swaddling mists, puts on expressive lineaments, and becomes at length that most faultless, but also, alas! that incommunicable product of the human mind, a perfected design. On the approach to execution all is changed. The artist must now step down, don his working clothes, and become the artisan. He now resolutely commits his airy conception, his delicate Ariel, to the touch of matter; he must decide, almost in a breath, the scale, the style, the spirit, and the particularity of execution of his whole design.

The engendering idea of some works is stylistic; a technical preoccupation stands them instead of some robuster principle of life. And with these the execution is but play; for the stylistic problem is resolved beforehand, and all large originality of treatment wilfully foregone. Such are the verses, intricately designed, which we have learnt to admire, with a certain smiling admiration, at the hands of Mr. Lang and Mr. Dobson; such, too, are those canvases where dexterity or even breadth of plastic style takes the place of pictorial nobility of design. So, it may be remarked, it was easier to begin to write *Esmond* than *Vanity Fair*, since, in the first, the style was dictated by the nature of the plan; and Thackeray, a man probably of some indolence of mind, enjoyed and got good profit of this economy of effort. But the case is exceptional. Usually in all works of art that have been conceived from within outwards, and generously nourished from the author's mind, the moment in which he begins to execute is one of extreme perplexity and strain. Artists of indifferent energy and an imperfect devotion to their own ideal make this ungrateful effort once for all; and, having formed a style, adhere to it through life. But those of a higher order cannot rest content with a process which, as they continue to employ it, must infallibly degenerate toward the academic and the cut-and-dried. Every fresh work in which they embark is the signal for a fresh engagement of the whole forces of their mind; and the changing views which accompany the growth of their experience are marked by still more sweeping alterations in the manner of their art. So that criticism loves to dwell upon and distinguish the varying periods of a Raphael, a Shakespeare, or a Beethoven.

It is, then, first of all, at this initial and decisive moment when execution is begun, and thenceforth only in a less degree, that the ideal and the real do indeed, like good and evil angels, contend for the direction of the work. Marble, paint, and language, the pen, the needle, and the brush, all have their grossnesses, their ineffable impotences, their hours, if I may so express myself, of insubordination. It is the work and it is a great part of the delight of any artist to contend with these unruly tools, and now by brute energy, now by witty expedient, to drive and coax them to effect his will. Given these means, so laughably inadequate, and given the interest, the intensity, and the multiplicity of the actual sensation whose effect he is to render with their aid, the artist has one main and necessary resource which he must, in every case and upon any theory, employ. He must, that is, suppress much and omit more. He must omit what is tedious or irrelevant, and suppress what is tedious and necessary. But such facts as, in regard to the main design, subserve a variety of purposes, he will perforce and eagerly retain. And it is the mark of the very highest order of creative art to be woven exclusively of such. There, any fact that is registered is contrived a double or a treble debt to pay, and is at once an ornament in its place and a pillar in the main design. Nothing would find room in such a picture that did not serve, at once, to complete the composition, to accentuate the scheme of colour, to distinguish the planes of distance, and to strike the note of the selected sentiment; nothing would be allowed in such a story that did not, at the same time, expedite the progress of the fable, build up the characters, and strike home the moral or the philosophical design. But this is unattainable. As a rule, so far from building the fabric of our works exclusively with these, we are thrown into a rapture if we think we can muster a dozen or a score of them, to be the plums of our confection. And hence, in order that the canvas may be filled or the story proceed from point to point, other details must be admitted. They must be admitted, alas! upon a doubtful title; many without marriage robes. Thus any work of art, as it proceeds toward completion, too often—I had almost written always—loses in force and poignancy of main design. Our little air is swamped and dwarfed among hardly relevant orchestration; our little passionate story drowns in a deep sea of descriptive eloquence or slipshod talk.

But again, we are rather more tempted to admit those particulars which we know we can describe; and hence those most of all which, having been described very often, have grown to be conventionally treated in the practice of our art. These we choose, as the mason chooses the acanthus to adorn his capital, because they come naturally to the accustomed hand. The old stock incidents and accessories, tricks of workmanship and schemes of composition (all being admirably good, or they would long have been forgotten) haunt and tempt our fancy, offer us ready-made but not perfectly appropriate solutions for any problem that arises, and wean us from the study of nature and the uncompromising practice of art. To struggle, to face nature, to find fresh solutions, and give expression to facts which have not yet been adequately or not yet elegantly expressed, is to run a little upon the danger of extreme self-love. Difficulty sets a high price upon achievement; and the artist may easily fall into the error of the French naturalists, and consider any fact as welcome to admission if it be the ground of brilliant handiwork; or, again, into the error of the modern landscape-painter, who is apt to think that difficulty overcome and science well displayed can take the place of what is, after all, the one excuse and breath of art—charm. A little further, and he will regard charm in the light of an unworthy sacrifice to prettiness, and the omission of a tedious passage as an infidelity to art.

We have now the matter of this difference before us. The idealist, his eye singly fixed upon the greater outlines, loves rather to fill up the interval with detail of the conventional order, briefly touched, soberly suppressed in tone, courting neglect. But the realist, with a fine intemperance, will not suffer the presence of anything so dead as a convention; he shall have all fiery, all hot-pressed from nature, all charactered and notable, seizing the eye. The style that befits either of these extremes, once chosen, brings with it its necessary disabilities and dangers. The immediate danger of the realist is to sacrifice the beauty and significance of the whole to local dexterity, or, in the insane pursuit of completion, to immolate his readers under facts; but he comes in the last resort, and as his energy declines, to discard all design, abjure all choice, and, with scientific thoroughness, steadily to communicate matter which is not worth learning. The danger of the idealist is, of course, to become merely null and lose all grip of fact, particularity, or passion.

We talk of bad and good. Everything, indeed, is good which is conceived with honesty and executed with communicative ardour. But though on neither side is dogmatism fitting, and though in every case the artist must decide for himself, and decide afresh and yet afresh for each succeeding work and new creation; yet one thing may be generally said, that we of the last quarter of the nineteenth century, breathing as we do the intellectual atmosphere of our age, are more apt to err upon the side of realism than to sin in quest of the ideal. Upon that theory it may be well to watch and correct our own decisions, always holding back the hand from the least appearance of irrelevant dexterity, and resolutely fixed to begin no work that is not philosophical, passionate, dignified, happily mirthful, or, at the last and least, romantic in design.

EARLIER WORKS

EARLIER WORKS

JUVENILIA

I

HISTORY OF MOSES

THERE was a woman that had a child when all the babies were to be drowned and she was a good woman and she asked God how she could save her baby and God told her to make a baskets of rushes and put it in the water, hiding it in the rushes. Then Pharaoh's daughter was going to bathe in a certain place and as she went past she saw the cradle and asked her servants to go and bring it out and they did it. When they brought it out they lifted the thing up that was on the top and they saw a baby crying. Then they saw the child's sister that was standing far away and Pharaoh's daughter cried to her to come and when she came she told her to call a nurse for the baby and then she ran and brought the mother of it and she told the mother to take charge of it and to come to the palace and so she came.

Then Moses when he was grown up was sent away to show some wonders to the Israelites and God told him the things he was to do. He first told him to lay down his rod and when he laid it down it became a serpent. Then he told him to go and do it when he was with the Israelites and he said he would do it. Then God told him to put his hand into his breast and he did so and his hand became a leper, then he pulled it out and he put it in again and when he pulled it out it was just the way it was before. Then God told him to do that and he went away home to the house that he lived in and God told him that he would have to go to the Israelites. Then he went away to the Israelites.

One day Moses saw an Egyptian whipping an Israelite and he came and killed the Egyptian. It was not wrong of Moses to kill the Egyptian because he was doing harm to the Israelite for he was an Israelite too. After that God told Aaron and Moses to go up and try to make Pharaoh let the Israelites go away and then Aaron and Moses went up to speak to him and asked him if he would allow them to go and Pharaoh said no that he wouldn't. Then Aaron laid down the rod and behold it became a serpent. He took it by the tail and pulled it up and it turned into a rod. He put his hand into his breast and it became a leper and he put it in again and it was just as it was before. Then the Egyptians took all their rods and laid them down and they became serpents. Pharaoh said that he would let them go but he hardened his heart and would not. When Pharaoh was going to bathe at a certain place Aaron stretched his rod over the water and it became blood. Then Pharaoh went home in despair and he said he would let them go but he hardened his heart again. Then Aaron stretched out his rod and frogs came forth and crept over all the beds and eat up all the food and everything and he said he would let them go but he hardened his heart again.

Then the next plague was little insects called lice which went all over the country. After that he sent swarms of flies which buzzed about in the most horrible manner. Then boils came all over the people even over Pharaoh and his servants. After that came deaths of beasts and nearly all the beasts died. Then God sent hail and rain and fire and thunder and before he sent it he told Pharaoh and all his people to keep in their houses. After that it happened all the grass was taken away and all the leaves off the trees by locusts. Then it turned all darkness and it was all light beside the Israelites. And God said to the Israelites that they must get all ready and stand round at a table eating a lamb and spread the blood of the lamb on the lintels of their doors for that the angel of death was going to pass to kill all the babies but whoever has the blood on the lintels wouldn't have their babies killed. Then when the Egyptians had gone to bed thinking of no danger, the angel of death passed through and every baby even Pharaoh's first born was killed and there was a great cry over all the land. Then Pharaoh cried for Moses and Aaron as quickly as possible and he said that they must go away as fast as they could and they all went and took their bags of meat and their flocks and they asked the women of Egypt to give them gold and silver and they did so.

They came to a sea called the Red Sea, now don't suppose it was red like blood, so the black cloud stood still that had led them all the way and they encamped and soon they heard a great noise of horses and chariots and it was the Egyptians coming after them. They then told Moses to go and pray to God and he did so. Then God told Moses to stretch out his rod over the Red Sea and he did so. Lo and behold the waters went up on each side of a dry path like walls, then the Israelites went into the path to cross. After they had got a little way across the Egyptians came up and they saw a dry path and they determined to go over it. They had not got very far across when lo and behold to their terror the wheels of their chariots stuck like as if in mud as God poured down his wrath and the thunder roared and such lightnings as were never seen in Egypt (this is in line upon line). God told Moses to stretch his rod over the water and he did so and the walls of water came down upon the tops of the Egyptians and they were drowned.

Then the Israelites were very hungry and they began to speak to Moses about it. Then Moses prayed to God

and God told Moses that the Israelites were to get up
very early in the morning and they would see small
white things on the ground and they were to gather it
but they were not to gather any for to-morrow because
it would breed worms and stink and they could not eat
it but on Saturdays they were to gather some for Sundays because on Sundays they would not see any little
white things. So they rose up early in the morning and
they went out and they did see little white things and
they called it manna. It tasted like honey. Then they
were thirsty and they murmured against Moses and
against God and so Moses went to pray to God and
God told Moses to go up to a rock with a few men and
to strike the rock with his rod and water would come
out, so he did so and water came flowing forth. Then
they travelled on through the wilderness and they came
to a mount called Sinai. God told Moses to come up
to him in the mount and Moses went up. God told
Moses that he was to tell the Israelites to wash their
clothes for they were to hear him speaking on the third
day. They did so and on the third morning they heard
his voice and the trumpet sounded loud. And he was
to put railing round the mountain and he was not to
let any of the people touch the mountain or the rail-
ings. Moses stayed forty days and forty nights with
God and God gave him two tables of stone with ten
commandments written on them and the Israelites
thought the time so long they thought he was never to
come back so they asked Aaron to make them a golden
calf. He told them to give all their gold earrings and
things so he melted them and took it out and when it
was soft he cut it into the shape of a calf. Then he took
it and put it upon a high place and he said they should
have a great feast to-morrow and so they had a grand
feast and they danced round the calf and cried, " This
is the one who brought us out of Egypt," and Moses

was coming down at that time and he saw the Israelites dancing round the image and he broke the tables of stone because he was so angry and he came down very quickly and took the calf and melted it and ground it into powder and threw it into some water and made them drink it and God said that somebody must take a sword and kill some of them and Moses asked God not to kill the whole of them and said, " Remember what you promised to Jacob."

Then Moses went up into the mount again and God told him to make a tabernacle and he told him of two clever men which could help them, to carve wood and things. Their names were Bezaleel and Aholiab. When Moses went down they could not look upon him because he shone with the glory of God and he put a veil over his face. Then he told the Israelites that they were to make a tabernacle for God and Moses asked them for their gold and silver and all their beautiful things to make it of and they gave them. In the court of the tabernacle there was a brazen altar for offering lambs and oxes upon and there was a brazen basin a little farther in, in which the priests used to wash the dishes and their hands. Then in the inside in the holy place there was a golden altar for burning incense on and a candlestick which had seven lamps upon it. Then draw up the veil of the tabernacle, you will see the Holy of Holies and in it a large box of gold, the top of which was called the Mercy Seat and there was two gold angels that bent their wings over the top, in the inside there was Aaron's budding rod and the tables of stone. The Holy of Holies was a light place because the glory of God was in it.

After the Israelites left Mount Sinai they came to a place near Canaan and they sent twelve men to see what like it was. When they had come into it they saw a great vine and so they plucked a bunch of grapes and one man could not carry it so they took a long staff and tied the grapes to it and Caleb and Joshua carried it and the rest carried figs and pomegranates. Then when they came to the Israelites they asked what kind of place it was and they said that the cities had strong gates and walls and that the people were giants and they were just like grasshoppers beside them. Then the Israelites said no, they would never conquer them. Then Caleb and Joshua struck up and said yes they would for God would help them for the people in Canaan only worshipped images. But the people did not believe Caleb and Joshua and sat up all night moaning and crying. Then God was angry and said they would never come into Canaan but were to wander forty years in the wilderness, but their children when they grew up were to go into Canaan and Caleb and Joshua were to go. They travelled away from that place into the wilderness then they murmured and said to Moses, " Why did you bring us out of Egypt? Here we have neither water nor food." Then Moses prayed to God and God told him to take his rod and speak to the rock. Then Moses went away and took his rod and Aaron came with Moses and they said, " Here now ye rebels must we bring you water out of this rock," and Moses struck the rock with his rod and water came flowing forth and God said to Moses and Aaron that they should not go into Canaan but should die and Moses prayed to God and asked him if he might not go into it and God told him not to pray any more because he should not go into it but God said to Moses that he should not die as soon as Aaron.

Then when they came to a place in the wilderness there was a great lot of serpents and their mouths burned like fire and God sent them among them when they murmured and they bit them and it made them very ill and they said to Moses to pray to God that he might take away the serpents from them. Then God told Moses to take some brass and soften it in the fire and to cut it into the shape of one of the serpents and to put it upon a pole and to hold up the pole and the Israelites who looked at the serpent would get better. That should put us in mind of Jesus, because the old Serpent the Devil bit us, that means made us naughty and when we look at Jesus that makes us better—not to look at Jesus with our eyes but to look with praying. Then God took away the serpents and when the Israelites looked at the brazen serpent they were quite well.

Then God said to Moses that he would have to die and God sent Moses alone up to a high hill called Nebo where he could see the whole land of Canaan and God buried him in a valley in the land of Moab and nobody knows where Moses was buried to this day. And there was great weeping in all Israel for Moses.

II

THE BOOK OF JOSEPH

BY R. L. B. S.

THE AUTHOR OF " A HISTORY OF MOSES "

CHAPTER I

JOSEPH IS SOLD AS A SLAVE

Jacob of old married two wives; one of his wives was called Rachael & the other Leah. Rachael's eldest son was Joseph which I intend to found my story on. Well, Joseph was his father's favourite & so his father made him a coat of many colours. Joseph had eleven brothers & they envied him very much. Well, one day the brothers were feeding their sheep afar off & Joseph's father said to him that he was to go with some loaves to his brethern. When Joseph came to the place they were not there & he met a man when he was searching for them & the man said that his brethern had gone over to Dothan and when Joseph was very far off they saw him coming. Now Joseph had dreamt that he and his brethern had been out cutting corn in the fields and binding sheaves & it came to pass that all his brethern's sheaves bowed down to his sheaf & he told his dream to his brethern. And he also dreamed another dream. He thought he was a star and that the sun & the moon & 11 stars bowed down to him & he told that dream also to his brethern from which he derived the name of the dreamer. Well, when they saw him, they said among themselves " behold this dreamer cometh, come let us kill him " but Reuben said " do not slay him but put him into this pit here " by which means Reuben intended to get Joseph by stealth to his father, however this plan failed as you shall hear. Well, when Joseph came up to them, they laid hands upon him & cast him into the pit. Well, Reuben went away, but when he came back, he was alarmed when he came back by the following occurrence. When the other brethern had sat down to meat there came in sight some camels and mules with a lot of merchants with spices & they said among one another " let us sell him to those merchants." Well, when the merchants came up they asked how much they would give for him & they said three talents of silver. So they drew Joseph out of the pit & sold him to the merchants. And they carried him down to Egypt where they sold him to the captain of Pharoah's guard.

Well, the wife of Potiphar brought out false accusations against Joseph & got him put in prison. There happened to be in the jail the chief baker of Pharoah and the chief butler of Pharoah. Well, one night they each dreamt a dream & the butler & the baker knew not the meaning of it. When Joseph heard it he said he knew the meaning of it, he said that in three days the butler would be restored out of jail & would squeeze the grapes into the cup of Pharoah again. And as to the baker's dream, he said that in three days the baker would be hung upon a tree & the birds would pick his flesh & it came to pass as you shall hear, for in three days was Pharoah's birthday & all manner of justice was to be done that day, so the chief butler was restored and the chief baker was hanged. The Chief Butler did not remember Joseph but forgot him.

CHAPTER II

THE DREAM AND ITS INTERPRETATION

Now, it came to pass that Pharoah dreamt a dream & he dreamed that he stood by the water & there came out of the water 7 well fed fat kine & they grazed in a meadow & also there came up out of the water 7 lean ill favoured kine & they eat up the fat ones but seemed none the fatter of it. And Pharoah awoke & behold it was a dream & he fell asleep and dreamed again & behold he was standing by the water again & there came up out of the water 7 good ears of wheat on one stalk & also out of the same water there came 7 lean and ill favoured ears of wheat & they eat up the fat ones but were none the fatter of it & Pharoah awoke & behold it was a dream. In the morning he called all the magicians and wise men of Egypt, but they could not interpret it. Then the chief butler said, " I do remember my faults this day for when the chief baker & I displeased King Pharoah & he cast us both into prison & we both dreamed a dream & there happened to be an Hebrew lad with us in the jail & he interpreted our dream & it came to pass according to his interpretation." So Pharoah sent to the prison for Joseph & Joseph shaved and put on new raiment & came before Pharoah & Pharoah told him his dream & Joseph said the dream is one & he said that the 7 kine & the 7 ears were years & that 7 fat kine & full ears were years of plenty & the seven thin kine & blasted ears were years of famine & he told Pharoah to put a wise man over the nation & gather up a fifth of the corn during the years of plenty for store during the years of famine. This interpretation pleased Pharoah & he said, There is not a wiser man in the country than thou & he set him over the land & he got the second chariot to ride in & he put a chain round his neck & a ring on his finger & Pharoah's servants went before him saying, " bow the knee,"

CHAPTER III

THE FAMINE

Now, when the 7 years of plenty were come, Joseph took all the wheat & corn & barley from the fields round the cities & laid it up in barns. And behold the famine waxed sore over the face of the world & Joseph's brethern heard that there was corn in Egypt & came down on asses with sacks & they came unto Joseph for it was Joseph that sold the corn.

Now, Joseph knew his brethern, but they did not know him & he spoke roughly to them & said that they were spies come to spy the nakedness of the land & they said no, that they were 12 brethern & that the youngest was at home with their father & that one was not. But he would not believe them & said that they must bring down their brother to let him see him. And he took Simeon out of their midst & bound him & put him in jail & said that the others must go & bring down their brother. So they went their way & as one of them opened his sack, he found his bag of money on the top & they were sorely afraid at this & said, " What hath the Lord done to us." When they came home the others opened their sacks & they found their money, too. And when they told their father that Benjamin must go to Egypt, he was very sorry & said Joseph is not & Simeon is not & will ye take Benjamin away; if evil befals him ye will bring down my grey hairs with sorrow to the grave.

CHAPTER IV

JOSEPH MAKES HIMSELF KNOWN TO HIS BRETHERN &
HIS FATHER COMES DOWN TO EGYPT

And when the food which the brothers had brought
was exhausted, their father said, " Go up to the man
& buy some more corn that we may eat." They said
that the man had said that they should not see his face
again until their brother came down but Jacob did not
want him to go lest peradventure evil should befal him.
Then Judah said that he would answer for Benjamin's
safety with the life of his two sons & so their father
answered and said unto them " Take spices & almonds
& nuts & make a present unto the governor & take
also Benjamin with you & take double money." When
Joseph heard that his brothers had come he said, " Kill
and make ready for these men shall dine with me to-day
at noon."

When the brethern came in they were afraid and
talked at the door of Joseph's house to the keeper & he
said, " Do not be afraid. Your money is with me " and
they made the present ready against Joseph coming at
noon for they heard that they were to dine with him.
The keeper let Simeon out to them. When Joseph
came and looked and saw Benjamin, he said, " Is this
your younger brother that ye spake about" & he said
to Benjamin, " God be gracious unto thee, my son."
And Joseph made haste & went into his chamber &
wept & then he came out & restrained his feelings.
Then he said, " Lay bread." They set bread for Joseph
alone, for his brethern next, then for the Egyptians
who eat with him next all alone. For the Egyptians
may not eat bread with the Hebrews. Joseph commanded his steward to put his cup into the mouth of

the youngest's sack & he also commanded him to put their money in the mouths of their sacks & he said that he should run after them as soon as they were out of sight & ask them why they had stolen these things & why they had rewarded evil for good.

The steward did so & overtook them & he said unto them what he had been told, then they opened every one his sack, beginning at the eldest and ending at the youngest & the cup was found in Benjamin's sack & they came back & Joseph said unto them " What is this that ye have done? " and Judah came forward & told him that he had wished them to bring their youngest brother & that their father would hardly let them & that if he kept Benjamin, he would bring down their father's grey hairs with sorrow to the grave. Then Joseph wept & he said unto them, " I am Joseph whom ye sold unto Egypt, is my father yet alive? " & they were terrified & he said, be not grieved that ye sold me for I was sent here by God to save life. And Joseph told them to bring their father down in haste.

THE PENTLAND RISING

A PAGE OF HISTORY
1666

"A cloud of witnesses ly here,
Who for Christ's interest did appear."
Inscription on Battle-field at Rullion Green.

I

THE CAUSES OF THE REVOLT

"Halt, passenger; take heed what thou dost see,
This tomb doth show for what some men did die."
*Monument, Greyfriars' Churchyard, Edinburgh, 1661–1668.**

Two hundred years ago a tragedy was enacted in Scotland, the memory whereof has been in great measure lost or obscured by the deeper tragedies which followed it. It is, as it were, the evening of the night of persecution—a sort of twilight, dark indeed to us, but light as the noonday when compared with the midnight gloom which followed. This fact, of its being the very threshold of persecution, lends it, however, an additional interest.

The prejudices of the people against Episcopacy were " out of measure increased," says Bishop Burnet, " by the new incumbents, who were put in the place of the ejected preachers, and were generally very mean and despicable in all respects. They were the worst preachers I ever heard; they were ignorant to a reproach; and many of them were openly vicious. They were indeed the dregs and refuse of the northern parts. Those of them who rose above contempt or scandal were men of such violent tempers that they were as much hated as the others were despised."† It was little

* Theatre of Mortality, p. 10, Edin. 1713.

† History of my Own Times, beginning 1660, by Bishop Gilbert Burnet, p. 158.

to be wondered at, from this account, that the country-folk refused to go to the parish church, and chose rather to listen to outed ministers in the field. But this was not to be allowed, and their persecutors at last fell on the method of calling a roll of the parishioners' names every Sabbath and marking a fine of twenty shillings Scots to the name of each absenter. In this way very large debts were incurred by persons altogether unable to pay. Besides this, landlords were fined for their tenants' absences, tenants for their landlords', masters for their servants', servants for their masters', even though they themselves were perfectly regular in their attendance. And as the curates were allowed to fine with the sanction of any common soldier, it may be imagined that often the pretexts were neither very sufficient nor well proven.

When the fines could not be paid at once, bibles, clothes, and household utensils were seized upon, or a number of soldiers, proportionate to his wealth, were quartered on the offender. The coarse and drunken privates filled the houses with woe; snatched the bread from the children to feed their dogs; shocked the principles, scorned the scruples, and blasphemed the religion of their humble hosts; and when they had reduced them to destitution, sold the furniture, and burned down the roof-tree, which was consecrated to the peasants by the name of Home. For all this attention each of these soldiers received from his unwilling landlord a certain sum of money per day—three shillings sterling, according to " Naphtali." And frequently they were forced to pay quartering money for more men than were in reality " cessed " on them. At that time it was no strange thing to behold a strong man begging for money to pay his fines, and many others who were deep in arrears, or who had attracted attention in some other way, were forced to flee from

their homes, and take refuge from arrest and imprisonment among the wild mosses of the uplands.*

One example in particular we may cite:—

John Nielson, the Laird of Corsack, a worthy man,
was, unfortunately for himself, a Nonconformist. First
he was fined in four hundred pounds Scots, and then
through cessing he lost nineteen hundred and ninety-
three pounds Scots. He was next obliged to leave his
house and flee from place to place, during which wan-
derings he lost his horse. His wife and children were
turned out of doors, and then his tenants were fined till
they too were almost all ruined. As a final stroke,
they drove away all his cattle to Glasgow and sold
them.† Surely it was time that something were done
to alleviate so much sorrow, to overthrow such
tyranny.

About this time too there arrived in Galloway a person calling himself Captain Andrew Gray, and advising
the people to revolt. He displayed some documents
purporting to be from the northern Covenanters, and
stating that they were prepared to join in any enterprise commenced by their southern brethren. The
leader of the persecutors was Sir James Turner, an
officer afterwards degraded for his share in the matter.
" He was naturally fierce, but was mad when he was
drunk, and that was very often," said Bishop Burnet.
" He was a learned man, but had always been in armies,
and knew no other rule but to obey orders. He told
me he had no regard to any law, but acted, as he was
commanded, in a military way."‡

This was the state of matters, when an outrage was
committed which gave spirit and determination to the
oppressed countrymen, lit the flame of insubordination,

* Wodrow's Church History, book II, chap. i, sect. 1.
† Crookshank's Church History, 1751, 2nd edit., p. 202.
‡ Burnet, p. 348.

and for the time at least recoiled on those who perpe-
trated it with redoubled force.

II

THE BEGINNING

I love no warres,
I love no jarres,
    Nor strife's fire,
May discord cease,
Let's live in peace :
    This I desire.
	If it must be,
	Warre we must see
	    (So fates conspire),
	May we not feel
	The force of steel :
	    This I desire.

T. JACKSON, 1651.*

Upon Tuesday, November 13th, 1666, Corporal
George Deanes and three other soldiers set upon an old
man in the Clachan of Dalry, and demanded the payment of his fines. On the old man's refusing to pay,
they forced a large party of his neighbours to go with
them and thresh his corn. The field was a certain distance out of the clachan, and four persons, disguised as
countrymen, who had been out on the moors all night,
met this mournful drove of slaves, compelled by the
four soldiers to work for the ruin of their friend. However, chilled to the bone by their night on the hills, and
worn out by want of food, they proceeded to the village
inn to refresh themselves. Suddenly some people
rushed into the room where they were sitting, and told
them that the soldiers were about to roast the old man,
naked, on his own girdle. This was too much for them
to stand, and they repaired immediately to the scene of
this gross outrage, and at first merely requested that
the captive should be released. On the refusal of the
two soldiers who were in the front room, high words
were given and taken on both sides, and the other two

* Fuller's Historie of the Holy Warre. 4th edit. 1651.

rushed forth from an adjoining chamber and made at
the countrymen with drawn swords. One of the latter,
John M'Lellan of Barskob, drew a pistol and shot the
corporal in the body. The pieces of tobacco pipe with
which it was loaded, to the number of ten at least,
entered him, and he was so much disturbed that he
never appears to have recovered, for we find long afterwards a petition to the Privy Council requesting a pension for him. The other soldiers then laid down their
arms, the old man was rescued, and the rebellion was
commenced.*

And now we must turn to Sir James Turner's
memoirs of himself; for, strange to say, this extraordinary man was remarkably fond of literary composition,
and wrote, besides the amusing account of his own
adventures just mentioned, a large number of essays
and short biographies, and a work on war, entitled
" Pallas Armata." The following are some of the
shorter pieces: *Magick, Friendship, Imprisonment, Anger,
Revenge, Duells, Cruelty, A Defence of some of the Ceremonies of the English Liturgie, to wit—Bowing at the
Name of Jesus, The frequent repetition of the Lord'.
Prayer and Good Lord deliver us, Of the Doxologie, Of
Surplesses, Rotchets, Cannonicall Coats*, etc. From what
we know of his character we should expect *Anger* and
Cruelty to be very full and instructive. But what earthly
right he had to meddle with ecclesiastical subjects it is
hard to see.

Upon the 12th of the month he had received some
information concerning Gray's proceedings, but as it
was excessively indefinite in its character, he paid no
attention to it. On the evening of the 14th, Corporal
Deanes was brought into Dumfries, who affirmed
stoutly that he had been shot while refusing to sign the
Covenant—a story rendered singularly unlikely by the

* Wodrow, vol. II, p. 17.

after conduct of the rebels. Sir James instantly despatched orders to the cessed soldiers either to come to Dumfries, or meet him on the way to Dalry, and commanded the thirteen or fourteen men in the town with him to come at nine next morning to his lodging for supplies.

On the morning of Thursday the rebels arrived at Dumfries with 50 horse and 150 foot. Nielson of Corsack, and Gray, who commanded, with a considerable troop, entered the town, and surrounded Sir James Turner's lodging. Though it was between eight and nine o'clock, that worthy, being unwell, was still in bed, but rose at once and went to the window.

Nielson and some others cried—" You may have fair quarter." " I need no quarter," replied Sir James; " nor can I be a prisoner, seeing there is no war declared." On being told, however, that he must either be a prisoner, or die, he came down and went into the street in his nightshirt. Here Gray showed himself very desirous of killing him, but he was overruled by Corsack. However, he was taken away a prisoner, Captain Gray mounting him on his own horse, though, as Turner naïvely remarks, " there was a good reason for it, for he mounted himself on a farre better one of mine." A large coffer containing his clothes and money, together with all his papers, were taken away by the rebels. They robbed Master Chalmers, the Episcopalian minister of Dumfries, of his horses, drank the King's health at the market-cross, and then left Dumfries.*

* Sir J. Turner's Memoirs, pp. 148–150.

III

THE MARCH OF THE REBELS

" Stay, passenger, take notice what thou reads,
    At Edinburgh lie our bodies, here our heads :
    Our right hands stood at Lanark, these we want,
    Because with them we signed the Covenant."

Epitaph on a Tombstone at Hamilton.*

On Friday the 16th, Bailie Irvine of Dumfries came
to the Council at Edinburgh, and gave information
concerning this " horrid rebellion." In the absence of
Rothes, Sharpe presided—much to the wrath of some
members; and as he imagined his own safety endan-
gered, his measures were most energetic. Dalzell was
ordered away to the west, the guards round the city
were doubled, officers and soldiers were forced to take
the oath of allegiance, and all lodgers were commanded
to give in their names. Sharpe, surrounded with all
these guards and precautions, trembled—trembled as
he trembled when the avengers of blood drew him
from his chariot on Magus Muir,—for he knew how
he had sold his trust, how he had betrayed his charge,
and he felt that against him must their chiefest hatred
be directed, against him their direst thunderbolts be
forged. But even in his fear the apostate Presbyterian
was unrelenting, unpityingly harsh; he published in
his manifesto no promise of pardon, no inducement to
submission. He said, " If you submit not you must
die," but never added, " If you submit you may live! "†

Meantime the insurgents proceeded on their way.
At Carsphairn they were deserted by Captain Gray,
who, doubtless in a fit of oblivion, neglected to leave

* A Cloud of Witnesses, p. 376.
    † Wodrow, pp. 19, 20.

behind him the coffer containing Sir James's money.
Who he was is a mystery, unsolved by any historian;
his papers were evidently forgeries—that, and his final
flight, appear to indicate that he was an agent of the
Royalists, for either the King or the Duke of York was
heard to say—" That, if he might have his wish, he
would have them all turn rebels and go to arms."*

Upon the 18th day of the month they left Carsphairn
and marched onwards.

Turner was always lodged by his captors at a good
inn, frequently at the best of which their halting-place
could boast. Here many visits were paid to him by the
ministers and officers of the insurgent force. In his
description of these interviews he displays a vein of
satiric severity, admitting any kindness that was done
to him with some qualifying souvenir of former harsh-
ness, and gloating over any injury, mistake, or folly
which it was his chance to suffer or to hear. He appears,
notwithstanding all this, to have been on pretty good
terms with his cruel " phanaticks," as the following
extract sufficiently proves :—

" Most of the foot were lodged about the church or
churchyard, and order given to ring bells next morning
for a sermon to be preached by Mr. Welsh. Maxwell
of Morith, and Major M'Cullough invited me to heare
' that phanatick sermon ' (for soe they merrilie called
it). They said that preaching might prove an effectual
meane to turne me, which they heartilie wished. I answered to them that I was under guards, and that if
they intended to heare that sermon, it was probable I
might likewise, for it was not like my guards wold goe
to church and leave me alone at my lodgeings. Bot to
what they said of my conversion, I said, it wold be hard
to turne a Turner. Bot because I founde them in a
merrie humour, I said, if I did not come to heare Mr.

* A Hind Let Loose, p. 123.

Earlier Works

Welch preach, then they might fine me in fortie shil
lings Scots, which was duoble the suome of what I had
exacted from the phanatics."* This took place at Ochil-
tree, on the 22nd day of the month. The following is
recounted by this personage with malicious glee, and
certainly, if authentic, it is a sad proof of how chaff is
mixed with wheat, and how ignorant, almost impious,
persons were engaged in this movement; nevertheless
we give it, for we wish to present with impartiality all
the alleged facts to the reader:—

"Towards the evening Mr. Robinsone and Mr.
Crukshank gaue me a visite; I called for some ale pur-
poselie to heare one of them blesse it. It fell Mr.
Robinsone to seeke the blessing, who said one of the
most bombastick graces that ever I heard in my life.
He summoned God Allmightie very imperiouslie to be
their secondarie (for that was his language). 'And if,'
said he, ' thou wilt not be our Secondarie, we will not
fight for thee at all, for it is not our cause bot thy cause;
and if thou wilt not fight for our cause and thy oune
cause, then we are not obliged to fight for it. They say,'
said he, ' that Dukes, Earles and Lords are coming
with the King's General against us, bot they shall be
nothing bot a threshing to us.' This grace did more
fullie satisfie me of the folly and injustice of their cause,
than the ale did quench my thirst."†

Frequently the rebels made a halt near some road-
side ale-house, or in some convenient park, where
Colonel Wallace, who had now taken the command,
would review the horse and foot, during which time
Turner was sent either into the ale-house or round the
shoulder of a hill, to prevent him from seeing the disorders which were likely to arise. He was, at last, on
the 25th day of the month, between Douglas and
Lanark, permitted to behold their evolutions. " I found

* Turner, p. 163.　　† Turner, p. 198.

their horse did consist of four hundreth and fortie and
the foot of five hundreth and upwards. . . . The horse-
men were armed for most part with suord and pistoll,
some onlie with suord. The foot with musket, pike,
sith [scythe], forke and suord; and some with suords
great and long." He admired much the proficiency of
their cavalry, and marvelled how they had attained to
it in so short a time.*

At Douglas, which they had just left on the morning
of this great wapinshaw, they were charged—awful
picture of depravity!—with the theft of a silver spoon
and a nightgown. Could it be expected that while the
whole country swarmed with robbers of every description, such a rare opportunity for plunder should be lost
by rogues—that among a thousand men, even though
fighting for religion, there should not be one Achan in
the camp? At Lanark a declaration was drawn up
and signed by the chief rebels. In it occurs the
following:—

" The just sense whereof "—the sufferings of the
country—" made us choose, rather to betake ourselves
to the fields for self-defence, than to stay at home, bur-
dened daily with the calamities of others, and tortured
with the fears of our own approaching misery."†

The whole body, too, swore the Covenant, to which
ceremony the epitaph at the head of this chapter seems
to refer.

A report that Dalzell was approaching drove them
from Lanark to Bathgate, where, on the evening of
Tuesday the 26th, the wearied army stopped. But at
twelve o'clock the cry which served them for a trumpet
of, " Horse! horse! " and " Mount the prisoner! " re-
sounded through the night-shrouded town, and called

* Turner, p. 167.   † Wodrow, p. 29.

the peasants from their well-earned rest to toil onwards in their march. The wind howled fiercely over the moorland; a close, thick, wetting rain descended. Chilled to the bone, worn out with long fatigue, sinking to the knees in mire, onward they marched to destruction. One by one the weary peasants fell off from their ranks to sleep, and die in the rain-soaked moor, or to seek some house by the wayside wherein to hide till daybreak. One by one at first, then in gradually increasing numbers, till at last, at every shelter that was seen, whole troops left the waning squadrons, and rushed to hide themselves from the ferocity of the tempest. To right and left nought could be descried but the broad expanse of the moor, and the figures of their fellow-rebels, seen dimly through the murky night, plodding onwards through the sinking moss. Those who kept together—a miserable few—often halted to rest themselves, and to allow their lagging comrades to overtake them. Then onward they went again, still hoping for assistance, reinforcement, and supplies; onward again, through the wind, and the rain, and the darkness—onward to their defeat at Pentland, and their scaffold at Edinburgh. It was calculated that they lost one half of their army on that disastrous night march.

Next night they reached the village of Colinton, four miles from Edinburgh, where they halted for the last time.*

* Turner, Wodrow, and *Church History*, by James Kirkton, an outed minister of the period.

The Pentland Rising

IV

RULLION GREEN

" From Covenanters with uplifted hands,
From remonstrators with associate bands,
Good Lord, deliver us."

Royalist Rhyme, Kirkton, p. 127.

Late on the fourth night of November, exactly twenty-four days before Rullion Green, Richard and George Chaplain, merchants in Haddington, beheld four men, clad like west country Whigamores, standing round some object on the ground. It was at the two-mile cross, and within that distance from their homes. At last, to their horror, they discovered that the recumbent figure was a livid corpse swathed in a blood-stained winding-sheet.* Many thought that this apparition was a portent of the deaths connected with the Pentland Rising.

On the morning of Thursday, the 28th of November, 1666, they left Colinton and marched to Rullion Green. There they arrived about sunset. The position was a strong one. On the summit of a bare heathery spur of the Pentlands are two hillocks, and between them lies a narrow band of flat marshy ground. On the highest of the two mounds—that nearest the Pentlands, and on the left hand of the main body—was the greater part of the cavalry, under Major Learmont; on the other Barskob and the Galloway gentlemen; and in the centre Colonel Wallace and the weak half-armed infantry. Their position was further strengthened by the depth of the valley below, and the deep chasm-like course of the Rullion Burn.

The sun, going down behind the Pentlands, cast

* Kirkton, p. 244.

golden lights and blue shadows on their snow-clad summits, slanted obliquely into the rich plain before them, bathing with rosy splendour the leafless, snow-sprinkled trees, and fading gradually into shadow in the distance. To the south, too, they beheld a deep-shaded amphitheatre of heather and bracken; the course of the Esk, near Penicuik, winding about at the foot of its gorge; the broad, brown expanse of Maw moss; and, fading into blue indistinctness in the south, the wild heath-clad Peeblesshire hills. In sooth, that scene was fair, and many a yearning glance was cast over that peaceful evening scene from the spot where the rebels awaited their defeat; and when the fight was over, many a noble fellow lifted his head from the blood-stained heather to strive with darkening eyeballs to behold that landscape, over which, as o'er his life and his cause, the shadows of night and of gloom were falling and thickening.

It was while waiting on this spot that the fear-inspiring cry was raised, " The enemy!—Here comes the enemy!"

Unwilling to believe their own doom—for our insurgents still hoped for success in some negotiations for peace which had been carried on at Colinton—they called out,—" They are some other of our own."

" They are too blacke " (i.e. too numerous), " fie! fie! for ground to draw up on," cried Wallace, fully realising the want of space for his men, and proving that it was not till after this time that his forces were finally arranged.*

First of all the battle was commenced by fifty royalist horse sent obliquely across the hill to attack the left wing of the rebels. An equal number of Learmont's men met them, and, after a struggle, drove them back.

* Kirkton.

The course of the Rullion Burn prevented almost all pursuit, and Wallace, on perceiving it, despatched a body of foot to occupy both the burn and some ruined sheep walls on the farther side.

Dalzell changed his position and drew up his army at the foot of the hill, on the top of which were his foes. He then despatched a mingled body of infantry and cavalry to attack Wallace's outpost, but they also were driven back. A third charge produced a still more disastrous effect, for Dalzell had to check the pursuit of his men by a reinforcement.

These repeated checks bred a panic in the lieutenant-general's ranks, for several of his men flung down their arms. Urged by such fatal symptoms, and by the approaching night, he deployed his men and closed in overwhelming numbers on the centre and right flank of the insurgent army. In the increasing twilight the burning matches of the fire-locks, shimmering on barrel, halbert, and cuirass, lent to the approaching army a picturesque effect, like a huge many-armed giant breathing flame into the darkness.

Placed on an overhanging hill, Welch and Semple cried aloud, " The God of Jacob! The God of Jacob! " and prayed with uplifted hands for victory.*

But still the royalist troops closed in.

Captain John Paton was observed by Dalzell, who determined to capture him with his own hands. Accordingly, he charged forward presenting his pistols. Paton fired, but the balls hopped off Dalzell's buff coat and fell into his boot. With the superstition peculiar to his age, the Nonconformist concluded that his adversary was rendered bullet-proof by enchantment, and pulling some small silver coins from his pocket, charged his pistol therewith. Dalzell, seeing this and supposing, it

* Turner.

is likely, that Paton was putting in larger balls, hid behind his servant, who was killed.*

Meantime the outposts were forced, and the army of Wallace was enveloped in the embrace of a hideous boa-constrictor—tightening, closing, crushing every semblance of life from the victim enclosed in his toils. The flanking parties of horse were forced in upon the centre, and though, as even Turner grants, they fought with desperation, a general flight was the result.

But when they fell there was none to sing their coronach or wail the death-wail over them. Those who sacrificed themselves for the peace, the liberty, and the religion of their fellow-countrymen, lay bleaching in the field of death for long, and when at last they were buried by charity, the peasants dug up their bodies, desecrated their graves, and cast them once more upon the open heath for the sorry value of their winding sheets!

Inscription on stone at Rullion Green:

Here
and near to
this place lyes the
reuerend Mr. John Crookshanks
and Mr. Andrew M'Cormock
ministers of the Gospel, and
about fifty other true covenanted Presbyterians who were
killed in this place in their own
innocent self-defence and defence of the Covenanted
Work of Reformation by
Thomas Dalzel of Bins
Upon 28 November
1666. Rev. 12. 11. Erected
September 28, 1738.

* Kirkton, p. 244.

The Pentland Rising

Back of stone :

> A Cloud of Witnesses ly here,
> Who for Christ's Interest did appear,
> For to restore true Liberty,
> O'erturned then by tyranny;
> And by proud Prelates who did Rage
> Against the Lord's own heritage;
> They sacrific'd were for the laws
> Of Christ their King, his noble cause,
> These heroes fought with great renown
> By falling got the Martyr's crown.*

V

A RECORD OF BLOOD

> "They cut his hands ere he was dead,
> And after that struck off his head.
> His blood under the altar cries,
> For vengeance on Christ's enemies."
>
> *Epitaph on Tomb at Longcross of Clermont.*†

Master Andrew Murray, an outed minister, residing in the Potterrow, on the morning after the defeat, heard the sounds of cheering and the march of many feet beneath his window. He gazed out. With colours flying, and with music sounding, Dalzell victorious entered Edinburgh. But his banners were dyed in blood, and a band of prisoners were marched within his ranks. The old man knew it all. That martial and triumphant strain was the death-knell of his friends and of their cause, the rust-hued spots upon the flags were the tokens of their courage and their death, and the prisoners were the miserable remnant spared from death in battle to die

* Kirkton, p. 246.
† Cloud of Witnesses, p. 389. Edin. 1765.

upon the scaffold. Poor old man! he had outlived all joy. Had he lived longer he would have seen increasing torment and increasing woe; he would have seen the clouds, then but gathering in the mist, cast a more than midnight darkness o'er his native hills, and have fallen a victim to those bloody persecutions which, later, sent their red memorials to the sea by many a burn. By a merciful Providence all this was spared to him—he fell beneath the first blow: and ere four days had passed since Rullion Green, the aged minister of God was gathered to his fathers.*

When Sharpe first heard of the rebellion, he applied to Sir Alexander Ramsay, the Provost, for soldiers to guard his house. Disliking their occupation, the soldiers gave him an ugly time of it. All the night through they kept up a continuous series of " alarms and incursions," cries of " Stand! " " Give fire! " etc., which forced the prelate to flee to the castle in the morning, hoping there to find the rest which was denied him at home.† Now, however, when all danger to himself was past, Sharpe came out in his true colours, and scant was the justice likely to be shown to the foes of Scotch Episcopacy when the Primate was by. The prisoners were lodged in Haddo's Hole, a part of St. Giles's Cathedral, where, by the kindness of Bishop Wishart, to his credit be it spoken, they were amply supplied with food.‡

Some people urged, in the council, that the promise of quarter which had been given on the field of battle should protect the lives of the miserable men. Sir John Gilmore, the greatest lawyer, gave no opinion—certainly a suggestive circumstance,—but Lord Lee declared that this would not interfere with their legal trial; so " to bloody executions they went."‖ To the

* Kirkton, p. 247.   † Ibid, p. 254.
‡ Ibid, p. 247.   ‖ Ibid, pp. 247, 248.

The Pentland Rising

number of thirty they were condemned and executed; while two of them, Hugh M'Kail, a young minister, and Nielson of Corsack, were tortured with the boots.

The goods of those who perished were confiscated, and their bodies were dismembered and distributed to different parts of the country; " the heads of Major M'Culloch and the two Gordons," it was resolved, says Kirkton, " should be pitched on the gate of Kirkcudbright; the two Hamiltons and Strong's head should be affixed at Hamilton, and Captain Arnot's sett on the Watter Gate at Edinburgh. The armes of all the ten, because they hade with uplifted hands renewed the Covenant at Lanark, were sent to the people of that town to expiate that crime, by placing these armes on the top of the prison."* Among these was John Nielson, the Laird of Corsack, who saved Turner's life at Dumfries; in return for which service, Sir James attempted, though without success, to get the poor man reprieved. One of the condemned died of his wounds between the day of condemnation and the day of execution. " None of them," says Kirkton, " would save their life by taking the declaration and renouncing the Covenant, though it was offered to them. . . . But never men died in Scotland so much lamented by the people, not only spectators, but those in the country. When Knockbreck and his brother were turned over, they clasped each other in their armes, and so endured the pangs of death. When Humphrey Colquhoun died, he spoke not like an ordinary citizen, but like a heavenly minister, relating his comfortable Christian experiences, and called for his Bible, and laid it on his wounded arm, and read John iii. 8, and spoke upon it to the admiration of all. But most of all, when Mr. M'Kail died, there was such a lamentation as was never known in Scotland before;

* Kirkton, p. 248.

117

not one dry cheek upon all the street, or in all the
numberless windows in the mercate place."*

The following passage from this speech speaks for
itself and its author:—

" Hereafter I will not talk with flesh and blood, nor
think on the world's consolations. Farewell to all my
friends, whose company hath been refreshful to me in
my pilgrimage. I have done with the light of the sun
and the moon; welcome eternal light, eternal life, everlasting love, everlasting praise, everlasting glory. Praise
to Him that sits upon the throne, and to the Lamb for
ever! Bless the Lord, O my soul, that hath pardoned
all my iniquities in the blood of His Son, and healed
all my diseases. Bless Him, oh! all ye His angels, that
excel in strength, ye ministers that do His pleasure.
Bless the Lord, O my soul! "†

After having ascended the gallows-ladder he again
broke forth in the following words of touching eloquence:

"And now I leave off to speak any more to creatures,
and begin my intercourse with God, which shall never
be broken off. Farewell father and mother, friends and
relations! Farewell the world and all delights! Farewell meat and drink! Farewell sun, moon, and stars!
Welcome God and Father! Welcome sweet Jesus
Christ, the Mediator of the new covenant! Welcome
blessed Spirit of grace, and God of all consolation!
Welcome glory! Welcome eternal life! Welcome
Death!"‡

At Glasgow, too, where some were executed, they
caused the soldiers to beat the drums and blow the

* Kirkton, p. 249.
† Naphtali, Glasg. 1721, p. 205.
‡ Wodrow, p. 59.

trumpets on their closing ears. Hideous refinement of revenge! Even the last words which drop from the lips of a dying man—words surely the most sincere and the most unbiassed which mortal mouth can utter—even these were looked upon as poisoned and as poisonous. "Drown their last accents," was the cry, "lest they should lead the crowd to take their part, or at least to mourn their doom!"* But, after all, perhaps it was more merciful than one would think—unintentionally so, of course; perhaps the storm of harsh and fiercely jubilant noises, the clanging of trumpets, the rattling of drums, and the hootings and jeerings of an unfeeling mob, which were the last they heard on earth, might, when the mortal fight was over, when the river of death was passed, add tenfold sweetness to the hymning of the angels, tenfold peacefulness to the shores which they had reached.

Not content with the cruelty of these executions, some even of the peasantry, though these were confined to the shire of Mid-Lothian, pursued, captured, plundered, and murdered the miserable fugitives who fell in their way. One strange story have we of these times of blood and persecution: Kirkton, the historian, and popular tradition tell us alike, of a flame which often would arise from the grave, in a moss near Carnwath, of some of those poor rebels; of how it crept along the ground; of how it covered the house of their murderer; and of how it scared him with its lurid glare.

Hear Daniel Defoe:†

"If the poor people were by these insupportable violences made desperate, and driven to all the extremities of a wild despair, who can justly reflect on them when they read in the word of God 'That oppres-

* Kirkton, p. 246.
† Defoe's Hist. of the Church.

sion makes a wise man mad '? And therefore were there no other original of the insurrection known by the name of the Rising of Pentland, it was nothing but what the intolerable oppressions of those times might have justified to all the world, nature having dictated to all people a right of defence when illegally and arbitrarily attacked in a manner not justifiable either by the laws of nature, the laws of God, or the laws of the country."

Bear this remonstrance of Defoe's in mind, and though it is the fashion of the day to jeer and to mock, to execrate and to contemn the noble band of Covenanters, though the bitter laugh at their old-world religious views, the curl of the lip at their merits, and the chilling silence on their bravery and their determination, are but too rife through all society; be charitable to what was evil, and honest to what was good about the Pentland insurgents, who fought for life and liberty, for country and religion, on the 28th of November, 1666, now just two hundred years ago.

Edinburgh, 28th Nov. 1866.

COLLEGE PAPERS

I

EDINBURGH STUDENTS IN 1824

On the 2nd of January, 1824, was issued the prospectus of the *Lapsus Linguæ ; or, the College Tatler ;* and on the 7th the first number appeared. On Friday the 2nd of April "*Mr. Tatler* became speechless." Its history was not all one success; for the editor (who applies to himself the words of Iago, " I am nothing if I am not critical ") overstepped the bounds of caution, and found himself seriously embroiled with the powers that were. There appeared in No. xvi. a most bitter satire upon Sir John Leslie, in which he was compared to Falstaff, charged with puffing himself, and very prettily censured for publishing only the first volume of a class-book, and making all purchasers pay for both. Sir John Leslie took up the matter angrily, visited Carfrae the publisher, and threatened him with an action, till he was forced to turn the hapless *Lapsus* out of doors. The maltreated periodical found shelter in the shop of Huie, Infirmary Street; and No. xvii. was duly issued from the new office. No. xvii. beheld *Mr. Tatler's* humiliation, in which, with fulsome apology and not very credible assurances of respect and admiration, he disclaims the article in question, and advertises a new issue of No. xvi. with all objectionable matter omitted. This, with pleasing euphemism, he terms in a later advertisement, " a new and improved edition." This was the only remarkable adventure of *Mr. Tatler's* brief existence; unless we consider as such a silly Chaldee manuscript in imitation of *Blackwood*, and a letter of reproof from a divinity student on the impiety of the same dull effusion. He laments the near approach of his end in pathetic terms. " How shall we summon up sufficient courage," says he, " to look for the last time on our beloved little devil and his inestimable proof-sheet? How shall we be able to pass No. 14 Infirmary Street and feel that all its attractions are over? How shall we bid farewell for ever to that excellent man, with the long great-coat, wooden leg, and wooden board, who acts as our representative at the gate of *Alma Mater?*" But alas! he had no choice: *Mr. Tatler,* whose career, he says himself, had been successful, passed peacefully away, and has ever since dumbly implored " the bringing home of bell and burial."

Alter et idem. A very different affair was the *Lapsus Linguæ* from the *Edinburgh University Magazine.* The two prospectuses alone, laid side by side, would indicate the march of luxury and the repeal of the paper duty. The penny bi-weekly broadside of session 1823–4 was almost wholly dedicated to Momus. Epigrams, pointless letters, amorous verses, and University grievances are the continual burthen of the song. But *Mr. Tatler* was not without a vein of hearty humour; and his pages afford what is much better: to wit, a good picture of student life as it then was. The students of those polite days insisted on retaining their hats in the class-room. There was a cab-stance in front of the College; and " Carriage Entrance " was posted above the main arch, on what the writer pleases to call "coarse, unclassic boards." The benches of the Speculative then, as now, were red; but all other Societies (the Dialectic is the only survivor) met downstairs, in some rooms of which it is pointedly said that " nothing else could conveniently be made of them." However horrible these dungeons may have been, it is certain that they were paid for, and that far too heavily for the taste of session 1823–4, which found enough calls upon its purse for porter and toasted cheese at Ambrose's, or cranberry tarts and ginger-wine at Doull's. Duelling was still a possibility; so much so that when two medicals fell to fisticuffs in Adam Square, it was seriously hinted that single combat would be the result. Last and most wonderful of all, Gall and Spurzheim were in every one's mouth; and the Law student, after having exhausted Byron's poetry and Scott's novels, informed the ladies of his belief in phrenology. In the present day he would dilate on "*Red as a rose is she,*" and then mention that he attends Old Greyfriars', as a tacit claim to intellectual superiority. I do not know that the advance is much.

But *Mr. Tatler's* best performances were three short papers in which he hit off pretty smartly the idiosyncrasies of the "*Divinity,*" the "*Medical,*" and the "*Law*" of session 1823–4. The fact that there was no notice of the "*Arts*" seems to suggest that they stood in the same intermediate position as they do now—the epitome of student-kind. *Mr. Tatler's* satire is, on the whole, good-humoured, and has not grown superannuated in *all* its limbs. His descriptions may limp at some points, but there are certain broad traits that apply equally well to session 1870–71. He shows us the *Divinity* of the period—tall, pale, and slender—his collar greasy, and his coat bare about the seams—" his white neckcloth serving four days, and regularly turned the third,"—" the rim of his hat deficient in wool,"— and " a weighty volume of theology under his arm." He was the man to buy cheap " a snuff-box, or a dozen of pencils, or a six-bladed knife, or a quarter of a hundred quills," at any of the public sale-rooms. He was noted for cheap purchases, and for exceeding the legal tender in halfpence. He haunted " the darkest and remotest corner of the Theatre Gallery." He was to be seen issuing from " aërial lodging-houses." Withal, says mine author, " there were many good points about him: he paid his landlady's bill, read his Bible, went twice to church on Sunday, seldom swore, was not often tipsy, and bought the *Lapsus Linguæ*."

The *Medical*, again, " wore a white greatcoat, and consequently talked loud "—(there is something very delicious in that *consequently*). He wore his hat on one side. He was active, volatile, and went to the top of Arthur's Seat on the Sunday forenoon. He was as quiet in a debating society as he was loud in the streets. He was reckless and imprudent: yesterday he insisted on your sharing a bottle of claret with him (and claret was claret then, before the cheap-and-nasty treaty), and to-morrow he asks you for the loan of a penny to buy the last number of the *Lapsus*.

The student of *Law*, again, was a learned man. " He had turned over the leaves of Justinian's *Institutes*, and knew that they were written in Latin. He was well acquainted with the title-page of *Blackstone's Commentaries*, and *argal* (as the gravedigger in *Hamlet* says) he was not a person to be laughed at." He attended the Parliament House in the character of a critic, and could give you stale sneers at all the celebrated speakers. He was the terror of essayists at the Speculative or the Forensic. In social qualities he seems to have stood unrivalled. Even in the police-office we find him shining with undiminished lustre. " If a *Charlie* should find him rather noisy at an untimely hour, and venture to take him into custody, he appears next morning like a Daniel come to judgment. He opens his mouth to speak, and the divine precepts of unchanging justice and Scots Law flow from his tongue. The magistrate listens in amazement, and fines him only a couple of guineas."

Such then were our predecessors and their College Magazine. Barclay, Ambrose, Young Amos, and Fergusson were to them what the Café, the Rainbow, and Rutherford's are to us. An hour's reading in these old pages absolutely confuses us, there is so much that is similar and so much that is different; the follies and amusements are so like our own, and the manner of frolicking and enjoying are so changed, that one pauses and looks about him in philosophic judgment. The muddy quadrangle is thick with living students; but in our eyes it swarms also with the phantasmal white greatcoats and tilted hats of 1824. Two races meet: races alike and diverse. Two performances are played before our eyes; but the change seems merely of impersonators, of scenery, of costume. Plot and passion are the same. It is the fall of the spun shilling whether seventy-one or twenty-four has the best of it.

In a future number we hope to give a glance at the individualities of the present, and see whether the cast shall be head or tail—whether we or the readers of the *Lapsus* stand higher in the balance.

THE MODERN STUDENT CONSIDERED
GENERALLY

We have now reached the difficult portion of our task. *Mr. Tatler*, for all that we care, may have been as virulent as he liked about the students of a former day; but for the iron to touch our sacred selves, for a brother of the Guild to betray its most privy infirmities, let such a Judas look to himself as he passes on his way to the Scots Law or the Diagnostic, below the solitary lamp at the corner of the dark quadrangle. We confess that this idea alarms us. We enter a protest. We bind ourselves over verbally to keep the peace. We hope, moreover, that having thus made you secret to our misgivings, you will excuse us if we be dull, and set that down to caution which you might before have charged to the account of stupidity.

The natural tendency of civilisation is to obliterate those distinctions which are the best salt of life. All the fine old professional flavour in language has evaporated. Your very gravedigger has forgotten his avocation in his electorship, and would quibble on the Franchise over Ophelia's grave, instead of more appropriately discussing the duration of bodies under ground. From this tendency, from this gradual attrition of life, in which everything pointed and characteristic is being rubbed down, till the whole world begins to slip between our fingers in smooth undistinguishable sands, from this, we say, it follows that we must not attempt to join *Mr. Tatler* in his simple division of students into *Law, Divinity*, and *Medical*. Nowadays the faculties may shake hands over their follies; and, like Mrs. Frail and Mrs. Foresight (in *Love for Love*), they may stand in the doors of opposite class-rooms, crying: " Sister, Sister—Sister everyway! " A few restrictions, indeed, remain to influence the followers of individual branches of study. The *Divinity*, for example, must be an avowed believer; and as this, in the present day, is unhappily considered by many as a confession of weakness, he is fain to choose one of two ways of gilding the distasteful orthodox bolus. Some swallow it in a thin jelly of metaphysics; for it is even a credit to believe in God on the evidence of some crack-jaw philosopher, although it is a decided slur to believe in Him on His own authority. Others again (and this we think the worst method), finding German grammar a somewhat dry morsel, run their own little heresy as a proof of independence; and deny one of the cardinal doctrines that they may hold the others without being laughed at.

Besides, however, such influences as these, there is little more distinction between the faculties than the traditionary ideal, handed down through a long sequence of students, and getting rounder and more featureless at each successive session. The plague of uniformity has descended on the College. Students (and indeed all sorts and conditions of men) now require their faculty and character hung round their neck on a placard, like the scenes in Shakespeare's theatre. And in the midst of all this weary sameness, not the least common feature is the gravity of every face. No more does the merry medical run eagerly in the clear winter morning up the rugged sides of Arthur's Seat, and hear the church bells begin and thicken and die away below him among the gathered smoke of the city. He will not break Sunday to so little purpose. He no longer finds pleasure in the mere output of his surplus energy. He husbands his strength, and lays out walks, and reading, and amusement with deep consideration, so that he may get as much work and pleasure out of his body as he can, and waste none of his energy on mere impulse, or such flat enjoyment as an excursion in the country.

See the quadrangle in the interregnum of classes, in those two or three minutes when it is full of passing students, and we think you will admit that, if we have not made it " an habitation of dragons," we have at least transformed it into "a court for owls." Solemnity broods heavily over the enclosure; and wherever you seek it, you will find a dearth of merriment, an absence of real youthful enjoyment. You might as well try

"To move wild laughter in the throat of death,"

as to excite any healthy stir among the bulk of this staid company.

The studious congregate about the doors of the different classes, debating the matter of the lecture, or comparing note-books. A reserved rivalry sunders them. Here are some deep in Greek particles: there, others are already inhabitants of that land

"Where entity and quiddity,
    Like ghosts of defunct bodies fly—
    Where Truth in person does appear
    Like words congealed in northern air."

But none of them seem to find any relish for their studies—no pedantic love of this subject or that lights up their eyes—science and learning are only means for a livelihood, which they have considerably embraced and which they solemnly pursue. " Labour's pale priests," their lips seem incapable of laughter, except in the way of polite recognition of professorial wit. The stains of ink are chronic on their meagre fingers. They walk like Saul among the asses.

The dandies are not less subdued. In 1824 there was a noisy dapper dandyism abroad. Vulgar, as we should now think, but yet genial—a matter of white greatcoats and loud voices—strangely different from the stately frippery that is rife at present. These men are out of their element in the quadrangle. Even the small remains of boisterous humour, which still cling to any collection of young men, jar painfully on their morbid sensibilities; and they beat a hasty retreat to resume their perfunctory march along Princes Street. Flirtation is to them a great social duty, a painful obligation, which they perform on every occasion in the same chill official manner, and with the same commonplace advances, the same dogged observance of traditional behaviour. The shape of their raiment is a burthen almost greater than they can bear, and they halt in their walk to preserve the due adjustment of their trouser-knees, till one would fancy he had mixed in a procession of Jacobs. We speak, of course, for ourselves; but we would as soon associate with a herd of sprightly apes as with these gloomy modern beaux. Alas, that our Mirabels, our Valentines, even our Brummels, should have left their mantles upon nothing more amusing!

Nor are the fast men less constrained. Solemnity, even in dissipation, is the order of the day; and they go to the devil with a perverse seriousness, a systematic rationalism of wickedness that would have surprised the simpler sinners of old. Some of these men whom we see gravely conversing on the steps have but a slender acquaintance with each other. Their intercourse consists principally of mutual bulletins of depravity; and, week after week, as they meet they reckon up their items of transgression, and give an abstract of their downward progress for approval and encouragement. These folk form a freemasonry of their own. An oath is the shibboleth of their sinister fellowship. Once they hear a man swear, it is wonderful how their tongues loosen and their bashful spirits take enlargement, under the consciousness of brotherhood. There is no folly, no pardoning warmth of temper about them; they are as steady-going and systematic in their own way as the studious in theirs.

Not that we are without merry men. No. We shall not be ungrateful to those whose grimaces, whose ironical laughter, whose active feet in the *College Anthem* have beguiled so many weary hours and added a pleasant variety to the strain of close attention. But even these are too evidently professional in their antics. They go about cogitating puns and inventing tricks. It is their vocation, Hal. They are the gratuitous jesters of the class-room; and, like the clown when he leaves the stage, their merriment too often sinks as the bell rings the hour of liberty, and they pass forth by the Post-Office, grave and sedate, and meditating fresh gambols for the morrow.

This is the impression left on the mind of any observing student by too many of his fellows. They seem all frigid old men; and one pauses to think how such an unnatural state of matters is produced. We feel inclined to blame for it the unfortunate absence of *University feeling* which is so marked a characteristic of our Edinburgh students. Academical interests are so few and far between—students, as students, have so little in common, except a peevish rivalry—there is such an entire want of broad college sympathies and ordinary college friendships, that we fancy that no University in the kingdom is in so poor a plight. Our system is full of anomalies. A, who cut B whilst he was a shabby student, curries sedulously up to him and cudgels his memory for anecdotes about him when he becomes the great so-and-so. Let there be an end of this shy, proud reserve on the one hand, and this shuddering fine-ladyism on the other; and we think we shall find both ourselves and the College bettered. Let it be a sufficient reason for intercourse that two men sit together on the same benches. Let the great A be held excused for nodding to the shabby B in Princes Street, if he can say, " That fellow is a student." Once this could be

brought about, we think you would find the whole
heart of the University beat faster. We think you would
find a fusion among the students, a growth of common
feelings, an increasing sympathy between class and
class, whose influence (in such a heterogeneous company as ours) might be of incalculable value in all
branches of politics and social progress. It would do
more than this. If we could find some method of
making the University a real mother to her sons—
something beyond a building full of class-rooms, a
Senatus and a lottery of somewhat shabby prizes—we
should strike a death-blow at the constrained and unnatural attitude of our Society. At present we are not a
united body, but a loose gathering of individuals, whose
inherent attraction is allowed to condense them into
little knots and coteries. Our last snowball riot read us
a plain lesson on our condition. There was no party
spirit—no unity of interests. A few, who were mis-
chievously inclined, marched off to the College of
Surgeons in a pretentious file; but even before they
reached their destination the feeble inspiration had died
out in many, and their numbers were sadly thinned.
Some followed strange gods in the direction of Drummond Street, and others slunk back to meek good-
boyism at the feet of the Professors. The same is visible
in better things. As you send a man to an English
University that he may have his prejudices rubbed off,
you might send him to Edinburgh that he may have
them ingrained—rendered indelible—fostered by sympathy into living principles of his spirit. And the reason
of it is quite plain. From this absence of University
feeling it comes that a man's friendships are always the
direct and immediate results of these very prejudices.
A common weakness is the best master of ceremonies
in our quadrangle: a mutual vice is the readiest introduction. The studious associate with the studious alone

—the dandies with the dandies. There is nothing to force them to rub shoulders with the others; and so they grow day by day more wedded to their own original opinions and affections. They see through the same spectacles continually. All broad sentiments, all real catholic humanity expires; and the mind gets gradually stiffened into one position—becomes so habituated to a contracted atmosphere, that it shudders and withers under the least draught of the free air that circulates in the general field of mankind.

Specialism in Society, then, is, we think, one cause of our present state. Specialism in study is another. We doubt whether this has ever been a good thing since the world began; but we are sure it is much worse now than it was. Formerly, when a man became a specialist, it was out of affection for his subject. With a somewhat grand devotion he left all the world of Science to follow his true love; and he contrived to find that strange pedantic interest which inspired the man who

> " Settled *Hoti's* business—let it be—
> Properly based *Oun*—
> Gave us the doctrine of the enclitic *De*,
> Dead from the waist down."

Nowadays it is quite different. Our pedantry wants even the saving clause of Enthusiasm. The election is now matter of necessity and not of choice. Knowledge is now too broad a field for your Jack-of-all-Trades; and, from beautifully utilitarian reasons, he makes his choice, draws his pen through a dozen branches of study, and behold—John the Specialist. That this is the way to be wealthy we shall not deny; but we hold that it is *not* the way to be healthy or wise. The whole mind becomes narrowed and circumscribed to one " punctual spot " of knowledge. A rank, unhealthy soil breeds a harvest of prejudices. Feeling himself above

others in his one little branch—in the classification of
toadstools, or Carthaginian history—he waxes great in
his own eyes and looks down on others. Having all his
sympathies educated in one way, they die out in every
other; and he is apt to remain a peevish, narrow, and
intolerant bigot. Dilettante is now a term of reproach;
but there is a certain form of dilettantism to which
no one can object. It is this that we want among our
students. We wish them to abandon no subject until
they have seen and felt its merit—to act under a general
interest in all branches of knowledge, not a commercial
eagerness to excel in one.

In both these directions our sympathies are consti-
pated. We are apostles of our own caste and our own
subject of study, instead of being, as we should, true
men and *loving* students. Of course both of these could
be corrected by the students themselves; but this is
nothing to the purpose; it is more important to ask
whether the Senatus or the body of alumni could do
nothing towards the growth of better feeling and wider
sentiments. Perhaps in another paper we may say
something upon this head.

One other word, however, before we have done.
What shall we be when we grow really old? Of yore,
a man was thought to lay on restrictions and acquire
new dead-weight of mournful experience with every
year, till he looked back on his youth as the very
summer of impulse and freedom. We please ourselves
with thinking that it cannot be so with us. We would
fain hope that, as we have begun in one way, we may
end in another; and that when we *are* in fact the
octogenarians that we *seem* at present, there shall be
no merrier men on earth. It is pleasant to picture us,
sunning ourselves in Princes Street of a morning, or
chirping over our evening cups, with all the merriment
that we wanted in youth.

DEBATING SOCIETIES

A debating society is at first somewhat of a disappointment. You do not often find the youthful Demosthenes chewing his pebbles in the same room with you; or, even if you do, you will probably think the performance little to be admired. As a general rule, the members speak shamefully ill. The subjects of debate are heavy; and so are the fines. The Ballot Question—oldest of dialectic nightmares—is often found astride of a somnolent sederunt. The Greeks and Romans, too, are reserved as sort of *general-utility* men, to do all the dirty work of illustration; and they fill as many functions as the famous waterfall scene at the *Princess's*, which I found doing duty on one evening as a gorge in Peru, a haunt of German robbers, and a peaceful vale in the Scottish borders. There is a sad absence of striking argument or real lively discussion. Indeed, you feel a growing contempt for your fellow-members; and it is not until you rise yourself to hawk and hesitate and sit shamefully down again, amid eleemosynary applause, that you begin to find your level and value others rightly. Even then, even when failure has damped your critical ardour, you will see many things to be laughed at in the deportment of your rivals.

Most laughable, perhaps, are your indefatigable strivers after eloquence. They are of those who " pursue with eagerness the phantoms of hope," and who, since they expect that " the deficiencies of last sentence will be supplied by the next," have been recommended by Dr. Samuel Johnson to " attend to the History of Rasselas, Prince of Abyssinia." They are characterised by a hectic hopefulness. Nothing damps them. They rise from the ruins of one abortive sentence, to launch forth into another with unabated vigour. They have all the manner of an orator. From the tone of their voice, you would expect a splendid period—and lo! a string of broken-backed, disjointed clauses, eked out with stammerings and throat-clearings. They possess the art (learned from the pulpit) of rounding an uneuphonious sentence by dwelling on a single syllable—of striking a balance in a top-heavy period by lengthening out a word into a melancholy quaver. Withal, they never cease to hope. Even at last, even when they have exhausted all their ideas, even after the would-be peroration has finally refused to perorate, they remain upon their feet with their mouths open, waiting for some further inspiration, like Chaucer's widow's son in the dung-hole, after

" His throat was kit unto the nekké bone,"

in vain expectation of that seed that was to be laid upon his tongue, and give him renewed and clearer utterance.

These men may have something to say, if they could only say it—indeed they generally have; but the next class are people who, having nothing to say, are cursed with a facility and an unhappy command of words, that makes them the prime nuisances of the society they affect. They try to cover their absence of matter by an unwholesome vitality of delivery. They look triumphantly round the room, as if courting applause, after a torrent of diluted truism. They talk in a circle, harping on the same dull round of argument, and returning again and again to the same remark with the same sprightliness, the same irritating appearance of novelty.

After this set, any one is tolerable; so we shall merely hint at a few other varieties. There is your man who is pre-eminently conscientious, whose face beams with sincerity as he opens on the negative, and who votes on the affirmative at the end, looking round the room with an air of chastened pride. There is also the irrelevant speaker, who rises, emits a joke or two, and then sits down again, without ever attempting to tackle the subject of debate. Again, we have men who ride pick-a-back on their family reputation, or, if their family have none, identify themselves with some well-known statesman, use his opinions, and lend him their patronage on all occasions. This is a dangerous plan, and serves oftener, I am afraid, to point a difference than to adorn a speech.

But alas! a striking failure may be reached without tempting Providence by any of these ambitious tricks. Our own stature will be found high enough for shame. The success of three simple sentences lures us into a fatal parenthesis in the fourth, from whose shut brackets we may never disentangle the thread of our discourse. A momentary flush tempts us into a quotation; and we may be left helpless in the middle of one of Pope's couplets, a white film gathering before our eyes, and our kind friends charitably trying to cover our disgrace by a feeble round of applause. *Amis lecteurs*, this is a painful topic. It is possible that we too, we, the "potent, grave, and reverend" editor, may have suffered these things, and drunk as deep as any of the cup of shameful failure. Let us dwell no longer on so delicate a subject.

In spite, however, of these disagreeables, I should recommend any student to suffer them with Spartan courage, as the benefits he receives should repay him an hundredfold for them all. The life of the debating society is a handy antidote to the life of the class-room and quadrangle. Nothing could be conceived more excellent as a weapon against many of those *peccant humours* that we have been railing against in the Jeremiad of our last *College Paper*—particularly in the field of intellect. It is a sad sight to see our heather-scented students, our boys of seventeen, coming up to College

with determined views—*roués* in speculation—having
gauged the vanity of philosophy or learned to shun it
as the middleman of heresy—a company of determined,
deliberate opinionists, not to be moved by all the
sleights of logic. What have such men to do with study?
If their minds are made up irrevocably, why burn the
" studious lamp " in search of further confirmation?
Every set opinion I hear a student deliver I feel a certain lowering of my regard. He who studies, he who
is yet employed in groping for his premises, should
keep his mind fluent and sensitive, keen to mark flaws,
and willing to surrender untenable positions. He should
keep himself teachable, or cease the expensive farce of
being taught. It is to further this docile spirit that we
desire to press the claims of debating societies. It is
as a means of melting down this museum of premature
petrifactions into living and impressionable soul that
we insist on their utility. If we could once prevail on
our students to feel no shame in avowing an uncertain
attitude towards any subject, if we could teach them
that it was unnecessary for every lad to have his
opinionette on every topic, we should have gone a far
way towards bracing the intellectual tone of the coming
race of thinkers; and this it is which debating societies
are so well fitted to perform.

We there meet people of every shade of opinion, and
make friends with them. We are taught to rail against
a man the whole session through, and then hob-a-nob
with him at the concluding entertainment. We find
men of talent far exceeding our own, whose conclusions
are widely different from ours; and we are thus taught
to distrust ourselves. But the best means of all towards
catholicity is that wholesome rule which some folk are
most inclined to condemn—I mean the law of *obliged
speeches*. Your senior member commands; and you must
take the affirmative or the negative, just as suits his best

137

convenience. This tends to the most perfect liberality. It is no good hearing the arguments of an opponent, for in good verity you rarely follow them; and even if you do take the trouble to listen, it is merely in a captious search for weaknesses. This is proved, I fear, in every debate; when you hear each speaker arguing out his own prepared *spécialité* (he never intended speaking, of course, until some remarks of, etc.), arguing out, I say, his own *coached-up* subject without the least attention to what has gone before, as utterly at sea about the drift of his adversary's speech as Panurge when he argued with Thaumaste, and merely linking his own prelection to the last by a few flippant criticisms. Now, as the rule stands, you are saddled with the side you disapprove, and so you are forced, by regard for your own fame, to argue out, to feel with, to elaborate completely, the case as it stands against yourself; and what a fund of wisdom do you not turn up in this idle digging of the vineyard! How many new difficulties take form before your eyes! how many superannuated arguments cripple finally into limbo, under the glance of your enforced eclecticism!

Nor is this the only merit of Debating Societies. They tend also to foster taste, and to promote friendship between University men. This last, as we have had occasion before to say, is the great requirement of our student life; and it will therefore be no waste of time if we devote a paragraph to this subject in its connection with Debating Societies. At present they partake too much of the nature of a *clique*. Friends propose friends, and mutual friends second them, until the society degenerates into a sort of family party. You may confirm old acquaintances, but you can rarely make new ones. You find yourself in the atmosphere of your own daily intercourse. Now, this is an unfortunate circumstance, which it seems to me might readily be rectified. Our

Debating Societies

Principal has shown himself so friendly towards all college improvements that I cherish the hope of seeing shortly realised a certain suggestion, which is not a new one with me, and which must often have been proposed and canvassed heretofore—I mean, a real *University Debating Society*, patronised by the Senatus, presided over by the Professors, to which every one might gain ready admittance on sight of his matriculation ticket, where it would be a favour and not a necessity to speak, and where the obscure student might have another object for attendance besides the mere desire to save his fines: to wit, the chance of drawing on himself the favourable consideration of his teachers. This would be merely following in the good tendency, which has been so noticeable during all this session, to increase and multiply student societies and clubs of every sort. Nor would it be a matter of much difficulty. The united societies would form a nucleus: one of the class-rooms at first, and perhaps afterwards the great hall above the library, might be the place of meeting. There would be no want of attendance or enthusiasm, I am sure; for it is a very different thing to speak under the bushel of a private club on the one hand, and, on the other, in a public place, where a happy period or a subtle argument may do the speaker permanent service in after life. Such a club might end, perhaps, by rivalling the " Union " at Cambridge or the " Union " at Oxford.

THE PHILOSOPHY OF UMBRELLAS*

It is wonderful to think what a turn has been given to our whole Society by the fact that we live under the sign of Aquarius—that our climate is essentially wet. A mere arbitrary distinction, like the walking-swords of yore, might have remained the symbol of foresight and respectability, had not the raw mists and dropping showers of our island pointed the inclination of Society to another exponent of those virtues. A ribbon of the Legion of Honour or a string of medals may prove a person's courage; a title may prove his birth; a professorial chair his study and acquirement; but it is the habitual carriage of the umbrella that is the stamp of Respectability. The umbrella has become the acknowledged index of social position.

Robinson Crusoe presents us with a touching instance of the hankering after them inherent in the civilised and educated mind. To the superficial, the hot suns of Juan Fernandez may sufficiently account for his quaint choice of a luxury; but surely one who had borne the hard labour of a seaman under the tropics for all these years could have supported an excursion after goats or a peaceful *constitutional* arm-in-arm with the nude Friday. No, it was not this: the memory of a vanished respectability called for some outward manifestation, and the result was—an umbrella. A pious castaway might have rigged up a belfry and solaced his Sunday mornings with the mimicry of church bells; but Crusoe was rather a moralist than a pietist, and his leaf-umbrella is as fine an example of the civilised mind

* " This paper was written in collaboration with James Walter Ferrier, and if reprinted this is to be stated, though his principal collaboration was to lie back in an easy-chair and laugh."—[R. L. S. *Oct.* 25, 1894.]

striving to express itself under adverse circumstances as we have ever met with.

It is not for nothing, either, that the umbrella has become the very foremost badge of modern civilisation —the Urim and Thummim of respectability. Its pregnant symbolism has taken its rise in the most natural manner. Consider, for a moment, when umbrellas were first introduced into this country, what manner of men would use them, and what class would adhere to the useless but ornamental cane. The first, without doubt, would be the hypochondriacal, out of solicitude for their health, or the frugal, out of care for their raiment; the second, it is equally plain, would include the fop, the fool, and the Bobadil. Anyone acquainted with the growth of Society, and knowing out of what small seeds of cause are produced great revolutions and wholly new conditions of intercourse, sees from this simple thought how the carriage of an umbrella came to indicate frugality, judicious regard for bodily welfare, and scorn for mere outward adornment, and, in one word, all those homely and solid virtues implied in the term RESPECTABILITY. Not that the umbrella's costliness has nothing to do with its great influence. Its possession, besides symbolising (as we have already indicated) the change from wild Esau to plain Jacob dwelling in tents, implies a certain comfortable provision of fortune. It is not everyone that can expose twenty-six shillings' worth of property to so many chances of loss and theft. So strongly do we feel on this point, indeed, that we are almost inclined to consider all who possess really well-conditioned umbrellas as worthy of the Franchise. They have a qualification standing in their lobbies; they carry a sufficient stake in the common-weal below their arm. One who bears with him an umbrella—such a complicated structure of whalebone, of silk, and of cane, that it becomes a very microcosm of modern industry—is necessarily a man of peace. A half-crown cane may be applied to an offender's head on a very moderate provocation; but a six-and-twenty shilling silk is a possession too precious to be adventured in the shock of war.

These are but a few glances at how umbrellas (in the general) came to their present high estate. But the true Umbrella-Philosopher meets with far stranger applications as he goes about the streets.

Umbrellas, like faces, acquire a certain sympathy with the individual who carries them: indeed, they are far more capable of betraying his trust; for whereas a face is given to us so far ready-made and all our power over it is in frowning, and laughing, and grimacing, during the first three or four decades of life, each umbrella is selected from a whole shopful, as being most consonant to the purchaser's disposition. An undoubted power of diagnosis rests with the practised Umbrella-Philosopher. O you who lisp and amble, and change the fashion of your countenances—you who conceal all these, how little do you think that you left a proof of your weakness in our umbrella-stand—that even now, as you shake out the folds to meet the thickening snow, we read in its ivory handle the outward and visible sign of your snobbery, or from the exposed gingham of its cover detect, through coat and waistcoat, the hidden hypocrisy of the *dickey* ! But alas! even the umbrella is no certain criterion. The falsity and the folly of the human race have degraded that graceful symbol to the ends of dishonesty; and while some umbrellas, from carelessness in selection, are not strikingly characteristic (for it is only in what a man loves that he displays his real nature), others, from certain prudential motives, are chosen directly opposite to the person's disposition. A mendacious umbrella is a sign of great moral degradation. Hypocrisy naturally shelters itself below a silk; while the fast youth goes to visit his religious friends armed with the decent and reputable gingham. May it not be said of the bearers of these inappropriate umbrellas that they go about the streets "with a lie in their right hand"?

The king of Siam, as we read, besides having a graduated social scale of umbrellas (which was a good thing), prevented the great bulk of his subjects from having any at all, which was certainly a bad thing. We should be sorry to believe that this Eastern legislator was a fool—the idea of an aristocracy of umbrellas is too philosophic to have originated in a nobody—and we have accordingly taken exceeding pains to find out the reason of this harsh restriction. We think we have succeeded; but, while admiring the principle at which he aimed, and while cordially recognising in the Siamese potentate the only man before ourselves who had taken a real grasp of the umbrella, we must be allowed to point out how unphilosophically the great man acted in this particular. His object, plainly, was to prevent any unworthy persons from bearing the sacred symbol of domestic virtues. We cannot excuse his limiting these virtues to the circle of his court. We must only remember that such was the feeling of the age in which he lived. Liberalism had not yet raised the war-cry of the working classes. But here was his mistake: it was a needless regulation. Except in a very few cases of hypocrisy joined to a powerful intellect, men, not by nature *umbrellarians*, have tried again and again to become so by art, and yet have failed—have expended their patrimony in the purchase of umbrella after umbrella, and yet have systematically lost them, and have finally, with contrite spirits and shrunken purses, given up their vain struggle, and relied on theft and borrowing for the remainder of their lives. This is the most remarkable fact that we have had occasion to notice; and

143

yet we challenge the candid reader to call it in question. Now, as there cannot be any *moral selection* in a mere dead piece of furniture—as the umbrella cannot be supposed to have an affinity for individual men equal and reciprocal to that which men certainly feel towards individual umbrellas—we took the trouble of consulting a scientific friend as to whether there was any possible physical explanation of the phenomenon. He was unable to supply a plausible theory, or even hypothesis; but we extract from his letter the following interesting passage relative to the physical peculiarities of umbrellas: " Not the least important, and by far the most curious property of the umbrella, is the energy which it displays in affecting the atmospheric strata. There is no fact in meteorology better established—indeed, it is almost the only one on which meteorologists are agreed —than that the carriage of an umbrella produces desiccation of the air; while if it be left at home, aqueous vapour is largely produced, and is soon deposited in the form of rain. No theory," my friend continues, " competent to explain this hygrometric law has yet been given (as far as I am aware) by Herschel, Dove, Glaisher, Tait, Buchan, or any other writer; nor do I pretend to supply the defect. I venture, however, to throw out the conjecture that it will be ultimately found to belong to the same class of natural laws as that agreeable to which a slice of toast always descends with the buttered surface downwards."

But it is time to draw to a close. We could expatiate much longer upon this topic, but want of space constrains us to leave unfinished these few desultory remarks—slender contributions towards a subject which has fallen sadly backwards, and which, we grieve to say, was better understood by the king of Siam in 1686 than by all the philosophers of to-day. If, however, we have awakened in any rational mind an interest in the symbolism of umbrellas—in any generous heart a more complete sympathy with the dumb companion of his daily walk—or in any grasping spirit a pure notion of respectability strong enough to make him expend his six-and-twenty shillings—we shall have deserved well of the world, to say nothing of the many industrious persons employed in the manufacture of the article.

V

THE PHILOSOPHY OF NOMENCLATURE

"How many Cæsars and Pompeys, by mere inspirations of the names, have been rendered worthy of them? And how many are there, who might have done exceeding well in the world had not their characters and spirits been totally depressed and Nicodemus'd into nothing?"—*Tristram Shandy*, vol. i. chap. xix.

Such were the views of the late Walter Shandy, Esq., Turkey merchant. To the best of my belief, Mr. Shandy is the first who fairly pointed out the incalculable influence of nomenclature upon the whole life —who seems first to have recognised the one child, happy in an heroic appellation, soaring upwards on the wings of fortune, and the other, like the dead sailor in his shotted hammock, haled down by sheer weight of name into the abysses of social failure. Solomon possibly had his eye on some such theory when he said that " a good name is better than precious ointment "; and perhaps we may trace a similar spirit in the compilers of the English Catechism, and the affectionate interest with which they linger round the catechumen's name at the very threshold of their work. But, be these as they may, I think no one can censure me for appending, in pursuance of the expressed wish of his son, the Turkey merchant's name to his system, and pronouncing, without further preface, a short epitome of the *Shandean Philosophy of Nomenclature*.

To begin, then: the influence of our name makes itself felt from the very cradle. As a schoolboy I remember the pride with which I hailed Robin Hood, Robert Bruce, and Robert le Diable as my namefellows; and the feeling of sore disappointment that fell on my heart when I found a freebooter or a general who did not share with me a single one of my numerous *prænomina*. Look at the delight with which two children find they have the same name. They are friends

146

from that moment forth; they have a bond of union stronger than exchange of nuts and sweetmeats. This feeling, I own, wears off in later life. Our names lose their freshness and interest, become trite and indifferent. But this, dear reader, is merely one of the sad effects of those "shades of the prison-house" which come gradually betwixt us and nature with advancing years; it affords no weapon against the philosophy of names.

In after life, although we fail to trace its working, that name which careless godfathers lightly applied to your unconscious infancy will have been moulding your character, and influencing with irresistible power the whole course of your earthly fortunes. But the last name, overlooked by Mr. Shandy, is no whit less important as a condition of success. Family names, we must recollect, are but inherited nicknames; and if the *sobriquet* were applicable to the ancestor, it is most likely applicable to the descendant also. You would not expect to find Mr. M'Phun acting as a mute, or Mr. M'Lumpha excelling as a professor of dancing. Therefore, in what follows, we shall consider names, independent of whether they are first or last. And to begin with, look what a pull *Cromwell* had over *Pym*—the one name full of a resonant imperialism, the other, mean, pettifogging, and unheroic to a degree. Who would expect eloquence from *Pym*—who would read poems by *Pym*—who would bow to the opinion of *Pym* ? He might have been a dentist, but he should never have aspired to be a statesman. I can only wonder that he succeeded as he did. Pym and Habakkuk stand first upon the roll of men who have triumphed, by sheer force of genius, over the most unfavourable appellations. But even these have suffered; and, had they been more fitly named, the one might have been Lord Protector, and the other have shared the laurels with Isaiah. In this matter we must not forget that all our great poets have borne great names. Chaucer, Spenser, Shakespeare, Milton, Pope, Wordsworth, Shelley— what a constellation of lordly words! Not a single commonplace name among them—not a Brown, not a Jones, not a Robinson; they are all names that one would stop and look at on a door-plate. Now, imagine if *Pepys* had tried to clamber somehow into the enclosure of poetry, what a blot would that word have made upon the list! The thing was impossible. In the first place, a certain natural consciousness that men have would have held him down to the level of his name, would have prevented him from rising above the Pepsine standard, and so haply withheld him altogether from attempting verse. Next, the booksellers would refuse to publish, and the world to read them, on the mere evidence of the fatal appellation. And now, before I close this section, I must say one word as to *punnable* names, names that stand alone, that have a significance and life apart from him that bears them. These are the bitterest of all. One friend of mine goes bowed and humbled through life under the weight of this misfortune; for it is an awful thing when a man's name is a joke, when he cannot be mentioned without exciting merriment, and when even the intimation of his death bids fair to carry laughter into many a home.

So much for people who are badly named. Now for people who are *too* well named, who go top-heavy from the font, who are baptised into a false position, and find themselves beginning life eclipsed under the fame of some of the great ones of the past. A man, for instance, called William Shakespeare could never dare to write plays. He is thrown into too humbling an apposition with the author of *Hamlet*. His own name coming after is such an anticlimax. " The plays of William Shakespeare? " says the reader—" O no! The plays of William Shakespeare Cockerill," and he throws the

148

book aside. In wise pursuance of such views, Mr. John Milton Hengler, who not long since delighted us in this favoured town, has never attempted to write an epic, but has chosen a new path, and has excelled upon the tight-rope. A marked example of triumph over this is the case of Mr. Dante Gabriel Rossetti. On the face of the matter, I should have advised him to imitate the pleasing modesty of the last-named gentleman, and confine his ambition to the sawdust. But Mr. Rossetti has triumphed. He has even dared to translate from his mighty name-father; and the voice of fame supports him in his boldness.

Dear readers, one might write a year upon this matter. A lifetime of comparison and research could scarce suffice for its elucidation. So here, if it please you, we shall let it rest. Slight as these notes have been, I would that the great founder of the system had been alive to see them. How he had warmed and brightened, how his persuasive eloquence would have fallen on the ears of Toby; and what a letter of praise and sympathy would not the editor have received before the month was out! Alas! the thing was not to be. Walter Shandy died and was duly buried, while yet his theory lay forgotten and neglected by his fellow-countrymen. But, reader, the day will come, I hope, when a paternal government will stamp out, as seeds of national weakness, all depressing patronymics, and when godfathers and godmothers will soberly and earnestly debate the interest of the nameless one, and not rush blindfold to the christening. In these days there shall be written a *Godfather's Assistant*, in shape of a dictionary of names, with their concomitant virtues and vices; and this book shall be scattered broadcast through the land, and shall be on the table of everyone eligible for godfathership, until such a thing as a vicious or untoward appellation shall have ceased from off the face of the earth.

SCIENTIFIC PAPERS

I

ON A NEW FORM OF INTERMITTENT LIGHT FOR LIGHTHOUSES

The necessity for marked characteristics in coast illumination increases with the number of lights. The late Mr. Robert Stevenson, my grandfather, contributed two distinctions, which he called respectively the *intermittent* and the *flashing* light. It is only to the former of these that I have to refer in the present paper. The intermittent light was first introduced at Tarbetness in 1830, and is already in use at eight stations on the coasts of the United Kingdom. As constructed originally, it was an arrangement by which a fixed light was alternately eclipsed and revealed. These recurrent occultations and revelations produce an effect totally different from that of the revolving light, which comes gradually into its full strength, and as gradually fades away. The changes in the intermittent, on the other hand, are immediate; a certain duration of darkness is followed at once and without the least gradation by a certain period of light. The arrangement employed by my grandfather to effect this object consisted of two opaque cylindric shades or extinguishers, one of which descended from the roof, while the other ascended from below to meet it, at a fixed interval. The light was thus entirely intercepted.

At a later period, at the harbour light of Troon, Mr. Wilson, C.E., produced an intermittent light by the use of gas, which leaves little to be desired and which is still in use at Troon harbour. By a simple mechanical contrivance, the gas-jet was suddenly lowered to the point of extinction, and, after a set period, as suddenly raised again. The chief superiority of this form of intermittent light is economy in the consumption of gas.

Intermittent Light for Lighthouses

In the original design, of course, the oil continues use-
lessly to illuminate the interior of the screens during
the period of occultation.

Mr. Wilson's arrangement has been lately resusci-
tated by Mr. Wigham of
Dublin, in connection with
his new gas-burner.

Gas, however, is inapplic-
able to many situations; and
it has occurred to me that
the desired result might be
effected with strict economy
with oil lights in the following manner:

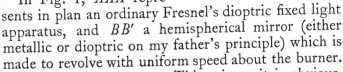

FIG. 1.

In Fig. 1, *AAA* repre-
sents in plan an ordinary Fresnel's dioptric fixed light
apparatus, and *BB'* a hemispherical mirror (either
metallic or dioptric on my father's principle) which is
made to revolve with uniform speed about the burner.

This mirror, it is obvious,
intercepts the rays of one
hemisphere, and, returning
them through the flame
(less loss by absorption,
etc.), spreads them equally
over the other. In this way
180° of light pass regularly
the eye of the seaman; and
are followed at once by
180° of darkness. As the
hemispherical mirror begins
to open the observer receives the full light, since the
whole lit hemisphere is illuminated with strict equality;
and as it closes again, he passes into darkness.

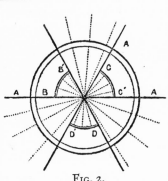

FIG. 2.

Other characteristics can be produced by different
modifications of the above. In Fig. 2 the original hemi-

spherical mirror is shown broken up into three different sectors, BB', CC', and DD'; so that with the same velocity of revolution the periods of light and darkness

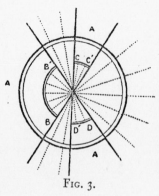

will be produced in quicker succession. In this figure (Fig. 2) the three sectors have been shown as subtending equal angles, but if one of them were increased in size and the other two diminished (as in Fig. 3), we should have one long steady illumination and two short flashes at each revolution. Again, the number of sectors may be increased; and by varying

FIG. 3.

both their number and their relative size, a number of additional characteristics are attainable.

Colour may also be introduced as a means of distinction. Coloured glass may be set in the alternate

spaces; but it is necessary to remark that these coloured sectors will be inferior in power to those which remain white. This objection is, however, obviated to a large extent (especially where the dioptric spherical mirror is used) by such an arrangement as is shown in Fig. 4; where the two

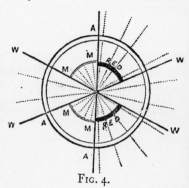

FIG. 4.

sectors, WW, are left unassisted, while the two with the red screens are reinforced respectively by the two sectors of mirror, MM.

Another mode of holophotally producing the intermittent light has been suggested by my father, and is shown in Fig. 5. It consists of alternate and opposite sectors of dioptric spherical mirror, *MM*, and of Fresnel's fixed light apparatus, *AA*. By the revolution of this composite frame about the burner, the same immediate alternation of light and darkness is produced, the first when the front of the fixed panel, and the second when the back of the mirror, is presented to the eye of the sailor.

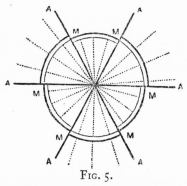

Fɪɢ. 5.

One advantage of the method that I propose is this, that while we are able to produce a plain intermittent light; an intermittent light of variable period, ranging from a brief flash to a steady illumination of half the revolution; and finally, a light combining the immediate occultation of the intermittent with combination and change of colour, we can yet preserve comparative lightness in the revolving parts, and consequent economy in the driving machinery. It must, however, be noticed, that none of these last methods are applicable to cases where more than one radiant is employed; for these cases, either my grandfather's or Mr. Wilson's contrivance must be resorted to.

ON THE THERMAL INFLUENCE
OF FORESTS

The opportunity of an experiment on a comparatively large scale, and under conditions of comparative isolation, can occur but rarely in such a science as Meteorology. Hence Mr. Milne Home's proposal for the plantation of Malta seemed to offer an exceptional opportunity for progress. Many of the conditions are favourable to the simplicity of the result; and it seemed natural that, if a searching and systematic series of observations were to be immediately set afoot, and continued during the course of the plantation and the growth of the wood, some light would be thrown on the still doubtful question of the climatic influence of forests.

Mr. Milne Home expects, as I gather, a threefold result: 1st, an increased and better-regulated supply of available water; 2nd, an increased rainfall; and, 3rd, a more equable climate, with more temperate summer heat and winter cold.* As to the first of these expectations, I suppose there can be no doubt that it is justified by facts; but it may not be unnecessary to guard against any confusion of the first with the second. Not only does the presence of growing timber increase and regulate the supply of running and spring water independently of any change in the amount of rainfall, but, as Boussingault found at Marmato,† denudation of forest is sufficient to decrease that supply, even when the rainfall has increased instead of diminished in amount. The second and third effects stand apart, therefore, from any question as to the utility of Mr. Milne Home's important proposal; they are both, per-

* *Jour. Scot. Met. Soc.*, New Ser., xxvi, 35.
† Quoted by Mr. Milne Home.

naps, worthy of discussion at the present time, but I wish to confine myself in the present paper to the examination of the third alone.

A wood, then, may be regarded either as a *superficies* or as a *solid*; that is, either as a part of the earth's surface slightly elevated above the rest, or as a diffused and heterogeneous body displacing a certain portion of free and mobile atmosphere. It is primarily in the first character that it attracts our attention, as a radiating and absorbing surface, exposed to the sun and the currents of the air; such that, if we imagine a plateau of meadow-land or bare earth raised to the mean level of the forest's exposed leaf-surface, we shall have an agent entirely similar in kind, although perhaps widely differing in the amount of action. Now, by comparing a tract of wood with such a plateau as we have just supposed, we shall arrive at a clear idea of the specialities of the former. In the first place, then, the mass of foliage may be expected to increase the radiating power of each tree. The upper leaves radiate freely towards the stars and the cold interstellar spaces, while the lower ones radiate to those above and receive less heat in return; consequently, during the absence of the sun, each tree cools gradually downward from top to bottom. Hence we must take into account not merely the area of leaf-surface actually exposed to the sky, but, to a greater or less extent, the surface of every leaf in the whole tree or the whole wood. This is evidently a point in which the action of the forest may be expected to differ from that of the meadow or naked earth; for though, of course, inferior strata tend to a certain extent to follow somewhat the same course as the mass of inferior leaves, they do so to a less degree—conduction, and the conduction of a very slow conductor, being substituted for radiation.

We come next, however, to a second point of difference. In the case of the meadow, the chilled air continues to lie upon the surface, the grass, as Humboldt says, remaining all night submerged in the stratum of lowest temperature; while in the case of trees, the coldest air is continually passing down to the space underneath the boughs, or what we may perhaps term the crypt of the forest. Here it is that the consideration of any piece of woodland conceived as a solid comes naturally in; for this solid contains a portion of the atmosphere, partially cut off from the rest, more or less excluded from the influence of wind, and lying upon a soil that is screened all day from isolation by the impending mass of foliage. In this way (and chiefly, I think, from the exclusion of winds), we have underneath the radiating leaf-surface a stratum of comparatively stagnant air, protected from many sudden variations of temperature, and tending only slowly to bring itself into equilibrium with the more general changes that take place in the free atmosphere.

Over and above what has been mentioned, thermal effects have been attributed to the vital activity of the leaves in the transudation of water, and even to the respiration and circulation of living wood. The whole actual amount of thermal influence, however, is so small that I may rest satisfied with the mere mention. If these actions have any effect at all, it must be practically insensible; and the others that I have already stated are not only sufficient validly to account for all the observed differences, but would lead naturally to the expectation of differences very much larger and better marked. To these observations I proceed at once. Experience has been acquired upon the following three points: 1, The relation between the temperature of the trunk of a tree and the temperature of the surrounding atmosphere; 2, The relation between the temperature of the air under a wood and the temperature of the air

utside; and 3, The relation between the temperature
of the air above a wood and the temperature of the air
above cleared land.

As to the first question, there are several independent
series of observations; and I may remark in passing,
what applies to all, that allowance must be made
throughout for some factor of specific heat. The results were as follows: The seasonal and monthly means
in the tree and in the air were not sensibly different.
The variations in the tree, in M. Becquerel's own observations, appear as considerably less than a fourth of
those in the atmosphere, and he has calculated, from
observations made at Geneva between 1796 and 1798,
that the variations in the tree were less than a fifth of
those in the air; but the tree in this case, besides being
of a different species, was seven or eight inches thicker
than the one experimented on by himself.* The variations in the tree, therefore, are always less than those in
the air, the ratio between the two depending apparently
on the thickness of the tree in question and the rapidity
with which the variations followed upon one another.
The times of the maxima, moreover, were widely
different: in the air, the maximum occurs at 2 p.m. in
winter, and at 3 p.m. in summer; in the tree, it occurs
in winter at 6 p.m., and in summer between 10 and
11 p.m. At nine in the morning in the month of June,
the temperatures of the tree and of the air had come to
an equilibrium. A similar difference of progression is
visible in the means, which differ most in spring and
autumn, and tend to equalise themselves in winter and
in summer. But it appears most strikingly in the case
of variations somewhat longer in period than the
daily ranges. The following temperatures occurred
during M. Becquerel's observations in the Jardin des
Plantes:

* *Atlas Météorologique de l'Observatoire Impérial,* 1867.

Date. 1859.					Temperature of the Air.		Temperature in the Tree.
Dec. 15	.	.	.	.	26·78°	.	32°
,, 16	.	.	.	.	19·76°	.	32°
,, 17	.	.	.	.	17·78°	.	31·46°
,, 18	.	.	.	.	13·28°	.	30·56°
,, 19	.	.	.	.	12·02°	.	28·40°
,, 20	.	.	.	.	12·54°	.	25·34°
,, 21	.	.	.	.	38·30°	.	27·86°
,, 22	.	.	.	.	43·34°	.	30·92°
,, 23	.	.	.	.	44·06°	.	31·46°

A moment's comparison of the two columns will make the principle apparent. The temperature of the air falls nearly fifteen degrees in five days; the temperature of the tree, sluggishly following, falls in the same time less than four degrees. Between the 19th and 20th the temperature of the air has changed its direction of motion, and risen nearly a degree; but the temperature of the tree persists in its former course, and continues to fall nearly three degrees farther. On the 21st there comes a sudden increase of heat, a sudden thaw; the temperature of the air rises twenty-five and a half degrees; the change at last reaches the tree, but only raises its temperature by less than three degrees; and even two days afterwards, when the air is already twelve degrees above freezing-point, the tree is still half a degree below it. Take, again, the following case:

Date. 1859.					Temperature of the Air.		Temperature in the Tree.
July 13	.	.	.	.	84·92°	.	76·28°
,, 14	.	.	.	.	82·58°	.	78·62°
,, 15	.	.	.	.	80·42°	.	77·72°
,, 16	.	.	.	.	79·88°	.	78·44°
,, 17	.	.	.	.	73·22°	.	75·92°
,, 18	.	.	.	.	68·54°	.	74·30°
,, 19	.	.	.	.	65·66°	.	70·70°

The same order reappears. From the 13th to the 9th the temperature of the air steadily falls, while the temperature of the tree continues apparently to follow the course of previous variations, and does not really begin to fall, is not really affected by the ebb of heat, until the 17th, three days at least after it had been operating in the air.* Hence we may conclude that all variations of the temperature of the air, whatever be their period, from twenty-four hours up to twelve months, are followed in the same manner by variations in the temperature of the tree; and that those in the tree are always less in amount and considerably slower of occurrence than those in the air. The *thermal sluggishness*, so to speak, seems capable of explaining all the phenomena of the case without any hypothetical vital power of resisting temperatures below the freezing-point, such as is hinted at even by Becquerel.

Réaumur, indeed, is said to have observed temperatures in slender trees nearly thirty degrees higher than the temperature of the air in the sun; but we are not informed as to the conditions under which this observation was made, and it is therefore impossible to assign to it its proper value. The sap of the ice-plant is said to be materially colder than the surrounding atmosphere; and there are several other somewhat incongruous facts, which tend, at first sight, to favour the view of some inherent power of resistance in some plants to high temperatures, and in others to low temperatures.† But such a supposition seems in the meantime to be gratuitous. Keeping in view the thermal redispositions, which must be greatly favoured by the ascent of the sap, and the difference between the condition as to temperature of such parts as the root, the heart of the trunk, and the extreme foliage, and never forgetting

* *Comptes Rendus de l'Académie*, 29th March, 1869.
† *Professor Balfour's Class Book of Botany*, Physiology, chap. xii, p. 670.

the unknown factor of specific heat, we may still regar
it as possible to account for all anomalies without th
aid of any such hypothesis. We may, therefore, I thin
disregard small exceptions, and state the result .
follows:

If, after every rise or fall, the temperature of the a
remained stationary for a length of time proportion
to the amount of the change, it seems probable—settin
aside all question of vital heat—that the temperature
the tree would always finally equalise itself with th
new temperature of the air, and that the range in tro
and atmosphere would thus become the same. Th
pause, however, does not occur: the variations follo
each other without interval; and the slow-conductin
wood is never allowed enough time to overtake th
rapid changes of the more sensitive air. Hence, so fi
as we can see at present, trees appear to be simply ba
conductors, and to have no more influence upon th
temperature of their surroundings than is fully ac
counted for by the consequent tardiness of the
thermal variations.

Observations bearing on the second of the thre
points have been made by Becquerel in France, by I
Cour in Jutland and Iceland, and by Rivoli at Poser
The results are perfectly congruous. Becquerel's obser
vations* were made under wood, and about a hundre
yards outside in open ground, at three stations in th
district of Montargis, Loiret. There was a differenc
of more than one degree Fahrenheit between the mea
annual temperatures in favour of the open ground. Th
mean summer temperature in the wood was from tw
to three degrees lower than the mean summer temper;
ture outside. The mean maxima in the wood were als
lower than those without by a little more than tw
degrees. Herr La Court† found the daily range cor

* *Comptes Rendus,* 1867 and 1869.   † See his paper.

sistently smaller inside the wood than outside. As far as regards the mean winter temperatures, there is an excess in favour of the forests, but so trifling in amount as to be unworthy of much consideration. Libri found that the minimum winter temperatures were not sensibly lower in Florence, after the Apennines had been denuded of forest, than they had been before.* The disheartening contradictoriness of his observations on this subject led Herr Rivoli to the following ingenious and satisfactory comparison.† Arranging his results according to the wind that blew on the day of observation, he set against each other the variation of the temperature under wood from that without, and the variation of the temperature of the wind from the local mean for the month:

Wind	N.	N.E.	E.	S.E.	S.	S.W.	W.	N.W.
Var. in Wood	+0·60	+0·26	+0·26	+0·04	−0·04	−0·20	+0·16	+0·07
Var. in Wind	−0·30	−2·60	−3·30	−1·20	+1·00	+1·30	+1·00	+1·00

From this curious comparison, it becomes apparent that the variations of the difference in question depend upon the amount of variations of temperature which take place in the free air, and on the slowness with which such changes are communicated to the stagnant atmosphere of woods; in other words, as Herr Rivoli boldly formulates it, a forest is simply a bad conductor. But this is precisely the same conclusion as we have already arrived at with regard to individual trees; and in Herr Rivoli's table, what we see is just another case of what we saw in M. Becquerel's—the different pro-

* *Annales de Chimie et de Physique*, xiv, 1830. A more detailed comparison of the climate in question would be a most interesting and important contribution to the subject.

† Reviewed in the *Austrian Meteorological Magazine*, vol. iv, p. 543

gression of temperatures. It must be obvious, however, that the thermal condition of a single tree must be different in many ways from that of a combination of trees and more or less stagnant air, such as we call a forest. And accordingly we find, in the case of the latter, the following new feature: The mean yearly temperature of woods is lower than the mean yearly temperature of free air, while they are decidedly colder in summer, and very little, if at all, warmer in winter. Hence, on the whole, forests are colder than cleared lands. But this is just what might have been expected from the amount of evaporation, the continued descent of cold air, and its stagnation in the close and sunless crypt of a forest; and one can only wonder here, as elsewhere, that the resultant difference is so insignificant and doubtful.

We now come to the third point in question, the thermal influence of woods upon the air above them. It will be remembered that we have seen reason to believe their effect to be similar to that of certain other surfaces, except in so far as it may be altered, in the case of the forest, by the greater extent of effective radiating area, and by the possibility of generating a descending cold current as well as an ascending hot one. M. Becquerel is (so far as I can learn) the only observer who has taken up the elucidation of this subject. He placed his thermometers at three points:* A and B were both about seventy feet above the surface of the ground; but A was at the summit of a chestnut tree, while B was in the free air, fifty feet away from the other. C was four or five feet above the ground, with a northern exposure; there was also a fourth station to the south, at the same level as this last, but its readings are very seldom referred to. After several years of observation, the mean temperature at A was found to be

* *Comptes Rendus,* 28th May, 1860.

between one and two degrees higher than that at *B*.
The order of progression of differences is as instructive
here as in the two former investigations. The maximum
difference in favour of station *A* occurred between
three and five in the afternoon, later or sooner according as there had been more or less sunshine, and ranged
sometimes as high as seven degrees. After this the
difference kept declining until sunrise, when there was
often a difference of a degree, or a degree and a half,
upon the other side. On cloudy days the difference
tended to a minimum. During a rainy month of April,
for example, the difference in favour of station *A* was
less than half a degree; the first fifteen days of May
following, however, were sunny, and the difference rose
to more than a degree and a half.* It will be observed
that I have omitted up to the present point all mention
of station *C*. I do so because M. Becquerel's language
leaves it doubtful whether the observations made at this
station are logically comparable with those made at the
other two. If the end in view were to compare the progression of temperatures above the earth, above a tree,
and in free air, removed from all such radiative and
absorptive influences, it is plain that all three should
have been equally exposed to the sun or kept equally
in shadow. As the observations were made, they give
us no notion of the relative action of the earth-surface
and forest-surface upon the temperature of the contiguous atmosphere; and this, as it seems to me, was
just the *crux* of the problem. So far, however, as they
go, they seem to justify the view that all these actions
are the same in kind, however they may differ in degree. We find the forest heating the air during the day,
and heating it more or less according as there has been
more or less sunshine for it to absorb, and we find it
also chilling it during the night; both of which are

* *Ibid.*, 20th May, 1861.

actions common to any radiating surface, and would be produced, if with differences of amount and time, by any other such surface raised to the mean level of the exposed foliage.

To recapitulate:

1st. We find that single trees appear to act simply as bad conductors.

2nd. We find that woods, regarded as solids, are, on the whole, slightly lower in temperature than the free air which they have displaced, and that they tend slowly to adapt themselves to the various thermal changes that take place without them.

3rd. We find forests regarded as surfaces acting like any other part of the earth's surface, probably with more or less difference in amount and progression, which we still lack the information necessary to estimate.

All this done, I am afraid that there can be little doubt that the more general climatic investigations will be long and vexatious. Even in South America, with extremely favourable conditions, the result is far from being definite. Glancing over the table published by M. Becquerel in his book on climates, from the observations of Humboldt, Hall, Boussingault, and others, it becomes evident, I think, that nothing can be founded upon the comparisons therein instituted; that all reasoning, in the present state of our information, is premature and unreliable. Strong statements have certainly been made; and particular cases lend themselves to the formation of hasty judgments. " From the Bay of Cupica to the Gulf of Guayaquil," says M. Boussingault, " the country is covered with immense forests and traversed by numerous rivers; it rains there almost ceaselessly; and the mean temperature of this moist district scarcely reaches 78·8° F. . . . At Payta commence the sandy deserts of Priura and Sechura; to the constant humidity of Choco succeeds almost at once an extreme of dryness; and the mean temperature of the coast increases at the same time by 1·8° F."* Even in this selected favourable instance it might be argued that the part performed in the change by the presence or absence of forest was comparatively small; there seems to have been, at the same time, an entire change of soil; and, in our present ignorance, it would be difficult to say by how much this of itself is able to affect the climate. Moreover, it is possible that the humidity of the one district is due to other causes besides the presence of wood, or even that the presence of wood is itself only an effect of some more general difference or combination of differences. Be that as it may, however, we have only to look a little longer at the table before referred to, to see how little weight can be laid on such special instances. Let us take five stations, all in this very district of Choco. Hacquita is eight hundred and twenty feet above Novita, and their mean temperatures are the same. Alto de Mombu, again, is five hundred feet higher than Hacquita, and the mean temperature has here fallen nearly two degrees. Go up another five hundred feet to Tambo de la Orquita, and again we find no fall in the mean temperature. Go up some five hundred farther to Chami, and there is a fall in the mean temperature of nearly six degrees. Such numbers are evidently quite untrustworthy; and hence we may judge how much confidence can be placed in any generalisation from these South American mean temperatures.

The question is probably considered too simply— too much to the neglect of concurrent influences. Until we know, for example, somewhat more of the comparative radiant powers of different soils, we cannot expect any very definite result. A change of temperature would

* Becquerel, *Climats*, p. 141.

certainly be effected by the plantation of such a marshy district as the Sologne, because, if nothing else were done, the roots might pierce the impenetrable subsoil, allow the surface-water to drain itself off, and thus dry the country. But might not the change be quite different if the soil planted were a shifting sand, which, *fixed* by the roots of the trees, would become gradually covered with a vegetable earth, and thus be changed from dry to wet? Again, the complication and conflict of effects arises, not only from the soil, vegetation, and geographical position of the place of the experiment itself, but from the distribution of similar or different conditions in its immediate neighbourhood, and probably to great distances on every side. A forest, for example, as we know from Herr Rivoli's comparison, would exercise a perfectly different influence in a cold country subject to warm winds, and in a warm country subject to cold winds; so that our question might meet with different solutions even on the east and west coasts of Great Britain.

The consideration of such a complexity points more and more to the plantation of Malta as an occasion of special importance; its insular position and the unity of its geological structure both tend to simplify the question. There are certain points about the existing climate, moreover, which seem specially calculated to throw the influence of woods into a strong relief. Thus, during four summer months, there is practically no rainfall. Thus, again, the northerly winds, when stormy, and especially in winter, tend to depress the temperature very suddenly; and thus, too, the southerly and south-westerly winds, which raise the temperature during their prevalence to from eighty-eight to ninety-eight degrees, seldom last longer than a few hours; insomuch that " their disagreeable heat and dryness may be escaped by carefully closing the windows and doors of apartments at their onset."* Such sudden and short variations seem just what is wanted to accentuate the differences in question. Accordingly, the opportunity seems one not lightly to be lost, and the British Association or this Society itself might take the matter up and establish a series of observations, to be continued during the next few years. Such a combination of favourable circumstances may not occur again for years; and when the whole subject is at a standstill for want of facts, the present occasion ought not to go past unimproved.

Such observations might include the following:

The observation of maximum and minimum thermometers in three different classes of situation—*videlicet*, in the areas selected for plantation themselves, at places in the immediate neighbourhood of those areas where the external influence might be expected to reach its maximum and at places distant from those areas where the influence might be expected to be least.

The operation of rain-gauges and hygrometers at the same three descriptions of locality.

In addition to the ordinary hours of observation, special readings of the thermometers should be made as often as possible at a change of wind and throughout the course of the short hot breezes alluded to already, in order to admit of the recognition and extension of Herr Rivoli's comparison.

Observation of the periods and forces of the land and sea breezes.

Gauging of the principal springs, both in the neighbourhood of the areas of plantation and at places far removed from those areas.

1873.

* Scoresby-Jackson's *Medical Climatology.*

WELLINGTON

Within easy memory of the fathers of our own generation, England possessed a man unique in history. The
greatest of English soldiers, his sword had been
sheathed for nearly fifty years; he had lived to be
cheered by the children of those who were born on the
day of his last engagement; the men who followed him
to victory were becoming few and his hand began to
grow more rarely to the pocket, in which, with hourly
generosity, he had always a guinea for a former comrade. He retired from the stage of the great wars
covered with honours, a duke of England, a count of
Portugal, a prince of Spain, a duke of Belgium; the
most conspicuous man in Europe, since Napoleon, the
previous observed of all observers had fallen before his
own stoutheartedness, and the loyalty of Marshal
Blücher. Thereupon he entered the second period of
his career, as the most despotic of English ministers,
capable in administration, not politically weather-wise,
ruling with a rod of iron the pitiful monarch whom
he was supposed to serve, and steadfastly indifferent to
popularity.

With the Reform Bill, he fell from this half-royal
power, and having so fallen, rose again almost at once
to a fresh station in the regard of his countrymen, as
the counsellor of all ministries and the recognised father
of the fatherland; so that, while he lived, the people
who had once broken his windows, escorted him about
the city with salutes and fondly pointed him out to their
young children; and when he came to die, the fall of
the ministry at home and the bloody rise of an empire
across the Channel were alike forgotten in the blow of
that national bereavement. It is proposed to study in
these pages the qualities of mind and character by
which he rose, and the nature of his singular devotion
to the service of his country, or—as he preferred to put

it, in words grown unfamiliar to our ears—the service of his King.

Mortier, Bessières, and Desaix were born in the year 1768; Murat, Davoust, Duroc, Suchet, the Clausel, and Junot, the Archduke Charles and the Englishmen Beresford and Rowland Hill between 1770 and 1772; and it is the distinction of the intervening year, 1769, to have given to the world Ney, Soult, Bonaparte, and Wellington. Thus, in the lapse of a lustre, there were born nearly a score of the men that grew most glorious in the long epic of the French Wars; and when the last shot was fired after Waterloo, the oldest of them still lacked some years of fifty.

Arthur Wellesley was the son of the second earl of Mornington. The Colley-Wellesleys, or the Cowley-Westleys (with other variants which I pass over) were a family of some standing in the matter of age. On the Irish side, their pedigree is graced with the names of several independent monarchs. It is more important that they were apparently related to the founders of Methodism; indeed it was as a Wesley that Arthur came into the world and grew to manhood, and the spelling was only changed to please the nice taste of the Marquess his brother. The stock at least was one of a certain virtue; they had pushed but recently into the Irish peerage, for certain services to the ministry which may be safely translated as the merging of votes; and Arthur's father was a man of taste and successfully cultivated that very graceful branch of music, once so popular, now seemingly so dead in England, the making of glees. The outbreak of artistic talent is usually the first sign of decay of the races; but with the house of Wellington this order was reversed, and the sons of the dilettante were men of action and affairs. Out of a family of nine, four became peers in their own right.

It was no great position to be the sixth son of a mushroom Irish peer; and in 1781 Lord Mornington died, leaving his affairs in confusion, and the position was thus rendered worse. But in these houses of the poor nobility, there was a strong clan feeling, and what would now seem to us a great effrontery of nepotism. Richard, the new Lord Mornington (since famous as the Marquess Wellesley), took up the load of his father and of his innumerable brothers and sisters with a good heart; and in one way and another he managed to carve out a position for them all. That the mother, a Hill of Seymour, must have been a woman of some stoicism, we may gather from the fact that she had forgotten the place of the birth of her first-born and both the place and date of that of Arthur. Perhaps dazzled by the parts and address of Richard she despaired of Arthur. He was a heavy, silent, sheepish, blank-faced lad; he displayed no taste for arms, nor indeed for anything but to play the fiddle; he made no friends, he was helplessly dull in society; and when a lady took him in her carriage to a picnic, she was so bored by the lad that she evaded him on the return, and the future duke drove back with the musicians. In after days he laughed with the lady over this incident.

What was to be done with this incubus—one of a very poor family ambitious to rise? He might now be clapped to a desk in a tea merchant's office or slapped upon a cattle ranch in Texas.

THE LATE SAM BOUGH, R.S.A.

A Cumberland man, and born in the legendary city of Carlisle, Sam Bough (as he delighted to be called) died in Edinburgh on November 19, aged fifty-seven. This is not only a loss to art, but the disappearance of a memorable type of man. Spectacled, burly in his rough clothes, with his solid, strong, and somewhat common gait, his was a figure that commanded notice even on the street. He affected rude and levelling manners; his geniality was formidable, above all for those whom he considered too fine for their company; and he delivered jests from the shoulder like buffets. He loved to put himself in opposition, to make startling, and even brutal speeches, and trample proprieties under foot. But this, although it troubled the amenities of his relations, was no more than a husk, an outer man, partly of habit, partly of affectation; and inside the burr there was a man of warm feelings, notable powers of mind, and much culture, which was none the less genuine because it was not of the same character, not altogether concerned in the same fields of knowledge, as that training which usually appropriates the name. Perhaps he was a little disappointed with himself, and partly because he loathed fustian, partly because he did not succeed in living consistently up to the better and more beautiful qualities of his nature, he did himself injustice in the world, and paraded his worst qualities with something like a swagger. To borrow a metaphor from the stage with which he was so long connected, he preferred to play his worst part because he imagined he could play it best. It was only when you got him alone, or when, in company, something occurred to call up a generous contempt, that you became clearly aware of his sterling, upright, and human character. Such manifestations his friends were as little willing to forget as he seemed shy of offering them. He would then display a sneering enmity for all that he thought mean or bad, and a quiet and genuine delight in all that he thought good. To students he was even exceptionally kind and helpful. He had an open hand, and came readily forth from his cynical out-works at any tale of sorrow. He had read much and wisely; and his talk was not only witty in itself, but enriched with the wit and eloquence of others. He played the violin, sang with spirit, and had a remarkable gift of telling stories. It was a delight to hear him when he spoke of Carlisle, Cumberland, and John Peel, the famous hunter; or when he narrated his own experience—cobbling shoes beside his father, gipsying among the moors to sketch, working in the docks as a porter, or painting scenes and sometimes taking a part at local theatres. As we say of books that they are readable, we may say of his talk that it was eminently *hearable*. He could broider romance into his narratives and you were none the wiser; they would all hold water; they had the grit and body of reality, the unity of a humorous masterpiece; and the talents of the novelist and the comedian were pressed together into the service of your entertainment.

His sentiment for nature was strong and just; but he avoided the subject in words and let his brush speak for him.

He was a massive, heavy painter, and liked broad effects of light. His colour was apt to be a little cold and dead. Yet he had a remarkable understanding of sunlight and certain aspects of summer atmosphere in the North, which perhaps lent themselves to the defect of his treatment. He was proud of his drawing and certainly rendered the significance of natural forms. Among his more important works in oil I may mention *Shipbuilding on the Clyde, Borrowdale, Canty Bay, St. Monans, Kirkwall,* and *London from Shooter's Hill.* But his name is more eminently connected with the practice of water-colours. The man's unshaken courage and great muscular power seem to have more directly found expression in this field. It was a sight to see him attack a sketch, peering boldly through his spectacles and, with somewhat tremulous fingers, flooding the page with colour; for a moment it was an indescribable hurly-burly, and then chaos would become ordered and you would see a speaking transcript: his method was an act of dashing conduct like the capture of a fort in war. I have seen one of these sketches in particular, a night-piece on a headland, where the atmosphere of tempest, the darkness and the mingled spray and rain, are conveyed with remarkable truth and force. It was painted to hang near a Turner; and in answer to some words of praise—" Yes, lad," said he, " I wasn't going to look like a fool beside the old man."

His activity was indefatigable; he worked from nature; he worked in the studio; even at home he would have a piece at his elbow to work upon in the intervals of music and conversation. By many it was supposed that this industry had a commercial motive, and injured the quality of his production; and it is true that Sam Bough was preoccupied about material necessities, and had a rooted horror of debt; but he thoroughly enjoyed his art, and, perhaps, still more the practice of it; and although there was an impression of power in the man and his work that led hasty judgments to expect more than ever he accomplished, the best that he has left is probably the best that he could do.

CRITICISMS

I

ON LORD LYTTON'S *FABLES IN SONG*

It seems as if Lord Lytton, in this new book of his, had found the form most natural to his talent. In some ways, indeed, it may be held inferior to *Chronicles and Characters*; we look in vain for anything like the terrible intensity of the night-scene in *Irene*, or for any such passages of massive and memorable writing as appeared, here and there, in the earlier work, and made it not altogether unworthy of its model, Hugo's *Legend of the Ages*. But it becomes evident, on the most hasty retrospect, that this earlier work was a step on the way towards the later. It seems as if the author had been feeling about for his definite medium, and was already, in the language of the child's game, growing hot. There are many pieces in *Chronicles and Characters* that might be detached from their original setting, and embodied, as they stand, among the *Fables in Song*.

For the term Fable is not very easy to define rigorously. In the most typical form some moral precept is set forth by means of a conception purely fantastic, and usually somewhat trivial into the bargain; there is something playful about it, that will not support a very exacting criticism, and the lesson must be apprehended by the fancy at half a hint. Such is the great mass of the old stories of wise animals or foolish men that have amused our childhood. But we should expect the fable, in company with other and more important literary forms, to be more and more loosely, or at least largely, comprehended as time went on, and so to degenerate in conception from this original type. That depended for much of its piquancy on the very fact that it was fantastic: the point of the thing lay in a sort of humorous inappropriateness; and it is natural enough that

174

pleasantry of this description should become less common, as men learn to suspect some serious analogy underneath. Thus a comical story of an ape touches us quite differently after the proposition of Mr. Darwin's theory. Moreover, there lay, perhaps, at the bottom of this primitive sort of fable, a humanity, a tenderness of rough truths; so that at the end of some story, in which vice or folly had met with its destined punishment, the fabulist might be able to assure his auditors, as we have often to assure tearful children on the like occasions, that they may dry their eyes, for none of it was true.

But this benefit of fiction becomes lost with more sophisticated hearers and authors: a man is no longer the dupe of his own artifice, and cannot deal playfully with truths that are a matter of bitter concern to him in his life. And hence, in the progressive centralisation of modern thought, we should expect the old form of fable to fall gradually into desuetude, and be gradually succeeded by another, which is a fable in all points except that it is not altogether fabulous. And this new form, such as we should expect, and such as we do indeed find, still presents the essential character of brevity; as in any other fable also, there is, underlying and animating the brief action, a moral idea; and as in any other fable, the object is to bring this home to the reader through the intellect rather than through the feelings; so that, without being very deeply moved or interested by the characters of the piece, we should recognise vividly the hinges on which the little plot revolves. But the fabulist now seeks analogies where before he merely sought humorous situations. There will be now a logical nexus between the moral expressed and the machinery employed to express it. The machinery, in fact, as this change is developed, becomes less and less fabulous. We find ourselves in presence of quite a serious, if quite a miniature, division of creative literature; and sometimes we have the lesson embodied in a sober, everyday narration, as in the parables of the New Testament, and sometimes merely the statement or, at most, the collocation of significant facts in life, the reader being left to resolve for himself the vague, troublesome, and not yet definitely moral sentiment which has been thus created. And step by step with the development of this change, yet another is developed: the moral tends to become more indeterminate and large. It ceases to be possible to append it in a tag, to the bottom of the piece, as one might write the name below a caricature; and the fable begins to take rank with all other forms of creative literature, as something too ambitious, in spite of its miniature dimensions, to be resumed in any succinct formula without the loss of all that is deepest and most suggestive in it.

Now it is in this widest sense that Lord Lytton understands the term; there are examples in his two pleasant volumes of all the forms already mentioned, and even of another which can only be admitted among fables by the utmost possible leniency of construction. *Composure, Et Cætera,* and several more, are merely similes poetically elaborated. So, too, is the pathetic story of the grandfather and grandchild: the child, having treasured away an icicle and forgotten it for ten minutes, comes back to find it already nearly melted, and no longer beautiful: at the same time, the grandfather has just remembered and taken out a bundle of love-letters, which he too had stored away in years gone by, and then long neglected; and, behold! the letters are as faded and sorrowfully disappointing as the icicle. This is merely a simile poetically worked out; and yet it is in such as these, and some others to be mentioned further on, that the author seems at his best. Wherever

he has really written after the old model, there is something to be deprecated: in spite of all the spirit and
freshness, in spite of his happy assumption of that
cheerful acceptation of things as they are, which,
rightly or wrongly, we come to attribute to the ideal
fabulist, there is ever a sense as of something a little
out of place. A form of literature so very innocent and
primitive looks a little overwritten in Lord Lytton's
conscious and highly coloured style. It may be bad
taste, but sometimes we should prefer a few sentences
of plain prose narration, and a little Bewick by way of
tail-piece. So that it is not among those fables that con-
form most nearly to the old model, but one had nearly
said among those that most widely differ from it, that
we find the most satisfactory examples of the author's
manner.

In the mere matter of ingenuity, the metaphysical
fables are the most remarkable; such as that of the
windmill who imagined that it was he who raised the
wind; or that of the grocer's balance (" Cogito ergo
sum ") who considered himself endowed with free-will,
reason, and an infallible practical judgment; until, one
fine day, the police make a descent upon the shop, and
find the weights false and the scales unequal; and the
whole thing is broken up for old iron. Capital fables,
also, in the same ironical spirit, are *Prometheus Unbound*,
the tale of the vainglorying of a champagne-cork, and
Teleology, where a nettle justifies the ways of God to
nettles while all goes well with it, and, upon a change
of luck, promptly changes its divinity.

In all these there is still plenty of the fabulous if you
will, although, even here, there may be two opinions
possible; but there is another group, of an order of
merit perhaps still higher, where we look in vain for
any such playful liberties with Nature. Thus we have
Conservation of Force ; where a musician, thinking of a

certain picture, improvises in the twilight; a poet, hearing the music, goes home inspired, and writes a poem; and then a painter, under the influence of this poem, paints another picture, thus lineally descended from the first. This is fiction, but not what we have been used to call fable. We miss the incredible element, the point of audacity with which the fabulist was wont to mock at his readers. And still more so is this the case with others. *The Horse and the Fly* states one of the unanswerable problems of life in quite a realistic and straightforward way. A fly startles a cab-horse, the coach is overset; a newly married pair within and the driver, a man with a wife and family, are all killed. The horse continues to gallop off in the loose traces, and ends the tragedy by running over an only child; and there is some little pathetic detail here introduced in the telling, that makes the reader's indignation very white-hot against some one. It remains to be seen who that some one is to be: the fly? Nay, but on closer inspection, it appears that the fly, actuated by maternal instinct, was only seeking a place for her eggs: is maternal instinct, then, " sole author of these mischiefs all "? *Who's in the Right?* one of the best fables in the book, is somewhat in the same vein. After a battle has been won, a group of officers assemble inside a battery, and debate together who should have the honour of the success: the Prince, the general staff, the cavalry, the engineer who posted the battery in which they then stand talking, are successively named: the sergeant, who pointed the guns, sneers to himself at the mention of the engineer; and, close by, the gunner, who had applied the match, passes away with a smile of triumph, since it was through his hand that the victorious blow had been dealt. Meanwhile, the cannon claims the honour over the gunner; the cannon-ball, who actually goes forth on the dread mission, claims it over the

cannon, who remains idly behind; the powder reminds
the cannon-ball that, but for him, it would still be lying
on the arsenal floor; and the match caps the discussion:
powder, cannon-ball, and cannon would be all equally
vain and ineffectual without fire. Just then there comes
on a shower of rain, which wets the powder and puts
out the match, and completes this lesson of dependence,
by indicating the negative conditions which are as
necessary for any effect, in their absence, as is the
presence of this great fraternity of positive conditions,
not any one of which can claim priority over any other.
But the fable does not end here, as perhaps, in all
logical strictness, it should. It wanders off into a discussion as to which is the truer greatness, that of the
vanquished fire or that of the victorious rain. And the
speech of the rain is charming:

> " Lo, with my little drops I bless again
> And beautify the fields which thou didst blast!
> Rend, wither, waste, and ruin, what thou wilt,
> But call not Greatness what the Gods call Guilt.
> Blossoms and grass from blood in battle spilt,
> And poppied corn, I bring.
> 'Mid mouldering Babels, to oblivion built,
> My violets spring.
> Little by little my small drops have strength
> To deck with green delights the grateful earth."

And so forth, not quite germane (it seems to me) to the
matter in hand, but welcome for its own sake.

Best of all are the fables that deal more immediately
with the emotions. There is, for instance, that of *The
Two Travellers*, which is profoundly moving in conception, although by no means as well written as some
others. In this, one of the two, fearfully frost-bitten,
saves his life out of the snow at the cost of all that was
comely in his body; just as, long before, the other, who
has now quietly resigned himself to death, had violently

freed himself from Love at the cost of all that was finest and fairest in his character. Very graceful and sweet is the fable (if so it should be called) in which the author sings the praises of that " kindly perspective " which lets a wheatstalk near the eye cover twenty leagues of distant country, and makes the humble circle about a man's hearth more to him than all the possibilities of the external world. The companion fable to this is also excellent. It tells us of a man who had, all his life through, entertained a passion for certain blue hills on the far horizon, and had promised himself to travel thither ere he died, and become familiar with these distant friends. At last, in some political trouble, he is banished to the very place of his dreams. He arrives there overnight, and, when he rises and goes forth in the morning, there sure enough are the blue hills, only now they have changed places with him, and smile across to him, distant as ever, from the old home whence he has come. Such a story might have been very cynically treated; but it is not so done, the whole tone is kindly and consolatory, and the disenchanted man submissively takes the lesson, and understands that things far away are to be loved for their own sake, and that the unattainable is not truly unattainable, when we can make the beauty of it our own. Indeed, throughout all these two volumes, though there is much practical scepticism, and much irony on abstract questions, this kindly and consolatory spirit is never absent. There is much that is cheerful and, after a sedate fireside fashion, hopeful. No one will be discouraged by reading the book; but the ground of all this hopefulness and cheerfulness remains to the end somewhat vague. It does not seem to arise from any practical belief in the future either of the individual or the race, but rather from the profound personal contentment of the writer. This is, I suppose, all we must look for in the case. It is as much as we can expect if the fabulist shall prove a shrewd and cheerful fellow-wayfarer, one with whom the world does not seem to have gone much amiss, but who has yet laughingly learned something of its evil. It will depend much, of course, upon our own character and circumstances, whether the encounter will be agreeable and bracing to the spirits, or offend us as an ill-timed mockery. But where, as here, there is a little tincture of bitterness along with the good-nature, where it is plainly not the humour of a man cheerfully ignorant, but of one who looks on, tolerant and superior and smilingly attentive, upon the good and bad of our existence, it will go hardly if we do not catch some reflection of the same spirit to help us on our way. There is here no impertinent and lying proclamation of peace—none of the cheap optimism of the well-to-do; what we find here is a view of life that would be even grievous, were it not enlivened with this abiding cheerfulness, and ever and anon redeemed by a stroke of pathos.

It is natural enough, I suppose, that we should find wanting in this book some of the intenser qualities of the author's work; and their absence is made up for by much happy description after a quieter fashion. The burst of jubilation over the departure of the snow, which forms the prelude to *The Thistle*, is full of spirit and of pleasant images. The speech of the forest in *Sans Souci* is inspired by a beautiful sentiment for nature of the modern sort, and pleases us more, I think, as poetry should please us, than anything in *Chronicles and Characters*. There are some admirable felicities of expression here and there; as that of the hill, whose summit

" Did print
The azure air with pines."

Moreover, I do not recollect in the author's former

work any symptom of that sympathetic treatment of still life, which is noticeable now and again in the fables; and perhaps most noticeably, when he sketches the burned letters as they hover along the gusty flue,

"Thin, sable veils wherein a restless spark yet trembled."

But the description is at its best when the subjects are unpleasant, or even grisly. There are a few capital lines in this key on the last spasm of the battle before alluded to. Surely nothing could be better, in its own way, than the fish in *The Last Cruise of the Arrogant*, "the shadowy, side-faced, silent things," that come butting and staring with lidless eyes at the sunken steam-engine. And although in yet another, we are told pleasantly enough how the water went down into the valleys, where it set itself gaily to saw wood, and on into the plains, where it would soberly carry grain to town; yet the real strength of the fable is when it deals with the shut pool in which certain unfortunate raindrops are imprisoned among slugs and snails, and in the company of an old toad. The sodden contentment of the fallen acorn is strangely significant; and it is astonishing how unpleasantly we are startled by the appearance of her horrible lover, the maggot.

And now for the last word, about the style. This is not easy to criticise. It is impossible to deny to it rapidity, spirit and a full sound; the lines are never lame, and the sense is carried forwards with an uninterrupted, impetuous rush. But it is not equal. After passages of really admirable versification, the author falls back upon a sort of loose, cavalry manner, not unlike the style of some of Mr. Browning's minor pieces, and almost inseparable from wordiness, and an easy acceptation of somewhat cheap finish. There is nothing here of that compression which is the note of a really sovereign style. It is unfair, perhaps, to set a not remarkable passage from Lord Lytton side by side with one of the signal masterpieces of another, and a very perfect poet; and yet it is interesting, when we see how the portraiture of a dog, detailed through thirty-odd lines, is frittered down and finally almost lost in the mere laxity of the style, to compare it with the clear, simple, vigorous delineation that Burns, in four couplets, has given us of the ploughman's collie. It is interesting, at first, and then it becomes a little irritating; for when we think of other passages so much more finished and adroit, we cannot help feeling that with a little more ardour after perfection of form, criticism would have found nothing left for her to censure. A similar mark of precipitate work is the number of adjectives tumultuously heaped together, sometimes to help out the sense, and sometimes (as one cannot but suspect) to help out the sound of the verses. I do not believe, for instance, that Lord Lytton himself would defend the lines in which we are told how Laocoön " Revealed to *Roman* crowds, now *Christian* grown, That *Pagan* anguish which, in *Parian* stone, the *Rhodian* artist," and so on. It is not only that this is bad in itself; but that it is unworthy of the company in which it is found; that such verses should not have appeared with the name of a good versifier like Lord Lytton. We must take exception also, in conclusion, to the excess of alliteration. Alliteration is so liable to be abused that we can scarcely be too sparing of it; and yet it is a trick that seems to grow upon the author with years. It is a pity to see fine verses, such as some in *Demos*, absolutely spoiled by the recurrence of one wearisome consonant.

SALVINI'S *MACBETH*

Salvini closed his short visit to Edinburgh by a performance of *Macbeth*. It was, perhaps, from a sentiment of local colour that he chose to play the Scottish
usurper for the first time before Scotsmen; and the
audience were not insensible of the privilege. Few
things, indeed, can move a stronger interest than to see
a great creation taking shape for the first time. If it
is not purely artistic, the sentiment is surely human.
And the thought, that you are before all the world, and
have the start of so many others as eager as yourself, at
least keeps you in a more unbearable suspense before
the curtain rises, if it does not enhance the delight with
which you follow the performance and see the actor
" bend up each corporal agent " to realise a masterpiece
of a few hours' duration. With a player so variable as
Salvini, who trusts to the feeling of the moment for so
much detail, and who, night after night, does the same
thing differently but always well, it can never be safe
to pass judgment after a single hearing. And this is
more particularly true of last week's *Macbeth* ; for the
whole third act was marred by a grievously humorous
misadventure. Several minutes too soon the ghost of
Banquo joined the party, and, after having sat helpless
a while at a table, was ignominiously withdrawn. Twice
was this ghostly Jack-in-the-box obtruded on the stage
before his time; twice removed again; and yet he
showed so little hurry when he was really wanted, that,
after an awkward pause, Macbeth had to begin his
apostrophe to empty air. The arrival of the belated
spectre in the middle, with a jerk that made him nod
all over, was the last accident in the chapter, and worthily topped the whole. It may be imagined how lamely
matters went throughout these cross-purposes.

Salvini's Macbeth

In spite of this, and some other hitches, Salvini's *Macbeth* had an emphatic success. The creation is worthy of a place beside the same artist's *Othello* and *Hamlet*. It is the simplest and most unsympathetic of the three; but the absence of the finer lineaments of *Hamlet* is redeemed by gusto, breadth, and a headlong unity. Salvini sees nothing great in Macbeth beyond the royalty of muscle, and that courage which comes of strong and copious circulation. The moral smallness of the man is insisted on from the first, in the shudder of uncontrollable jealousy with which he sees Duncan embracing Banquo. He may have some Northern poetry of speech, but he has not much logical understanding. In his dealings with the supernatural powers he is like a savage with his fetich, trusting them beyond bounds while all goes well, and whenever he is crossed, casting his belief aside and calling " fate into the list." For his wife, he is little more than an agent, a frame of bone and sinew for her fiery spirit to command. The nature of his feeling towards her is rendered with a most precise and delicate touch. He always yields to the woman's fascination; and yet his caresses (and we know how much meaning Salvini can give to a caress) are singularly hard and unloving. Sometimes he lays his hand on her as he might take hold of anyone who happened to be nearest to him at a moment of excitement. Love has fallen out of this marriage by the way, and left a curious friendship. Only once—at the very moment when she is showing herself so little a woman and so much a high-spirited man—only once is he very deeply stirred towards her; and that finds expression in the strange and horrible transport of admiration, doubly strange and horrible on Salvini's lips—" Bring forth men-children only! "

The murder scene, as was to be expected, pleased the audience best. Macbeth's voice, in the talk with his wife, was a thing not to be forgotten; and when he spoke of his hangman's hands he seemed to have blood in his utterance. Never for a moment, even in the very article of the murder, does he possess his own soul. He is a man on wires. From first to last it is an exhibition of hideous cowardice. For, after all, it is not here, but in broad daylight, with the exhilaration of conflict, where he can assure himself at every blow he has the longest sword and the heaviest hand, that this man's physical bravery can keep him up; he is an unwieldy ship, and needs plenty of way on before he will steer.

In the banquet scene, while the first murderer gives account of what he has done, there comes a flash of truculent joy at the "twenty trenchèd gashes" on Banquo's head. Thus Macbeth makes welcome to his imagination those very details of physical horror which are so soon to turn sour in him. As he runs out to embrace these cruel circumstances, as he seeks to realise to his mind's eye the reassuring spectacle of his dead enemy, he is dressing out the phantom to terrify himself; and his imagination, playing the part of justice, is to "commend to his own lips the ingredients of his poisoned chalice." With the recollection of Hamlet and his father's spirit still fresh upon him, and the holy awe with which that good man encountered things not dreamt of in his philosophy, it was not possible to avoid looking for resemblances between the two apparitions and the two men haunted. But there are none to be found. Macbeth has a purely physical dislike for Banquo's spirit and the "twenty trenchèd gashes." He is afraid of he knows not what. He is abject, and again blustering. In the end he so far forgets himself, his terror, and the nature of what is before him, that he rushes upon it as he would upon a man. When his wife tells him he needs repose there is something really childish in the way he looks about the room, and seeing

186

nothing with an expression of almost sensual relief, plucks up heart enough to go to bed. And what is the upshot of the visitation? It is written in Shakespeare, but should be read with the commentary of Salvini's voice and expression:—"*O! siam nell' opra ancor fanciulli*,"—" We are yet young indeed." Circle below circle. He is looking with horrible satisfaction into the mouth of hell. There may still be a prick to-day; but to-morrow conscience will be dead, and he may move untroubled in this element of blood.

In the fifth act we see this lowest circle reached; and it is Salvini's finest moment throughout the play. From the first he was admirably made up, and looked Macbeth to the full as perfectly as ever he looked Othello. From the first moment he steps upon the stage you can see this character is a creation to the fullest meaning of the phrase; for the man before you is a type you know well already. He arrives with Banquo on the heath, fair and red-bearded, sparing of gesture, full of pride and the sense of animal well-being, and satisfied after the battle like a beast who has eaten his fill. But in the fifth act there is a change. This is still the big, burly, fleshly, handsome-looking Thane; here is still the same face which in the earlier acts could be superficially good-humoured and sometimes royally courteous. But now the atmosphere of blood, which pervades the whole tragedy, has entered into the man and subdued him to its own nature; and an indescribable degradation, a slackness and puffiness, has overtaken his features. He has breathed the air of carnage, and supped full of horrors. Lady Macbeth complains of the smell of blood on her hand: Macbeth makes no complaint—he has ceased to notice it now; but the same smell is in his nostrils. A contained fury and disgust possesses him. He taunts the messenger and the doctor as people would taunt their mortal enemies.

And, indeed, as he knows right well, everyone is his
enemy now, except his wife. About her he questions
the doctor with something like a last human anxiety;
and, in tones of grisly mystery, asks him if he can
" minister to a mind diseased." When the news of her
death is brought him, he is staggered and falls into a
seat; but somehow it is not anything we can call grief
that he displays. There had been two of them against
God and man; and now, when there is only one, it
makes perhaps less difference than he had expected.
And so her death is not only an affliction, but one more
disillusion; and he redoubles in bitterness. The speech
that follows, given with tragic cynicism in every word,
is a dirge, not so much for her as for himself. From
that time forth there is nothing human left in him,
only " the fiend of Scotland," Macduff's " hell-hound,"
whom, with a stern glee, we see baited like a bear and
hunted down like a wolf. He is inspired and set above
fate by a demoniacal energy, a lust of wounds and
slaughter. Even after he meets Macduff his courage
does not fail; but when he hears the Thane was not
born of woman, all virtue goes out of him; and though
he speaks sounding words of defiance, the last combat
is little better than a suicide.

The whole performance is, as I said, so full of gusto
and a headlong unity; the personality of Macbeth is
so sharp and powerful; and within these somewhat
narrow limits there is so much play and saliency that,
so far as concerns Salvini himself, a third great success
seems indubitable. Unfortunately, however, a great
actor cannot fill more than a very small fraction of the
boards; and though Banquo's ghost will probably be
more seasonable in his future apparitions, there are
some more inherent difficulties in the piece. The company at large did not distinguish themselves. Macduff,
to the huge delight of the gallery, out-Macduff'd the

average ranter. The lady who filled the principal female part has done better on other occasions, but I fear she has not metal for what she tried last week. Not to succeed in the sleep-walking scene is to make a memorable failure. As it was given, it succeeded in being wrong in art without being true to nature.

And there is yet another difficulty, happily easy to reform, which somewhat interfered with the success of the performance. At the end of the incantation scene the Italian translator has made Macbeth fall insensible upon the stage. This is a change of questionable propriety from a psychological point of view; while in point of view of effect it leaves the stage for some moments empty of all business. To remedy this, a bevy of green ballet-girls came forth and pointed their toes about the prostrate king. A dance of High Church curates, or a hornpipe by Mr. T. P. Cooke, would not be more out of the key; though the gravity of a Scots audience was not to be overcome, and they merely expressed their disapprobation by a round of moderate hisses, a similar irruption of Christmas fairies would most likely convulse a London theatre from pit to gallery with inextinguishable laughter. It is, I am told, the Italian tradition; but it is one more honoured in the breach than the observance. With the total disappearance of these damsels, with a stronger Lady Macbeth, and, if possible, with some compression of those scenes in which Salvini does not appear, and the spectator is left at the mercy of Macduffs and Duncans, the play would go twice as well, and we should be better able to follow and enjoy an admirable work of dramatic art.

BAGSTER'S *PILGRIM'S PROGRESS*

I have here before me an edition of the *Pilgrim's Progress*, bound in green, without a date, and described as "illustrated by nearly three hundred engravings, and memoir of Bunyan." On the outside it is lettered "Bagster's Illustrated Edition," and after the author's apology, facing the first page of the tale, a folding pictorial "Plan of the Road" is marked as "drawn by the late Mr. T. Conder," and engraved by J. Basire. No further information is anywhere vouchsafed; perhaps the publishers had judged the work too unimportant; and we are still left ignorant whether or not we owe the woodcuts in the body of the volume to the same hand that drew the plan. It seems, however, more than probable. The literal particularity of mind which, in the map, laid down the flower-plots in the devil's garden, and carefully introduced the court-house in the town of Vanity, is closely paralleled in many of the cuts; and in both, the architecture of the buildings and the disposition of the gardens have a kindred and entirely English air. Whoever he was, the author of these wonderful little pictures may lay claim to be the best illustrator of Bunyan.* They are not only good illustrations like so many others; but they are like so few, good illustrations of Bunyan. Their spirit, in defect and quality, is still the same as his own. The designer also has lain down and dreamed a dream, as literal, as quaint, and almost as apposite as Bunyan's; and text and pictures make but the two sides of the same homespun yet

* The illustrator was, in fact, a lady, Miss Eunice Bagster, eldest daughter of the publisher, Samuel Bagster ; except in the case of the cuts depicting the fight with Apollyon, which were designed by her brother, Mr. Jonathan Bagster. The edition was published in 1845. I am indebted for this information to the kindness of Mr. Robert Bagster, the present managing director of the firm.—[ED.]

impassioned story. To do justice to the designs, it will be necessary to say, for the hundredth time, a word or two about the masterpiece which they adorn.

All allegories have a tendency to escape from the purpose of their creators; and as the characters and incidents become more and more interesting in themselves, the moral, which these were to show forth, falls more and more into neglect. An architect may command a wreath of vine leaves round the cornice of a monument; but if, as each leaf came from the chisel, it took proper life and fluttered freely on the wall, and if the vine grew, and the building were hidden over with foliage and fruit, the architect would stand in much the same situation as the writer of allegories. The *Faëry Queen* was an allegory, I am willing to believe; but it survives as an imaginative tale in incomparable verse. The case of Bunyan is widely different; and yet in this also Allegory, poor nymph, although never quite forgotten, is sometimes rudely thrust against the wall. Bunyan was fervently in earnest; with " his fingers in his ears, he ran on," straight for his mark. He tells us himself, in the conclusion to the first part, that he did not fear to raise a laugh; indeed, he feared nothing, and said anything; and he was greatly served in this by a certain rustic privilege of his style, which, like the talk of strong uneducated men, when it does not impress by its force, still charms by its simplicity. The mere story and the allegorical design enjoyed perhaps his equal favour. He believed in both with an energy of faith that was capable of moving mountains. And we have to remark in him, not the parts where inspiration fails and is supplied by cold and merely decorative invention, but the parts where faith has grown to be credulity, and his characters become so real to him that he forgets the end of their creation. We can follow him step by step into the trap which he lays for himself by his own entire good faith and triumphant literality of vision, till the trap closes and shuts him in an inconsistency. The allegories of the Interpreter and of the Shepherds of the Delectable Mountains are all actually performed, like stage-plays, before the pilgrims. The son of Mr. Greatgrace visibly " tumbles hills about with his words." Adam the First has his condemnation written visibly on his forehead, so that Faithful reads it. At the very instant the net closes round the pilgrims, " the white robe falls from the black man's body." Despair " getteth him a grievous crab-tree cudgel "; it was in " sunshiny weather " that he had his fits; and the birds in the grove about the House Beautiful, " our country birds," only sing their little pious verses " at the spring, when the flowers appear and the sun shines warm." " I often," says Piety, " go out to hear them; we also oft-times keep them tame on our house." The post between Beulah and the Celestial City sounds his horn, as you may yet hear in country places. Madam Bubble, that " tall, comely dame, something of a swarthy complexion, in very pleasant attire, but old," " gives you a smile at the end of each sentence "—a real woman she; we all know her. Christiana dying " gave Mr. Stand-fast a ring," for no possible reason in the allegory, merely because the touch was human and affecting. Look at Great-heart, with his soldierly ways, garrison ways, as I had almost called them; with his taste in weapons; his delight in any that " he found to be a man of his hands "; his chivalrous point of honour, letting Giant Maul get up again when he was down, a thing fairly flying in the teeth of the moral; above all, with his language in the inimitable tale of Mr. Fearing: " I thought I should have lost my man " —" chicken-hearted "—" at last he came in, and I will say that for my lord, he carried it wonderful lovingly to him." This is no Independent minister; this is a stout, honest, big-busted ancient, adjusting his shoulder-belts, twirling his long moustaches as he speaks. Last and most remarkable, " My sword," says the dying Valiant-for-Truth, he in whom Great-heart delighted, " my sword I give to him that shall succeed me in my pilgrimage *and my courage and skill to him that can get it.*" And after this boast, more arrogantly unorthodox than was ever dreamed of by the rejected Ignorance, we are told that " all the trumpets sounded for him on the other side."

In every page the book is stamped with the same energy of vision and the same energy of belief. The quality is equally and indifferently displayed in the spirit of the fighting, the tenderness of the pathos, the startling vigour and strangeness of the incidents, the natural strain of the conversations, and the humanity and charm of the characters. Trivial talk over a meal, the dying words of heroes, the delights of Beulah or the Celestial City, Apollyon, and my Lord Hategood, Great-heart, and Mr. Worldly Wiseman, all have been imagined with the same clearness, all written of with equal gusto and precision, all created in the same mixed element, of simplicity that is almost comical, and art that, for its purpose, is faultless.

It was in much the same spirit that our artist sat down to his drawings. He is by nature a Bunyan of the pencil. He, too, will draw anything, from a butcher at work on a dead sheep, up to the courts of Heaven. "A Lamb for Supper " is the name of one of his designs, " Their Glorious Entry " of another. He has the same disregard for the ridiculous, and enjoys somewhat of the same privilege of style, so that we are pleased even when we laugh the most. He is literal to the verge of folly. If dust is to be raised from the unswept parlour, you may be sure it will " fly abundantly " in the picture. If Faithful is to lie " as dead " before Moses, dead he shall lie with a warrant—dead and stiff like granite; nay (and here the artist must enhance upon the symbolism of the author), it is with the identical stone tables of the law that Moses fells the sinner. Good and bad people, whom we at once distinguish in the text by their names, Hopeful, Honest, and Valiant-for-Truth on the one hand, as against By-ends, Sir Having Greedy, and the Lord Old-man on the other, are in these drawings as simply distinguished by their costume. Good people, when not armed *cap-à-pie*, wear a speckled tunic girt about the waist, and low hats, apparently of straw. Bad people swagger in tail-coats and chimney-pots, a few with knee-breeches, but the large majority in trousers, and for all the world like guests at a garden-party. Worldly Wiseman alone, by some inexplicable quirk, stands before Christian in laced hat, embroidered waistcoat, and trunk-hose. But above all examples of this artist's intrepidity, commend me to the print entitled " Christian Finds it Deep." "A great darkness and horror," says the text, have fallen on the pilgrim; it is the comfortless death-bed with which Bunyan so strikingly concludes the sorrows and conflicts of his hero. How to represent this worthily the artist knew not; and yet he was determined to represent it somehow. This was how he did: Hopeful is still shown to his neck above the water of death; but Christian has bodily disappeared, and a blot of solid blackness indicates his place.

As you continue to look at these pictures, about an inch square for the most part, sometimes printed three or more to the page, and each having a printed legend of its own, however trivial the event recorded, you will soon become aware of two things: first, that the man can draw, and, second, that he possesses the gift of an imagination. " Obstinate reviles," says the legend; and you should see Obstinate reviling. " He warily retraces his steps"; and there is Christian, posting through the plain, terror and speed in every muscle. "Mercy yearns to go" shows you a plain interior with packing going forward, and, right in the middle, Mercy yearning to go—every line of the girl's figure yearning. In "The Chamber called Peace" we see a simple English room, bed with white curtains, window valance and door, as may be found in many thousand unpretentious houses; but far off, through the open window, we behold the sun uprising out of a great plain, and Christian hails it with his hand:

> "Where am I now! is this the love and care
> Of Jesus, for the men that pilgrims are!
> Thus to provide! That I should be forgiven!
> And dwell already the next door to heaven!"

A page or two further, from the top of the House Beautiful, the damsels point his gaze towards the Delectable Mountains: "The Prospect," so the cut is ticketed—and I shall be surprised, if on less than a square of paper you can show me one so wide and fair. Down a cross-road on an English plain, a cathedral city outlined on the horizon, a hazel shaw upon the left, comes Madam Wanton dancing with her fair enchanted cup, and Faithful, book in hand, half pauses. The cut is perfect as a symbol: the giddy movement of the sorceress, the uncertain pose of the man struck to the heart by a temptation, the contrast of that even plain of life whereon he journeys with the bold, ideal bearing of the wanton—the artist who invented and portrayed this had not merely read Bunyan, he had also thoughtfully lived. The Delectable Mountains— I continue skimming the first part—are not on the whole happily rendered. Once, and once only, the note is struck, when Christian and Hopeful are seen coming, shoulder-high, through a thicket of green shrubs—box, perhaps, or perfumed nutmeg; while behind them,

Earlier Works

domed or pointed, the hills stand ranged against the sky. A little further, and we come to that masterpiece of Bunyan's insight into life, the Enchanted Ground; where, in a few traits, he has set down the latter end of such a number of the would-be good; where his allegory goes so deep that, to people looking seriously on life, it cuts like satire. The true significance of this invention lies, of course, far out of the way of drawing; only one feature, the great tedium of the land, the growing weariness in well-doing, may be somewhat represented in a symbol. The pilgrims are near the end: " Two Miles Yet," says the legend. The road goes ploughing up and down over a rolling heath; the wayfarers, with outstretched arms, are already sunk to the knees over the brow of the nearest hill; they have just passed a milestone with the cipher two; from over-head a great, piled, summer cumulus, as of a slumber-ous summer afternoon, beshadows them: two miles! it might be hundreds. In dealing with the Land of Beulah the artist lags, in both parts, miserably behind the text, but in the distant prospect of the Celestial City more than regains his own. You will remember when Christian and Hopeful " with desire fell sick." "Effect of the Sunbeams " is the artist's title. Against the sky, upon a cliffy mountain, the radiant temple beams upon them over deep, subjacent woods; they, behind a mound, as if seeking shelter from the splendour—one prostrate on his face, one kneeling, and with hands ecstatically lifted—yearn with passion after that im-mortal city. Turn the page, and we behold them walk-ing by the very shores of death; Heaven, from this nigher view, has risen half-way to the zenith, and sheds a wider glory; and the two pilgrims, dark against that brightness, walk and sing out of the fullness of their hearts. No cut more thoroughly illustrates at once the merit and the weakness of the artist. Each pilgrim sings with a book in his grasp—a family Bible at the least for bigness; tomes so recklessly enormous that our second impulse is to laughter. And yet that is not the first thought, nor perhaps the last. Something in the attitude of the manikins—faces they have none, they are too small for that—something in the way they swing these monstrous volumes to their singing, some-thing perhaps borrowed from the text, some subtle differentiation from the cut that went before and the cut that follows after—something, at least, speaks clearly of a fearful joy, of Heaven seen from the death-bed, of the horror of the last passage no less than of the glorious coming home. There is that in the action of one of them which always reminds me, with a differ-ence, of that haunting last glimpse of Thomas Idle, travelling to Tyburn in the cart. Next come the Shining Ones, wooden and trivial enough; the pilgrims pass into the river; the blot already mentioned settles over and obliterates Christian. In two more cuts we behold them drawing nearer to the other shore; and then, between two radiant angels, one of whom points up-wards, we see them mounting in new weeds, their former lendings left behind them on the inky river. More angels meet them; Heaven is displayed, and if no better, certainly no worse, than it has been shown by others—a place, at least, infinitely populous and glorious with light—a place that haunts solemnly the hearts of children. And then this symbolic draughts-man once more strikes into his proper vein. Three cuts conclude the first part. In the first the gates close, black against the glory struggling from within. The second shows us Ignorance—alas! poor Arminian!— hailing, in a sad twilight, the ferryman Vain-Hope; and in the third we behold him, bound hand and foot, and black already with the hue of his eternal fate, carried high over the mountain-tops of the world by two angels of the anger of the Lord. "Carried to Another Place," the artist enigmatically names his plate—a terrible design.

Wherever he touches on the black side of the supernatural his pencil grows more daring and incisive. He has many true inventions in the perilous and diabolic; he has many startling nightmares realised. It is not easy to select the best; some may like one and some another; the nude, depilated devil bounding and casting darts against the Wicket Gate; the scroll of flying horrors that hang over Christian by the Mouth of Hell; the horned shade that comes behind him whispering blasphemies; the daylight breaking through that rent cave-mouth of the mountains and falling chill adown the haunted tunnel; Christian's further progress along the causeway, between the two black pools, where, at every yard or two, a gin, a pitfall, or a snare awaits the passer-by—loathsome white devilkins harbouring close under the bank to work the springes, Christian himself pausing and pricking with his sword's point at the nearest noose, and pale discomfortable mountains rising on the farther side; or yet again, the two ill-favoured ones that beset the first of Christian's journey, with the frog-like structure of the skull, the frog-like limberness of limbs—crafty, slippery, lustful-looking devils, drawn always in outline as though possessed of a dim, infernal luminosity. Horrid fellows are they, one and all; horrid fellows and horrific scenes. In another spirit that Good-Conscience "to whom Mr. Honest had spoken in his lifetime," a cowled, grey, awful figure, one hand pointing to the heavenly shore, realises, I will not say all, but some at least of the strange impressiveness of Bunyan's words. It is no easy nor pleasant thing to speak in one's lifetime with Good-Conscience; he is an austere, unearthly friend, whom maybe Torquemada knew; and the folds of his raiment are not merely claustral, but have something of the horror of the pall. Be not afraid, however; with the hand of that appearance Mr. Honest will get safe across.

Yet perhaps it is in sequences that this artist best displays himself. He loves to look at either side of a thing: as, for instance, when he shows us both sides of the wall—" Grace Inextinguishable " on the one side, with the devil vainly pouring buckets on the flame, and " The Oil of Grace " on the other, where the Holy Spirit, vessel in hand, still secretly supplies the fire. He loves, also, to show us the same event twice over, and to repeat his instantaneous photographs at the interval of but a moment. So we have, first, the whole troop of Pilgrims coming up to Valiant, and Great-heart to the front, spear in hand and parleying; and the next, the same cross-roads, from a more distant view, the convoy now scattered and looking safely and curiously on, and Valiant handing over for inspection his " right Jerusalem blade." It is true that his designer has no great care after consistency: Apollyon's spear is laid by, his quiver of darts will disappear, whenever they might hinder the designer's freedom; and the fiend's tail is blobbed or forked at his good pleasure. But this is not unsuitable to the illustration of the fervent Bunyan, breathing hurry and momentary inspiration. He, with his hot purpose, hunting sinners with a lasso, shall himself forget the things that he has written yesterday. He shall first slay Heedless in the Valley of the Shadow, and then take leave of him talking in his sleep, as if nothing had happened, in an arbour on the Enchanted Ground. And again, in his rhymed prologue, he shall assign some of the glory of the siege of Doubting Castle to his favourite Valiant-for-Truth, who did not meet with the besiegers till long after, at that dangerous corner by Deadman's Lane. And, with all inconsistencies and freedoms, there is a power shown in these sequences of cuts: a power of

joining on one action or one humour to another; a
power of following out the moods, even of the dismal
subter-human fiends engendered by the artist's fancy;
a power of sustained continuous realisation, step by
step, in nature's order, that can tell a story, in all its
ins and outs, its pauses and surprises, fully and figura-
tively, like the art of words.

One such sequence is the fight of Christian and
Apollyon—six cuts, weird and fiery, like the text. The
pilgrim is throughout a pale and stockish figure; but
the devil covers a multitude of defects. There is no
better devil of the conventional order than our artist's
Apollyon, with his mane, his wings, his bestial legs,
his changing and terrifying expression, his infernal
energy to slay. In cut the first you see him afar off,
still obscure in form, but already formidable in suggestion. Cut the second, " The Fiend in Discourse,"
represents him, not reasoning, railing rather, shaking
his spear at the pilgrim, his shoulder advanced, his tail
writhing in the air, his foot ready for a spring, while
Christian stands back a little, timidly defensive. The
third illustrates these magnificent words: " Then
Apollyon straddled quite over the whole breadth of
the way, and said, I am void of fear in this matter: pre-
pare thyself to die; for I swear by my infernal den that
thou shalt go no farther: here will I spill thy soul! And
with that he threw a flaming dart at his breast." In the
cut he throws a dart with either hand, belching pointed
flames out of his mouth, spreading his broad vans, and
straddling the while across the path, as only a fiend can
straddle who has just sworn by his infernal den. The
defence will not be long against such vice, such flames,
such red-hot nether energy. And in the fourth cut, to
be sure, he has leaped bodily upon his victim, sped by
foot and pinion, and roaring as he leaps. The fifth shows
the climacteric of the battle; Christian has reached

nimbly out and got his sword, and dealt that deadly home-thrust, the fiend still stretched upon him, but " giving back, as one that had received his mortal wound." The raised head, the bellowing mouth, the paw clapped upon the sword, the one wing relaxed in agony, all realise vividly these words of the text. In the sixth and last, the trivial armed figure of the pilgrim is seen kneeling with clasped hands on the betrodden scene of contest and among the shivers of the darts; while just at the margin the hinder quarters and the tail of Apollyon are whisking off, indignant and discomfited.

In one point only do these pictures seem to be unworthy of the text, and that point is one rather of the difference of arts than the difference of artists. Throughout his best and worst, in his highest and most divine imaginations as in the narrowest sallies of his sectarianism, the human-hearted piety of Bunyan touches and ennobles, convinces, accuses the reader. Through no art besides the art of words can the kindness of a man's affections be expressed. In the cuts you shall find faithfully parodied the quaintness and the power, the triviality and the surprising freshness of the author's fancy; there you shall find him outstripped in ready symbolism and the art of bringing things essentially invisible before the eyes: but to feel the contact of essential goodness, to be made in love with piety, the book must be read and not the prints examined.

Farewell should not be taken with a grudge; nor can I dismiss in any other words than those of gratitude a series of pictures which have, to one at least, been the visible embodiment of Bunyan from childhood up, and shown him, through all his years, Great-heart lungeing at Giant Maul, and Apollyon breathing fire at Christian, and every turn and town along the road to the Celestial City, and that bright place itself, seen as to a stave of music, shining afar off upon the hill-top, the candle of the world.

*SCOTTISH RIVERS**

Dr. John Brown calls this, in his pleasant preface to it, a delightful book; and Dr. John Brown is a good judge. A delightful book it certainly is, and delightful in no ordinary way. Although it is not thirty years since the author left it unfinished at his death, it is already in some sense an antiquity. The style is farther away from us than many styles older in date. There is throughout a sort of ponderous editorial levity, that has now gone somewhat into disuse. We are saluted as " gentle reader " and " gentlest of all readers." Social gossip about men and things and perpetual compliments to the nobility and gentry, by whose estates the river may chance to go, speak to us of a time when Scotland was to some extent a separate country and an author could address himself to a Scottish public, almost small enough to deserve the name of a clique and with a clique's special knowledge and special readiness to be pleased. In speaking to us as he does, we feel that the author is treating us as one of the family. His garrulousness has all the character of personal intercourse. We begin to regard his " old and much valued friend General Sir James Russel," as an old and much valued friend of our own; at least, we are sure the author would be glad to give us an introduction, not only to him, but to all the friends and acquaintances who come in his way, and so frank us, for a whole holiday, from one country house to another, all over Tweeddale and the valley of the Tyne.

This is just one of the qualities that make the book delightful. It is in no literary sense, it is merely from

* Scottish Rivers. By the late Sir Thomas Dick Lauder, Baronet, author of the " Morayshire Floods," etc. With illustrations by the Author and a Preface by John Brown, M.D., author of " Rab and his Friends," etc. (Edinburgh : Edmonston and Douglas, 1874.)

the pleasure of making a lovable acquaintance and going through interesting scenery, that we can accord it merit. We have called the style editorial; indeed, it is not unlike that of a provincial editor's description of the annual games, with just such little touches of personal compliment as the editor would deal out to his distinguished fellow-townsmen and the various successful competitors. Now, at a first sight, one would have thought that a book like this would depend almost entirely upon style; that a book which merely promises to set forth to us, with appropriate gossip, the changeful character of the valley of one river after another, if it failed in the point of vivid descriptive writing, would be a failure altogether. But we have a proof to the contrary before us. *Scottish Rivers* is a delightful book, in virtue of the delightful character of the author and the delightful character of his subject. It is all about things that are in themselves agreeable. The natural heart of man is made happy by hearing that the wild cattle of Ettrick Forest *were three times the size of those kept at Chillingham;* and all the more, perhaps, if we do not know what that was—there is the more rein for picturesque imagination. We should be very sorry for anyone who did not care to hear about Thomas the Rhymer and the Black Dwarf; about border-rievers, fugitive Jacobites, and hunted Covenanters. The breath of Walter Scott has gone out over these dry bones of old Scotch history; the work of imagination is done to our hand; and as we turn over these leaves, just as when we follow the actual course of the rivers themselves, we are accompanied by the pageant world of the Waverley Novels, and *Marmion*, and the *Lay of the Last Minstrel.*

Moreover, there is a great deal of quotation in the book; not only Scott, but all manner of old ballads and old songs, take the tale, now and again, out of the mouth of the author; and the pages are pleasantly broken up and lightened with these snatches of verse. It is the fashion nowadays to run down this good old custom of quotation; we write prose so admirably, it seems, that these scraps would give even pain to the cultured reader, as an interruption to the sustained measure of the sentences. It may be so, but there is something to be said on the other side; and we greet some familiar passage when we find it in another man's book, like a friend in strange company.

The great point, however, in this book upon Scottish rivers, is the sincerity of the author's own delight in the stories he repeats, the verses he quotes, the scenery and the animals he seeks to describe to us. It is by this sense of enjoyment that the whole book is kept alive. Sometimes it crops out in one way, sometimes in another, sometimes it is his passion for fishing that adds gusto to what he has to say of a place—as for example: " Below Kirkurd, the Tairth runs through a series of valuable water meadows, in a deep and uniform stream, resembling in character an English river; and," he adds, " we are much mistaken if it be not full of fine fat trouts." One can hear the smack of the lips in these words. His whole past life has been so pleasant; he has such a host of sunny recollections, that the one jostles the other and they come tumbling forth together in a happy confusion: his basket is so full of those " fine fat trouts " of the memory, that it is a sight to see him empty it before us. Even fishing is passed by in superior ecstasies: " This is one of the most beautiful parts of the Tweed," he says, " and well do we remember the day when, wandering in our boyhood up hither from Melrose, we found ourselves for the first time in the midst of scenery so grand and beautiful. The rod was speedily put up, and the fly-book was exchanged for the sketch-book. We wandered about from point to point, now and then reclining on the grass, and sometimes, from very wantonness, wading into the shallows of the clear stream; and so we passed away some hours of luxurious idleness, the pleasure of which we shall never cease to remember."

Is not that passage enough to convince the reader? He will find the book full of the like. He will find that this man, not very wise perhaps, certainly not very cunning in words, had a great faculty of pleasurable recollection, that he noticed things more closely than most of us, and liked them better, and that he could speak of what he thus observed and loved in a plain diffuse way that is full of gusto and most truly human.

And the last thing to be thought of, is that the book was written during the author's final illness. " What a place for linnets' nests and primroses in the lovely springtime of the year! " he exclaims, as the name Blackford Hill comes from under his pen. Would one not fancy that he was a schoolboy with forty spring-times before him? It is easy, after this, to believe what Lord Cockburn said of him, that " his dying deserves to be remembered, for it reconciles one to the act."

*A QUIET CORNER OF ENGLAND**

"A building," says Mr. Champneys, "can never be like a picture, complete within the limits of its frame and independent of influences beyond. It must be studied upon its own site, and under all the conditions of history, landscape and neighbourhood." We may amplify this idea a little, or rather put it in terms a little more general: The author wishes people to look at what they see with their eyes open, and not isolate special things artificially, and look at these only to the exclusion of the others. He is not one of those who say they are looking at a church when they are looking, in truth, at a church, complicated with a confusion of roofs and chimneys, connecting itself naturally with the sweep of the street that leads up to it, and relieved against the blue distance and the bright sky on the horizon. A building is a building, indeed, but it is much more. It makes or mars the landscape, it completes or nullifies the profile of a town upon a hill-top. I have in my eye two notable instances. In one, a block of high barracks, built in late days upon the battlements of an old citadel, falls admirably into harmony with the situation, and carries up into the sky-line the sentiment of the steep rock upon which the place is founded; so that, although a commonplace structure in itself, it has become the most impressive, and I had almost said the most romantic, feature of the pile. In the other, a monumental tower of some architectural pretensions has been put upon a poor hill, the last buttress of a grand wall of mountains; and those who remember the

* A Quiet Corner of England : Studies of Landscape and Architecture in Winchelsea, Rye, and the Romney Marsh. By Basil Champneys, B.A., Architect. With numerous Illustrations by Alfred Dawson. (London : Seeley, Jackson, and Halliday, 1874.)

hill before it was thus burthened, the whole scene before it was thus burlesqued and stultified, can alone
appreciate the evil that has been effected.

The most delicate shades of religion may be traced
between the sentiment of a building and the sentiment
of its surroundings. And in no place is this religion so
delicate and amiable, at least for Englishmen, as in
quiet corners of England, such as the one Mr. Champneys has set himself to realise for us. He was moved,
he tells us, by " a jealous desire that the modest and
homely landscape and architecture of our own country
should receive more general appreciation." He has
been justly irritated at that very pinchbeck and undis-
criminating enthusiasm which inspires so many of the
readers of the Continental Bradshaw and the followers
after Mr. Cook.

" Those," he says, " whose association with either
landscape or art is more or less occasional, naturally find
grandeur more effective than modesty, scale more easy
to appreciate than sentiment. But such emotions as
are engendered exclusively by gorgeous effects are
apt to be sensational, and are neither so wholesome
nor so enduring as those which arise in a homely
atmosphere. Moreover, familiarity with the more
specious is apt to render the more modest permanently
insipid."

There is a great deal of truth in this, and yet I should
be inclined to regard this exclusive preference for Alps
and Pyramids as entirely exotic to the heart of Englishmen. If this tare has grown up among us, it is because
an enemy came by night and sowed it—many enemies
rather: the whole generation of small poets and small
romantic travellers—and because better husbandmen
have been remiss and let the good seed lie idle. And
so we may have all hope of the ultimate success of books
such as this, and the better spirit of which they are the

sign. The English are a docile people in such matters: they will gladly learn from Mr. Champneys that there is a sentiment in Romney Marsh as well as in the Pyrenees; this acquisition will make it an easier task for some one else to prove to them the beauty of some other out-of-the-way corner or beaten track; and so line upon line, precept upon precept, they will become intelligently reconciled to the fashion of their own country, and learn, perhaps, some more refined conception of natural loveliness than a very big hill of no particular shape with some white snow upon the top of it.

The district chosen by Mr. Champneys is one of somewhat romantic geographical conditions. Out of a bay on the old coast line, still strongly marked and easily recognisable for a coast line, the sea has gone back step by step, leaving behind it a great flat. This flat is Romney Marsh. The chief note of the district is its amphibiousness; and this is capitally realised for us in the book. Traces of the retiring waters are nowhere wanting. You can recognise what was once an island by the constrained grouping together of trees and houses; and what was once an estuary or lagoon, by bridges and stepping-stones now left high and dry for ever. On the horizon, ships in full sail seem mixed together with stationary trees and haystacks.

" The more subtile effects," says Mr. Champneys, " are as those upon the sea. You see the storm gathering in the distance, and it sweeps over the ground self-contained, solid, and detached, neither distorted nor delayed by any prominence; the wind blows steady and undiverted; and the countryman who shows you a circuitous path to some distant object on the open plain, has some story to tell of former perils by sea. The farmers keep a few boats, and the retired sailors become farmers or farm labourers, and the old houses far inland are specially and elaborately planned for hiding smuggled goods. Moreover, the sea, though from the dead level it is actually unseen, is constantly present to the imagination as a haunting influence, and to the senses as a bright horizon of reflected light; and the seashore is marked here and there by a few white-washed cottages and a flagstaff."

This is very good, and there is more of a like quality. Altogether, what with Mr. Champneys' description and some of Mr. Dawson's illustrations—that, for instance, opposite page 12 and that at the foot of page 61— Romney Marsh becomes very distinct and familiar to our minds before we have finished the little volume.

Of the various buildings that are brought out for us against this background, the various bits of architectural detail criticised—architectural detail of all sorts and descriptions down to the carpentry of certain prison doors at Rye, and a glazed cupboard from the inn at New Romney—I propose to say nothing. There is much to interest the reader: and here again some of Mr. Dawson's etchings are worthy of all praise. But one must avoid falling into the manner of those *critiques de critiques* that have stirred the scorn of Baudelaire, and many others who had a better right, perhaps, to be scornful in such a case. So, without entering into any of the more particular points here dealt with, it will be enough to say that all the criticism bears the stamp of strong personality. Mr. Champneys is no more open to all the pleasurable details of art than angry against those whom he considers as art's banded enemies, and he is a very plain dealer when angry. Indeed, some of the most entertaining passages of the volume are those in which he has suffered his righteous indignation to carry him away, and refers with truculent irony to " the refined and interesting zeal of Protestantism," or regrets the rashness which led him to " anticipate that a Conservative Government would extend to our most valuable monuments some portion of that tenderness which it is supposed to show for abuses."

VI

BÉRANGER

Pierre Jean de Béranger, the national song-writer of
France, was born at Paris on the 19th of August, 1780.
The aristocratic particle before the name was a piece
of groundless vanity on the part of his father, which
the poet found useful as well as a distinction. He was
descended, in truth, from a tailor in the Rue Montor-
gueil. Of education, in the narrower sense, he had but
little. From the roof of his school he beheld the capture
of the Bastille, and this stirring memory was all that he
acquired. Later on he passed some time in a school of
Péronne, founded by one Bellenglise on the principles
of Rousseau, where the boys were formed into clubs
and regiments, and taught to play solemnly at politics
and war. Béranger was president of the club, made
speeches before such members of convention as passed
through Péronne, and drew up addresses to Tallien or
Robespierre at Paris. In the meanwhile he learned
neither Greek nor Latin—not even French, it would
appear; for it was after he had left school, from the
printer Laisney, that he acquired the elements of
grammar. His true education was of another sort. In
his childhood, shy, sickly, and skilful with his hands,
as he sat at home alone to carve cherry stones, he was
already forming for himself those habits of retirement
and patient elaboration which influenced the whole
tenor of his life and the character of all that he wrote.
At Péronne he learned of his good aunt to be a stout
republican; and from the doorstep of her inn, on quiet
evenings, he would listen to the thunder of the guns
before Valenciennes, and fortify himself in his passionate love of France and distaste for all things foreign.
Although he could never read Horace save in translation, he had been educated on Télémaque, Racine, and

the dramas of Voltaire, and taught from a child in the
tradition of all that is highest and most correct in
French.

After serving his aunt for some time in the capacity
of waiter, and passing some time also in the printing
office of one Laisney, he was taken to Paris by his
father. Here he saw much low speculation and many
low royalist intrigues. In 1802, in consequence of a
distressing quarrel, he left his father and began life for
himself in the garret of his ever-memorable song. For
two years he did literary hackwork when he could get
it, and wrote pastorals, epics, and all manner of
ambitious failures. At the end of that period (1804)
he wrote to Lucien Bonaparte, enclosing some of these
attempts. He was then in bad health, and in the last
stage of misery. His watch was pledged. His ward-
robe consisted of one pair of boots, one great-coat, one
pair of trousers with a hole in the knee, and " three
bad shirts which a friendly hand wearied itself in en-
deavouring to mend." The friendly hand was that of
Judith Frère, with whom he had been already more or
less acquainted since 1796, and who continued to be
his faithful companion until her death, three months
before his own, in 1857. She must not be confounded
with the Lisette of the songs; the pieces addressed to
her (*La Bonne Vieille, Maudit Printemps*, etc.) are in a
very different vein. Lucien Bonaparte interested himself in the young poet, transferred to him his own pension of 1000 francs from the Institute, and set him to
work on a *Death of Nero*. Five years later, through the
same patronage, although indirectly, Béranger became
a clerk in the University at a salary of another thousand.

Meanwhile he had written many songs of convivial
occasions, and " to console himself under all misfortune "; some, according to M. Boiteau, had already
been published by his father; but he set no great store

on them himself; and it was only in 1812, while watching by the sick-bed of a friend, that it occurred to him to write down the best he could remember. Next year he was elected to the *Caveau Moderne*, and his reputation as a song-writer began to spread. Manuscript copies of *Les Gueux*, *Le Sénateur*, above all of *Le Roi d'Yvetot*, a satire against Napoleon, whom he was to magnify so much in the sequel, passed from hand to hand with acclamation. It was thus that all his best works went abroad; one man sang them to another over all of France. He was the only poet of modern times who could altogether have dispensed with printing.

His first collection escaped censure. " We must pardon many things to the author of *Le Roi d'Yvetot*," said Louis XVIII. The second (1821) was more daring. The apathy of the Liberal camp, he says, had convinced him of the need of some bugle call of awakening. This publication lost him his situation in the University, and subjected him to a trial, a fine of 500 francs, and an imprisonment of three months. Imprisonment was a small thing for Béranger. At Sainte Pélagie he occupied a room (it had just been quitted by Paul Louis Courier), warm, well-furnished, and preferable in every way to his own poor lodging, where the water froze on winter nights. He adds, on the occasion of his second imprisonment, that he found a certain charm in this quiet, claustral existence, with its regular hours and long evenings alone over the fire. This second imprisonment of nine months, together with a fine and expenses amounting to 1,100 francs, followed on the appearance of his fourth collection. The Government proposed through Lafitte that, if he would submit to judgment without appearing or making defences, he should only be condemned in the smallest penalty. But his public spirit made him refuse the proposal; and he would not even ask permission to pass his term of imprisonment in a *maison de santé*, although his health was more than usually feeble at the time. When you " have taken your stand in a contest with the Government, it seems to me," he wrote, " ridiculous to complain of the blows it inflicts on you, and impolitic to furnish it with any occasion of generosity." His first thought in La Force was to alleviate the condition of the other prisoners.

In the revolution of July he took no inconsiderable part. Copies of his song, *Le Vieux Drapeau*, were served out to the insurgent crowd. He had been for long the intimate friend and adviser of the leading men; and during the decisive week his counsels went a good way towards shaping the ultimate result. "As for the republic, that dream of my old life," he wrote in 1831, " I did not wish it should be given us a second time unripe." Louis Philippe, hearing how much the song-writer had done towards his elevation, expressed a wish to see and speak with him; but Béranger refused to present himself at court, and used his favour only to ask a place for a friend, and a pension for Rouget de Lisle, author of the famous *Marseillaise*, who was now old and poor, and whom he had been already succouring for five years.

In 1848, in spite of every possible expression of his reluctance, he was elected to the assembly, and that by so large a number of votes (4471) that he felt himself obliged to accept the office. Not long afterwards, and with great difficulty, he obtained leave to resign. This was the last public event of Béranger's life. He continued to polish his songs in retirement, visited by nearly all the famous men of France. He numbered among his friends: Chateaubriand, Thiers, Lafitte, Michelet, Lamennais, Mignet. Nothing could exceed the amiability of his private character; so poor a man has rarely been so rich in good actions; he was always ready to receive help from his friends when he was in need, and always forward to help others. His correspondence is full of wisdom and kindness, with a smack of Montaigne, and now and then a vein of pleasantry that will remind the English reader of Charles Lamb. He occupied some of his leisure in preparing his own memoirs, and a certain treatise on *Social and Political Morality*, intended for the people, a work he had much at heart, but judged at last to be beyond his strength. He died on July 16th, 1857. It was feared that his funeral would be the signal for some political disturbance; but the Government took immediate measures, and all went quietly. The Streets of Paris were lined with soldiers and full of townsfolk, silent and uncovered. From time to time cries arose: " Honneur, honneur à Béranger!"

The songs of Béranger would scarcely be called songs in English. They are elaborate, written in a clear and sparkling style, full of wit and incision. It is not so much for any lyrical flow as for the happy turn of the phrase that they claim superiority. Whether the subject be gay or serious, light or passionate, the medium remains untroubled. The special merits of the songs are merits to be looked for rather in English prose than in English verse. He worked deliberately, never wrote more than fifteen songs a year and often less, and was so fastidious that he has not preserved a quarter of what he finished. " I am a good little bit of a poet," he says himself, " clever in the craft, and a conscientious worker, to whom old airs and a modest choice of subjects (*le coin où je me suis confiné*), have brought some success." Nevertheless, he makes a figure of importance in literary history. When he first began to cultivate the *chanson*, this minor form lay under some contempt, and was restricted to slight subjects, and a humorous guise of treatment. Gradually he filled these little chiselled toys of verbal perfection with ever more and

more of sentiment. From a date comparatively early he
had determined to sing for the people. It was for this
reason that he fled, as far as possible, the houses of his
influential friends, and came back gladly to the garret
and the street corner. Thus it was, also, that he came
to acknowledge obligations to Émile Debraux, who
had often stood between him and the masses as interpreter, and given him the key-note of the popular
humour. Now, he had observed in the songs of the
sailors, and all who labour, a prevailing note of sadness; and so, as he grew more masterful in this sort of
expression, he sought more and more after what is
deep, serious, and constant in the thoughts of common
men. The evolution was slow; and we can see in his
own works examples of every stage, from that of witty
indifference in fifty pieces of the first collection, to that
of grave and even tragic feeling in *Les Souvenirs du
Peuple* or *Le Vieux Vagabond*. And this innovation involved another, which was as a sort of prelude to the
great romantic movement. For the *chanson*, as he says
himself, opened up to him a path in which his genius
could develop itself at ease; he escaped, by this literary
postern, from strict academical requirements, and had
at his disposal the whole dictionary, four-fifths of
which, according to La Harpe, were forbidden to the
use of more regular and pretentious poetry. If he still
kept some of the old vocabulary, some of the old
imagery, he was yet accustoming people to hear moving
subjects treated in a manner more free and simple than
heretofore; so that his was a sort of conservative reform, preceding the violent revolution of Victor Hugo
and his army of uncompromising romantics. He
seemed himself to have had glimmerings of some such
idea; but he withheld his full approval of the new movement on two grounds;—first, because the romantic
school misused somewhat brutally the delicate organism

of the French language; and second, as he wrote to Sainte-Beuve in 1882, because they adopted the motto of "Art for Art," and set no object of public usefulness before them as they wrote. For himself (and this is the third point of importance) he had a strong sense of political responsibility. Public interest took a far higher place in his estimation than any private passion or favour. He had little toleration for those erotic poets who sing their own loves and not the common sorrows of mankind, " who forget," to quote his own words, " beside their mistress those who labour before the Lord." Hence it is so many of his pieces are political, and so many, in the later times at least, inspired with a socialistic spirit of indignation and revolt. It is by this socialism that he becomes truly modern, and touches hands with Burns.

The following books may be consulted: *Ma Biographie* (his own memoirs); *Vie de Béranger*, edited by Paul Boiteau, 1861; *Correspondance de Béranger*, edited by Paul Boiteau, 4 vols., 1861; *Béranger et Lamennais* by Napoléon Peyrat, 1857; *Quarante-cinq lettres de Béranger publiées par Madame Louise Colet* (almost worthless), 1857; *Béranger, ses amis, ses ennemis, et ses critiques*, by A. Arnould, 2 vols., 1864; J. Janin, *Béranger et son Temps*, 2 vols., 1866; also Sainte-Beuve's *Portraits contemporains*, vol. i.

VII

THE WORKS OF EDGAR ALLAN POE*

With just so much of the author's works before us, it would be too soon to speak definitely of his character, either as a man or a writer; and hence, although Mr. Ingram's memoir is prefixed duly enough, to the first volume, I do not think it falls to be considered here in detail. Mr. Ingram has done his best to clear Poe's name from the calumnies of Rufus Griswold (a gentleman, grim by name, who makes so repulsive a figure in literary history, that he might well have been coined in the morbid fancy of his victim); but when all is said, it is not in the power of man to make Poe altogether sympathetic. I cannot find it in my heart to like either his portrait or his character; though it is possible we see him more or less refracted through the strange medium of his works, yet I do fancy that we can detect, alike in these, in his portrait, and in the facts of his life as now most favourably told, a certain jarring note, a taint of something that we do not care to dwell upon or find a name for.

The tales themselves are all before us in these two volumes; and though Mr. Ingram does not tell us whether they are there printed in chronological order, I fancy we shall not be mistaken in regarding some of the last stories in the second volume as being also among the last he wrote. There is no trace, in these, of the brilliant and often solid workmanship of his better moments. The stories are ill-conceived and written carelessly. There is much laughter; but it is a very ghastly sort of laughter at best—the laughter of those, in his own words, " who laugh, but smile no

* The Works of Edgar Allan Poe. Edited by John H. Ingram. Vols. I and II containing the Collected Tales. (London and Edinburgh : Adam and Charles Black, 1874.)

more." He seems to have lost respect for himself, for his art, and for his audience. When he dealt before with horrible images, he dealt with them for some definite enough creative purpose, and with a certain measure and gravity suitable to the occasion; but he scatters them abroad in these last tales with something of the ghoul or the furious lunatic that surpasses what one had imagined to oneself of Hell. There is a duty to the living more important than any charity to the dead; and it would be criminal in the reviewer to spare one harsh word in the expression of his own loathing and horror lest, by its absence, another victim should be permitted to soil himself with the perusal of the infamous *King Pest*. He who could write *King Pest* had ceased to be a human being. For his own sake, and out of an infinite compassion for so lost a spirit, one is glad to think of him as dead. But if it is pity that we feel towards Poe, it is certainly not pity that inspires us as we think of Baudelaire, who could sit down in cold blood, and dress out in suitable French this pointless farrago of horrors. There is a phase of contempt that, if indulged, transcends itself and becomes a phase of passionate self-satisfaction; so for the weal of our own spirits, it is better to think no more of Baudelaire or *King Pest*.

It is not the fashion of Poe's earlier tales to be pointless, however it may be with these sorry ones of the end. Pointlessness is, indeed, the very last charge that could be brought reasonably against them. He has the true story-teller's instinct. He knows the little nothings that make stories or mar them. He knows how to enhance the significance of any situation, and give colour and life to seeming irrelevant particulars. Thus, the whole spirit of *The Cask of Amontillado* depends upon Fortunato's carnival costume of cap and bells and motley. When Poe had once hit upon this device of

dressing the victim grotesquely he had found the key
to the story; and so he sends him with uneven steps
along the catacombs of the Montresors, and the last
sound we hear out of the walled-up recess is the jingling
of the bells upon his cap. Admirable, also, is the use he
makes of the striking clock at Prince Prospero's feast,
in *The Masque of the Red Death*. Each time the clock
struck (the reader will remember), it struck so loudly
that the music and dancing must cease perforce until
it had made an end; as the hours ran on towards midnight, these pauses grew naturally longer; the maskers
had the more time to think and look at one another,
and their thoughts were none the more pleasant. Thus,
as each hour struck there went a jar about the assem-
blage; until, as the reader will remember, the end
comes suddenly. Now, this is quite legitimate; no one
need be ashamed of being frightened or excited by such
means; the rules of the game have been respected;
only, by the true instinct of the story-teller he has told
his story to the best advantage, and got full value for
his imaginations. This is not so always, however; for
sometimes he will take a high note falsetto; sometimes,
by a sort of conjuring trick, get more out of his story
than he has been able to put into it; and, while the
whole garrison is really parading past us on the
esplanade, continue to terrify us from the battlements
with sham cannon and many fierce-looking shakos
upon broom-sticks. For example, in *The Pit and the
Pendulum*, after having exhausted his bedevilled imagination in the conception of the pendulum and the red-
hot collapsing walls, he finds he can figure forth
nothing more horrible for the pit; and yet the pit was
to be the crowning horror. This is how he effects his
purpose:—"Amid the thought of the fiery destruction
that impended, the idea of the coolness of the well came
over my soul like balm. I rushed to its deadly brink.

I threw my straining vision below. The glare from the enkindled roof illumined its inmost recesses. Yet for a wild moment did my spirit refuse to comprehend the meaning of what I saw. At length it forced—it wrestled its way into my soul—it burned itself upon my shuddering reason. Oh, for a voice to speak! oh, horror! oh, any horror but this!"

And that is all. He knows no more about the pit than you or I do. It is pure imposture, a piece of audacious, impudent thimble-rigging; and yet, even with such bugs as these he does manage to frighten us. You will find the same artifice repeated in *Hans Pfaal*, about the mysteries of the moon; and again, though with a difference, in the abrupt conclusion of *Arthur Gordon Pym*. His imagination is a willing horse; but three times, as you see, he has killed it under him by over-riding, and come limping to the post on foot. With what a good grace does he not turn these failures to advantage, and make capital out of each imaginative bankruptcy! Even on a critical retrospect it is hard to condemn him as he deserves; for he cheats us with gusto.

After this knowledge of the stage, this cleverness at turning a story out, perhaps the most striking of Poe's peculiarities is an almost incredible insight into the debatable region between sanity and madness. *The Imp of the Perverse*, for example, is an important contribution to morbid psychology; so, perhaps, is *The Man of the Crowd*; *Berenice*, too, for as horrible as it is, touches a chord in one's own breast, though perhaps it is a chord that had better be left alone; and the same idea recurs in *The Tell-Tale Heart*. Sometimes we can go with him the whole way with a good conscience; sometimes—instead of saying, " Yes, this is how I should be if I were just a little more mad than ever I was "—we can say frankly, " This is what I am." There is one passage of analysis in this more normal vein, in the story of *Ligeia*, as to the expression of Ligeia's eyes. He tells us how he felt ever on the point of understanding their strange quality, and ever baffled at the last moment, just as, " in our endeavours to recall to memory something long forgotten, we often find ourselves upon the very verge of remembrance, without being able in the end to remember "; and how, in streams of running water, in the ocean, in the falling of a meteor, in the glances of unusually aged people, in certain sounds from stringed instruments, in certain passages from books, in the commonest sights and sensations of the universe, he found ever and anon some vague inexplicable analogy to the expression and the power of these loved eyes. This, at least, or the like of it, we all know. But, in general, his subtlety was more of a snare to him than anything else. "*Nil sapientiæ odiosius*," he quotes himself from Seneca, "*nil sapientiæ odiosius acumine nimio*." And though it is delightful enough in the C. Auguste Dupin trilogy—it was Baudelaire who called it a trilogy—yet one wearies in the long run of this strain of ingenuity; one begins to marvel at the absence of the good homespun motives and sentiments that do the business of the everyday world; although the demonstrator is clever, and the cases instructive and probably unique, one begins to weary of going round this madhouse, and longs for the society of some plain harmless person, with business habits and a frock coat, and nerves not much more shattered than the majority of his plain and harmless contemporaries. Nor did this exaggerated insight make him wearisome only; it did worse than that—it sometimes led him astray. Thus, in *The Pit and the Pendulum*, when the hero has been condemned, " the sound of the inquisitorial voices," he says, " seemed merged in one dreamy indeterminate hum. It conveyed to my soul the idea of *revolution*, perhaps from its association in fancy with the burr of a mill-wheel." Now, it wants but a moment's reflection to prove how much too clever Poe has been here, how far from true reason he has been carried by this *nimium acumen*. For—the man being giddy—the "idea of revolution" must have preceded the merging of the inquisitorial voices into an indeterminate hum, and most certainly could not have followed it as any fanciful deduction. Again, as before in the matter of effect, one cannot help fearing that some of the subtlety is fustian. To take an example of both sorts of imagination—the fustian and the sincere—from the same story, *Arthur Gordon Pym* : the four survivors on board the brig *Grampus* have lashed themselves to the windlass, lest they should be swept away; as one of them, having drawn his lashings too tight, is ready to yield up his spirit for a long while, is nearly cut in two, indeed, by the cord about his loins. "No sooner had we removed it, however," Poe goes on, "than he spoke and seemed to experience instant relief—being able to move with much greater ease than Parker or myself" (two who had not tied themselves so closely). *"This was no doubt owing to the loss of blood."* Now, whether medically correct or not, this is, on the face of it, sincerely imagined. Whether or not in fact, it is correct in art, Poe evidently believed it true; evidently it appeared to him that thus, and not otherwise, the thing would fall out. Now turn a page back, and we shall find in the description of the visions that went before Pym while thus bound, something to be received very much more deliberately. "I now remember," he writes, "that in all which passed before my mind's eye *motion*, was a predominant idea. Thus I never fancied any stationary object, such as a house, a mountain, or anything of that kind; but windmills, ships, large birds, balloons, people on horseback, carriages driving furiously, and similar moving objects presented themselves in endless succession." This may be true; it may be the result of great erudition in the thoughts of people in such sore straits; but the imagination does not adopt these details, they do not commend themselves to our acceptance, it is nowise apparent why stationary objects should *not* present themselves to the fancy of a man tied to the windlass of a dismantled brig; and, this being so, the whole passage, as art, stands condemned. If it be mere careless fancy (as it seems), it is fustian of the most unpardonable sort; if it be erudition—well then, it may be erudition, but never art. Things are fit for art so far only as they are both true and apparent. To make what I mean clear; Mr. Ruskin, in some one or other of his delightful books, quotes and approves a poet (I think it was Homer) who said of a brave man that he was as brave as a fly; and proceeds, in his usual happy manner, to justify the epithet. The fly, he tells us, is in very deed the most madly courageous of all created beings. And therefore the simile is good—excellently good. And yet the reader's instinct would tell him, I am sure, that the simile is a vile simile. Let him prefer his instinct before Mr. Ruskin's natural history. For, though it be based on what is true, this comparison is not based upon a truth that is apparent; it does not commend itself to our acceptance; it is not art.

I have spoken at so great a length of these matters of method and detail, that no room remains to me to speak of the larger question—a question avoided also by Baudelaire on the same plea of want of space—why it is that these subjects interested Poe's imagination—a question difficult of solution, indeed, but not insoluble with time. Nor have I left myself room to speak of what is perhaps still more important, the relation between Poe and his far greater and better compatriot,

Hawthorne. That there is a consanguinity, that the two saw the world in a fashion not altogether dissimilar, that some of the short stories of Hawthorne seem inspired by Poe, and some of Poe's short stories seem to be an echo of Hawthorne—all this is beyond question; but all this I can do no more than indicate.

Nor should the reader be surprised if a criticism upon Poe is mostly negative, and rather suggests new doubts than resolves those already existing; for it is Poe's merit to carry people away, and it is his besetting sin that he wants altogether such scrupulous honesty as guides and restrains the finished artist. He was, let us say it with all sorrow, not conscientious. Hunger was ever at his door, and he had too imperious a desire for what we call nowadays the sensational in literature. And thus the critic (if he be more conscientious than the man he is criticising) dare not greatly praise lest he should be thought to condone all that is unscrupulous and tinsel in these wonderful stories. They are to be praised by him in one way only—by recommending those that are least objectionable. If anyone wishes to be excited, let him read, under favourable circumstances, *The Gold Bug, The Descent into the Maelström, The Cask of Amontillado, The Oval Portrait,* and the three stories about C. Auguste Dupin, the philosophical detective. If he should then decide to read more, he may go on, but warily; there are trap-doors and spring-guns in these two volumes, there are gins and pitfalls; and the precipitate reader may stumble unawares upon some nightmare not easily to be forgotten.

One word on the services of Mr. Ingram. This edition has evidently been a labour of love with him. Let us hope, in the next two volumes which are to complete the series, he may extend some of his love and labour to the scraps of French which Poe was so fond of scattering about his pages. There are some deplorable errors abroad in the two that are under consideration—errors I should like to make clear to Mr. Ingram, some fine evening, over what he would call, or suffer his printers to call, a *flacon* of *Clos de Vougeot*.

VIII

*THE POETS AND POETRY OF SCOTLAND**

It is somewhat too much the fashion to pat Scottish literature on the back. Inhabitants of South Britain are pleased to commend verses, which, short of a miraculous gift of tongues, it is morally impossible they should comprehend. It may interest these persons to learn that Burns wrote a most difficult and crude *patois* (or sub-*patois*, if they prefer): that there are not so very many people alive in Scotland who could read his works without a furtive reference to the margin; and consequently, that an Englishman need not be ashamed to confess he can make nothing out of the vernacular poems except a raucous gibberish—which, it is the honest belief of the present reviewer, is about the measure of his achievement. It is partly to this that we must attribute the exaggerated favour of *The Cotter's Saturday Night*, by no means one of his best poems, but one of the most easily understood; partly to this, and partly to the Scottish predilection for religious literature.

But even the least intelligent condescension of the South Briton is better than the hysterical praise with which Mr. Grant Wilson bedaubs his native literature—praise which reads all the more hysterical, that it is gravely written, without adjectives, without points of admiration, in the most convinced and matter-of-fact tone conceivable. Scottish literature, he tells us, contains " a body of poetry and song than which there is none superior in the literature of any land, ancient or modern." Barbour's *Bruce*, " in clearness and simplicity must rank before either Chaucer or Gower; and

* The Poets and Poetry of Scotland, from the Earliest to the Present Time ; comprising characteristic selections from the Works of the more noteworthy Scottish Poets ; with Biographical and Critical Notices. By James Grant Wilson. Vol. I, 1219 to 1776 ; (London : Blackie and Co., 1876).

Earlier Works

in elevation of sentiment Pinkerton does not hesitate to prefer it to both Dante and Petrarch." Dunbar's *Dance of Sevin Deidly Sins* " is equal in its way to anything in Spenser," and his *Justis betuix the Tailzour and Sowtar*, " as droll as anything in Scarron or Rabelais." Mr. Wilson thinks that Burns spoke with " somewhat too much extravagance " when he called the *Gentle Shepherd* " the most glorious poem ever written "; but he seems quite to agree with Allan Cunningham in thinking " Willie was a wanton wag," the most original of lyrics. And this barbarous galimanfry or hotch-potch of indiscriminate laudation does not come fairly to the boil, until we hear that Falconer's *Shipwreck* placed its author " in the front rank of Scottish poets." What? alongside of Barbour who surpassed Dante, Chaucer, and Petrarch, cheek by jowl with Dunbar who was the equal of Spenser and Rabelais, and arm in arm with the unique Hamilton of Gilbertfield, for whom it had been reserved since the foundation of the world to write the most original lyric on record! Was there ever such irreverent hurly-burly of names, such a profane morris-dance of great men and little poetasters? Whaur's Wully Shakespeare noo? let us exclaim, and write it in the richest vernacular for English consonants.

And not only (to make an end of fault-finding), not only has Mr. Wilson made himself a mouthpiece for all that the perfervid genius of the Scots has ever found to say in praise of itself, but he has been somewhat hasty and inexact in his historical enquiries. Certainly in 1414 the English King Henry IV. did not take James I. along with him on his second expedition to France. If for no other reason, Henry IV. had then been some time dead. And certainly Mr. Wilson ought not to have printed Lapraik's " When I upon thy bosom lean." They are shocking bad verses, whatever Burns may have thought. And besides, good or bad,

228

they are not Lapraik's. They are a bungling plagiarism from an English piece in the *Weekly Magazine*; and the really lamentable manner in which they have suffered in the stealing is the last article in the charge against   "the odd kind rhiel aboot Muir-kirk."

We have convicted him on two counts; not being able to write himself, and not knowing what was good in other people's verses. Again, the fable of the *Eagle and Robin Redbreast* should certainly have appeared in the collection, but as certainly, I apprehend, should not have appeared under the name of Alexander Scot. "Ar. Scot " was the signature with which Allan Ramsay chose to send abroad his forgeries; it contains, it will be seen, his initials and a declaration of his nationality, which is characteristic of the race. The fable in question, which is here attributed to the " Scottish Anacreon," and the *Vision* which has been rightly enough placed among the selections from Ramsay, both appeared for the first time in the *Evergreen* under the same signature of "Ar. Scot." And, unless Mr. Grant Wilson has some other light unknown to me on the matter, I cannot understand upon what principle he has separated them. Either they are both by Scot, or both by Ramsay. There is no third way. And, as a matter of fact, I believe they are both Ramsay's.

But Mr. Grant Wilson is not without qualifications for the task he has set himself to do. Of course, all anthologies make bad blood. Of course, one is far more sorry for the good things left out, than pleased that so many have been put in. I am inconsolable for Drummond's sonnet, beginning " In vain I haunt the cold and silver springs." Where is *Auld Lang Syne* ? What strange blindness fell upon Mr. Wilson when he began to make his selections out of Scott? Scott, of all men, is the man to gain in a properly made anthology. And here he has not gained; here he has cruelly lost. The death of Marmion has been printed, the admirable battle scene immediately preceding is left out. And of all those inspired fragments of song he scattered here and there about the pages of novels, we have no more than the barest representation. On the whole, however, the selection is well done. There might have been a little less of what is Scots in no real sense, and the same principle which led Mr. Wilson to include Susanna Blamyre might have led him, not without advantage, to leave some others out. She was English by birth, but wrote in the Scottish spirit; these others were born Scots, but aped the English manner just well enough to fall between two stools. And, indeed, they will not long detain the reader—they are so dead and so dead-heavy—and he will pass on to what is genuinely national in the collection, to the specimen of that merry, coarse, and somewhat prosaic poetry which began with James I. and is yet scarcely cold.

Christ's Kirk on the Green is a direct descendant of the *Canterbury Tales*, and its best successors are all more or less in the same vein. A clear stream of narration, a plentiful scarcity of serious images and similes, a sort of dry slyness, a gross, unflinching realism in humorous disquisition or description—these are notes common to almost all that is good in Scotch poetry. Even when an author seeks to move pity, it is not by strong language that he sets about the task, but by dramatic truth. In the simplest words, he makes his characters say what they might have said and do what they might have done. He relies entirely on the inherent pathos of the situation. He does not seek to heighten or idealise. He is no Shakespeare, only a sort of provincial Boccaccio at the most.

All this is fairly well illustrated in the volume under review. Here also the reader will find that gem of a poem, Alexander Hume's *Day Estivall.* In speaking of such work, one must beware of the Grant Wilson school of oratory. Let an earnest recommendation here suffice.

A point of curiosity is the rest of Burns's ode about Washington, some of which appears already in his Correspondence. It is a very poor performance, but interesting as another testimony to the profound sympathy of Burns for all democratic movements. Why does Mr. Wilson tell us no more about the history of the piece; and why (since we are at fault-finding once more) does he not give us explicit notice when a piece is original and when it is a translation from the Gaelic?

IX

JULES VERNE'S STORIES*

A new vein in story-telling, discovered, I believe, by
Edgar Allan Poe, has been worked with almost devilish
ingenuity by the clever Frenchman whose name stands
at the head of this article. His heroes are in advance
of contemporary science like Von Rempelen; they are
bound for the Pole like Arthur Gordon Pym; they go
to the moon like Hans Pfaal, and descend the Maelström like the Norway fisher. But on the bare idea of
such strange chances, Jules Verne has engrafted a
wealth of most persuasive detail. He has fenced them
in with instances and calculations, not much more trust-
worthy, perhaps, than the calculation in *Mokeanna*, but
mighty reassuring to unscientific readers. Moreover,
he has a sort of prosaic pedestrian quality of imagination, eminently fitted to win belief of nineteenth-
century readers. These tales of his are not true, but
they do not seem to fall altogether under the heading
of impossible. He could easily have made stranger
stories if he had liked; but it is not strangeness that he
follows after with his discreet and daring pen. He likes
just to outstrip the possible, and no more: to go one
step beyond his generation, one step outside the habit-
able world; and to do all this drily and solidly, as
though he had originally prepared his facts for a learned
Society, and only by an afterthought turned them to
account in a fantastic tale. *Joanne-Hoffman* Pierre
Véron called him in the *Panthéon de Poche* : to parody
the phrase in English—Murray's Guide Books edited
by Edgar Allan Poe. It is this mixture, this opposition

* Jules Verne's Stories. 1. Adventures of Three Englishmen and
Three Russians. 2. Five Weeks in a Balloon. 3. A Floating City.
4. The Blockade Runners. 5. From the Earth to the Moon. 6. Around
the Moon. 7. Twenty Thousand Leagues under the Sea. 8. A Voyage
round the World. (London : Sampson Low and Co., 1876.)

of ends, that gives a peculiar and most original flavour
to his work. This teller of extravagant stories is quite
a practical man, it appears, with a taste for mechanics
that puts the most of us to shame. It is little wonder
if we extend some confidence, in this scientific age, to
a man who goes about to get the wind of us by such
purely scientific means. If we don't exactly believe in
the Gun Club's projectile, we cannot see why something of the same sort, or to the same end, should not
become practical in the course of years; and if Sir
Humphry Davy spoke tenderly of the Philosopher's
Stone, an outsider with a taste for the marvellous may
be allowed to indulge a secret foible for the submarine
boat.

I suspect the science throughout is very flimsy; not
that this compromises in any degree the super-excel-
lence of the tales. And I can't help fancying that, once
he has got his story fairly planned and put together,
Jules Verne careers on the paper with the most flagrant
and detestable vivacity. Of human nature it is certain
he knows nothing; and it is almost with a sense of relief
that one finds in these sophisticated days a good
trotting horse of an author who whistles by the way
and affects to know nothing of the mysteries of the
human heart. Once, indeed, he has gone out of his
way, and with perfect ill-success: his Captain Nemo, of
the undying hatred and the Scotch impromptus, is a
memorable warning. But his extraordinary stock-in-
trade consists of several somewhat time-worn dolls:
scientific people with bald heads, and humorous sea-
men of indescribable fidelity. His marionettes are all
athletic and all virtuous. I do not remember any bad
character in his gallery, or one who was afraid. " If I
sought to despair, I could not," says Professor Arron-
aux, referring to a very ticklish moment of his life.
And his confidence was not misplaced. Jules Verne has

the point of honour of a good ship-captain, and holds himself personally responsible for the lives of all the crew. A few anonymous persons may perish by the way, lest we should think too lightly of the perils; but so soon as a man has been referred to by name, he bears a charmed existence and will turn up at the last page in good health and animal spirits. Once or twice, as in *Captain Hatteras* or *The Survivors of the Chancellor*, Jules Verne sins against this principle, brings his stories to a bad end or tortures us too much upon the way, and then, I confess, he seems to me shallow and impertinent.

His characters being dolls, it is truly instructive to see how well he juggles with them. He has the knack of making stories to a nicety. He is as full of resources as one of his own heroes; his books are as accurately calculated as the lines of the *Nautilus*, or the partition-breaks of the projectile. Look, for instance, at the skill with which he keeps us interested during the eighty days of Phineas Fogg's journey round the world. He has Fix, the detective, on his trail from first to last— a continual excitement to the reader! And Fix serves yet another purpose; for the warrant which he expects at port after port keeps us always with one eye on London, and so helps us to realise the distance travelled. Another device for the same end, and even more ingenious, is the gas jet left burning by Passepartout in the hurry of departure. All around the world we are kept in irritating remembrance of this little flicker of light in Savile Row. We are continually sent back again in fancy to the starting-point; and on each occasion we spin the globe around between our fingers and take stock of the hero's progress. Similarly admirable is the treatment of the projectile during its perilous voyage. Everything is done to make us realise its new position as an independent world. It has a climate of its own.

The dead dog, thrown out of the scuttle, accompanies it on its journey as an obedient satellite. The cold of space through which it passes, the wandering meteors it encounters, the earth seen as a crescent on the wane —all these tell their story with convincing eloquence. If anything will help young imaginations to grapple with the difficult ideas of astronomy and conceive the world as one star among many, it seems to me it should be such a tale as this. For it is quite in a child's way. The projectile plays at being a world, just as the boy plays at being a soldier.

Everyone knows, of course, that the *Voyages Extraordinaires* are illustrated, and everyone has admired the designs of De Neuville and Riou. In themselves these pictures are a source of much delight; but I cannot help asking myself whether they do not harm the stories. I am sure a person who has already scampered over the illustrations to *Twenty Thousand Leagues under the Sea* loses a great deal of pleasure when he commences to read the dexterous commencement. And, if we had the three volumes of *The Mysterious Island* put all at once into our hands, how much of the mystery would remain? There might still be a few savoury claws to crack, but the body of the story would be ready broken to our hands. It is true there is another form of interest; and perhaps we find as much amusement, after we ourselves have the clue of the labyrinth, in watching the bewilderment of the characters, their rude expedients and blindfold guesses at the truth. And it is true, also, that mystery is rarely more than subordinate in the best of Jules Verne's tales. Such a book as *The Fur Country* will stand almost any test you like to put it to. For my own part, I first had the whole plot retailed to me by an enthusiastic admirer; some time after I fell upon the second volume and read it with such pleasure that I lost no time in procuring and reading the first. It would be difficult to pay a higher compliment to a book without any pretension to style, human nature, or philosophy, which offers no interest but the legitimate interest of the fable, and hinges for a great while on an elaborate mystery.

What a pity it is we were not all boys when these jolly—for I must use a schoolboy's word—jolly books appeared! I think I can fancy how the possessor of one of them will be worried and importuned by eager companions; and what a deal of new matter will be at the disposal of the dormitory storyteller.

X

NOCTES AMBROSIANÆ*

It was a fortunate idea to extricate from so much that
was purely local, purely temporary, and often enough
in ill humour, all that seemed permanently human in
Wilson's *Noctes*. Few people nowadays would take the
trouble to go through the fruit of these ten years of
high-pressure literary action. Of the few who did so,
most would feel a strange weariness and despair creep
over them among these warfares of the dead. Bygone
personalities have an odd smack of the grave; and we
feel moved to turn the tables on the high-stepping
satirist, and remind him, with something of the irony
of country headstones, that not only they, but he—not
only the rejected Whiglings, but the redoubtable Kit
North—point the moral of dust to dust.

But of the more perennial part, picked skilfully from
among the *detritus* of old literary and political convul-
sions, Mr. Skelton has erected what is perhaps the most
durable monument to Wilson's fame that we possess.
In it we find the immortal trio at their best throughout.
From beginning to end, their meetings are inspired and
sanctified by Bacchus and Apollo. North can always
lay aside his crutch; Tickler is always six feet high; and
the Shepherd is always the Shepherd. For how is it
possible to praise that adorable creation but in terms
of himself? He is the last expression of sophisticated
rusticity; at once a poet, a journalist, a Scotsman, and
a shepherd; oscillating between Burns and the *Daily
Telegraph* in things literary; and, in things moral,
occupying all sorts of intermediate stations between a
prize-fighter and Peden the Prophet. If it were lawful

---

* The Comedy of the Noctes Ambrosianæ. By Christopher North.
Selected and arranged by John Skelton, Advocate. (Edinburgh and
London : William Blackwood & Sons, 1876.)

to marry words of so incongruous a strain, we might classify him as a Presbyterian Faun.

And this book is not only welcome because it takes us on a visit to Wilson when he is in his best vein, but because Wilson in all his veins is the best antidote or at least the antithesis of much contemporary cant. Here is a book full of the salt of youth; a red-hot shell of animal spirits calculated, if anybody reads it, to set up a fine conflagration among the dry heather of present-day Phariseeism. Touch it as you will, it gives out shrewd galvanic shocks, which may perhaps brighten and shake up this smoke-dried and punctilious generation. Look at the profound animal sensuality, which breaks out in the praise of all sorts of exercise, and gloats, through near one-half the pages, over the details of eating and drinking. " O man," says the Shepherd to Tickler, " it wad be a great peety to dee wi' sic an appeteet! " Again, the Shepherd explains his own position immediately before dinner: " I'm nae glutton —nae gormandeezer—but a man o' a gude, a great appeteet—and for the next half-hour I shall be as perfectly happy as ony man in a' Scotland." And those who can read the " towsy tea " in the snuggery without an access of imaginary hunger must have something amiss with their digestions. Look at the grand inhumanity; see how they laugh over the two bagmen lost in the snow, for no better reason than that they were Cockneys, and wore false collars something delicately starched; or listen to them declaring that " any man may well lose patience to think of fools being sorry for the death of a fox." And then look at that curious and most Scottish enthusiasm which rages at large in all descriptive passages, and inspires such extravagant poetry and reasoning that one is never rightly sure whether it be in jest or earnest. Some of it is false fire, I daresay; but by far the most is the uncontrollable expression of the man's high spirits. If any other writer broke out into a fervent " Thank God that Nelson died at sea! " we should be not a little exercised as to his sanity; but in Wilson we like the extravagance, because we understand the man. And it all goes well enough with his copious and headlong style. For it is scarcely literature: at most, a sort of inspired talking, as it purports to be: and the fiction of Gurney the short-hand writer in the ear of Dionysius seems almost necessary to explain the existence of the book.

Wilson looked upon life with the positive acceptation of a man in excellent health; his heart seems never to have failed him over anything, however squalid or sad; but, squaring his elbows, he put it outside of himself in some easy and forcible pages. The man who wrote the Alderman's death, or the Shepherd's commentary over the oysters was certainly of no very dainty stomach. But it was to this same unscrupulous catholicity of taste that we owe masterpieces (after their fashion) like the dog-fight in the Guse Dubs, the execution of the mutineer, or those scathing pictures of depravity with which the Shepherd silences some sentimental aspirations after the improvement of the species.

XI

BYWAYS OF BOOK ILLUSTRATION

Here are two illustrated Japanese romances; one *Chiushingura, or the Loyal League,* translated into English by Mr. Dickins; the other *Les Fidèles Rônins,* rendered into French by M. Gausseron from the American edition of Messrs. Greey and Schiouichiro Saito. Each is an imaginative version of the story of the *Forty-seven Rônins,* the gem of Mr. Mitford's collection. No one who has read it once will be likely to forget that drama of clan fidelity; but it may be as well, in the interest of those who have not, to recapitulate the leading features. In 1701 the chief of a clan, insulted by his superior, fell upon him with his sword in the precincts of the palace, and was condemned in consequence to self-destruction. By the same edict, the lands and castle were forfeited to Government, and the clan dispersed. Now Kuranosuke, the Karô, or chief vassal of the clan, was a man of excellent conduct and courage —a man " worth millions." He gathered the clansmen together, as if to defend the castle; for that, it seems dimly to appear, would have been one way of doing honour to the *manes* of their chief. But this was not his genuine purpose. Explaining to the clan the vanity of any such defence, he laid before them a document binding the signatories to self-destruction, and to this sixty-three were prevailed upon to set their hands. Kuranosuke had now separated the wheat from the chaff; to the sixty-three he explained his true intention. The document was a blind; they were not to slay themselves, but to execute vengeance on their dead chieftain's enemy. To this desperate engagement forty-seven proved faithful. For something more than a year they watched the movements of their adversary, themselves hunted by spies, apart from their homes and

families, feigning recklessness and degradation, and
contemned by all for the apparent tameness with which
they had accepted the ruin and dishonour of their clan.
At length, when all suspicion had been lulled to sleep,
they carried the mansion of their powerful enemy by
night, put him to the sword in the midst of his guards,
and quietly resigned themselves into the hands of
justice. Then they could say, in the words of one of
the romances now before us, " We deserted our wives,
we abandoned our children, we left our aged folk un-
cared for, all to obtain this head." The authorities
condemned them as criminals to the pain of self-
destruction; but the people of Japan, both high and
low, greeted their achievement with an outburst of
applause; their memories are cherished to this day,
their story is become a theme for the novelist, and the
grave of Kuranosuke was honoured, only thirteen years
ago, with the most distinguished mark of Imperial
approval.

There is no form of conceit more common or silly
than to look down on barbarous codes of morals.
Barbarous virtues, the chivalrous point of honour, the
fidelity of the wild highlander or the two-sworded
Japanese, are of a generous example. We may question
the utility of what is done; the whole-hearted sincerity
of the actors shuts our mouth. Nor can that idea be
merely dishonourable for which men relinquish the
comforts and consideration of society, the love of wife
and child and parent, the light of the sun, and the pro-
tection of the laws. The seductions of life are strong in
every age and station; we make idols of our affections,
idols of our customary virtues; we are content to avoid
the inconvenient wrong and to forego the inconvenient
right with almost equal self-approval, until at last we
make a home for our conscience among the negative
virtues and the cowardly vices. A story like this of the

Rônins shakes about our ears the ramparts of our
crockery Jericho. We cry out for a while on the insufficiency of the men's motives or the barbarity of the
act. But our hearts soon begin to misgive us, and we
recognise at last that for no purpose under heaven,
however excellently just, could we collect forty-seven
of our relatives or neighbours to be thus contemptuous
of the terrors of death and of public opinion.

The historical incident, it will be seen, involves important moral issues. Nothing can be more instructive
than to observe the play of native imagination about a
theme of such a character; and in both of the volumes
under review we find the same quality of moral vigour.
It is from the moral rather than from the romantic side
—it is not as a feat of arms, not as a story of the sword,
but of pathetic duty—that the action has been strengthened. It is as a case of competition of duties, and the
continued triumph of the superior duty, the duty to
the clan, that the tale has been throughout considered
by the writers. Our duties here in England weaken as
they get farther from the hearth, until patriotism is but
a fitful and tepid consideration, and honesty to the
State a stretch of Quixotry. To these Japanese, on the
other hand, the clan came before the family; and both
of our authors have fixed upon that doctrine with
singular zest, and lavished a considerable wealth of
fancy in varying the conditions in which it is displayed.
To one character after another clan virtues are made
to clash with filial duty, with married love, with the becoming prudences of social life; and one after another
makes the nobler choice and goes forth to die. From
the point of view of literary art this is an error in design.
The main outline of the story already strikes the note
with epic brevity and force. A true artist might have
been content, in addition, to elaborate the figure of
Kuranosuke—a loyal Lorenzaccio—lulling his enemy's

suspicions by a life of heartless dissipation, divorcing
his beloved wife, pointed at with fingers as he went
reeling homeward from the tea-house, and conscious
through all his loathed carousals of the sad purity of
his heart and the tragic death that followed at his heels.
But our two authors go on to show us, in the history
of one Rônin after another, the same wrenching of the
family affections, the same incredible nobility of mind
in man and woman, Samurai and commoner. The
mother of Communal kills herself that her son may
pursue his duty with the lighter heart. The servants of
Kuranosuke are with difficulty restrained from suicide.
Honzo manœuvres to be killed. Gihei is eager to sacrifice his infant son. The Karô of the villain dies as gladly
for his master as the Karô of the beloved chieftain.
Something in this iteration sets the teeth on edge. We
grow weary of the triumph of clan duty as we grow
weary of the triumph of the point of honour in Cor-
neille's *Cid*. There is even something in this continual
return of the motive, this moral " air and variations,"
which faintly reminds us of the elaborate method of
such a book as *Quatre-vingt-treize*, and the manner of
Dumas had been more suitable in such a case than the
manner of Hugo. Indeed, I have a thought of regret
that this excellent fable never fell into the hands of the
author of the *Mousquetaires*. He could have given it the
fire and action which it somehow lacks; he would have
put some deviltry into the fighting; and his spirited,
boyish, but really adequate presentation of character
was excellently suited to so chivalrous a tale.

And yet these innumerable episodes are, in themselves, touching and pleasant. The good women, the
simple homes illuminated by respectful love, the honest
pieties which tempt the Rônins from the dark path of
duty, are dwelt upon and made amiable in our eyes.
The whole web of the men's lives is kind, courteous,

and elegant. They make verses with their wives; they make verses as they sight the sunny peak of Fuji on their way to death. The flowers of wild cherry are dear to them. When Kuranosuke allows one of the vassals to visit his family on the way to the catastrophe at Yeddo—an indulgence which he rigidly refuses himself—" The perfume of the flowering plum tree passes swiftly," says he. " Profit as best you may by these delightful moments." The vassal goes; after a day and half he reaches the miserable house to which his family has been reduced by the ruin of the clan and his own adherence to duty; at the door his wife is washing clothes, their baby on her back; and even as she washes she prattles to the child about her absent husband and his desired return. Truly a moment to wring the heart of a man who was looking at these things for the last time. And yet when he discloses his presence it seems she scarcely interrupts her task. " Oh, honourable husband! " she says, " how glad I am to see you! Mother has been very anxious on your account. Honourable mother, where are you? my husband has come home." The simplicity, the absence of exaggeration, the thought of her mother-in-law leaping out among the first—how amiable a family picture!

The first of our illustrations represents another of these family scenes. The husband has been long ill, threatened with blindness; the wife, the servant, and two children have made a long and painful journey to attend upon his wants; they find him in a crazy house full of tatters and patches; and there you behold the family united. The servant nurses the baby, the wife sits respectfully before her lord, the elder child is speaking: " Dear papa, do your eyes hurt you? I am so glad I came; now you will have somebody to rub your back! You know that's good for invalids." Perhaps the last idea is a reminiscence of his own; for both children have been down with smallpox on the journey, and are but just recovered. Here again, and in all these scenes, there is the same absence of caresses, so strange in the Western mind, the same affection understood and passed over in silence or with but a word. This wife, for instance, has undertaken a long journey to comfort her husband; she knows besides the certain death that awaits him ere long; yet on her arrival she first inquires after his health, and then, having elaborately saluted him on her knees, " My honourable husband," she says, " it is now many, many months since I have seen you. All the while I have sighed after the time when I should see your face again." This distance, this subjection of all relations to etiquette, is still more drolly illustrated when Rikiya comes with a message and is received by Konami, his betrothed. The one blushes like the plum tree, the other like the wild cherry: and the girl, forgetful of her manners, draws near to her betrothed. " Rikiya drew back with an offended air," it seems. " Hold! " he cried, " this is scarcely civil. All the world knows that when a message is to be received the forms of politeness ought to be rigidly observed." Well, every country has its custom. There were plenty of true marriages conducted from the altar to the grave according to these nice conventions. Our Rônins were accustomed to see their wives kneel before them and stoop their foreheads to the mat; but their hearts bled when they had to part with them. It was pity and love for his young wife that kept back one of the number on the night of the attack, until he had actually to be sent after and led away. And there could be no prettier marriage relation than that of the old Samurai who was a poet and had a poetess to wife. His last letter, written on the eve of battle, is a gem. "Although our separation is the result of a resolution of so old a standing, we both of us feel cruelly its sadness. During the day, you write, your affairs prevent you from dwelling on the thoughts of our misfortune, but, when the night comes, you think of me and cannot sleep. My poor dear wife, I feel even as you feel. . . . You tell me that you were pleased with my verses on the defile of Osaka. I have a great admiration for those you send me in your letters: and I hope, whenever you have a moment, you will write and send me more." And so he goes on advising her about her health, talking of old bereavements, and touching once on business; and ends by sending her a salted goose to make a soup of.

In this same letter, among other matters, there is a sketch of how the conspirators lived when they were all gathered together, waiting for their spring. The younger ones kept house, and served at table; they had sometimes leave of absence for the theatre. All were full of courage and even mirth; they all had nick-names; and the old poet, among others, was familiarly called " the doctor." Happy and simple ways: mirth, innocent pleasure, and innocent freedoms, prolonged up to the very margin of their voluntary grave.

Both in matter and illustrations the French version is the more interesting; unfortunately it is a translation of a translation, and is disfigured by the fatuous error of translating proper names. Messieurs Lebleu and Duval are not at all happily introduced to English readers under the style of Mr. The-Blue and Mr. Of-the-Vale; nor can a book be anything but arduous reading where the characters masquerade with such titles as Fortuné-Six, Récolte-Précoce, or Lac-Wisteria. Even the translator seems to have lost his head, for the Chevalier Petit-Bosquet loses his own name at an early page, and meets his death under the alias of Bosquet-Droit. Mr. Dickins's version of the other romance has a more outlandish smack, more of trick, colour and imagery of an alien language, society, and literature. His original besides is more fiery—fuller of fighting and brave words; but it is at the same time decidedly inferior; and *Chiushingura* is perhaps more curious than interesting. But it is interesting, too; both are interesting—first for their intrinsic merit, and secondly as a piece of foreign travel among strange scenes, manners, and virtues. Both in the text and illustrations a hundred little touches transport us into the houses, besides the busy shores, and on the mountain passes of Japan: —messengers shaken all day and night in flying litters; the hunter caught by rain, begging a light for his match-lock from the traveller who passes with a paper lantern; the rowdy coolies at the river ferry; the young man, on his way to die, hopefully saluting the hill Fuji on the day of his majority; the Samurai at home, with the pipe, the kettle, the glasses, and the two swords laid by upon the bamboo sword-rack; and behind and around all these, the well-known features of the scenery of Japan, the square sails of vessels putting out to sea, the black pines, the mountain summits, the congregated roofs of towns.

For both volumes all the illustrations have been designed and cut by natives, but in neither do they represent the highest order of Japanese work. The consummate generalisation, the singular clarity and elegance of design, are not here so conspicuous as in many of those enchanting picture-books that find their way to us from over seas, and are a joy for ever. The effect is sometimes a little scattered, the details too much insisted on. But the cuts in M. Quantin's book, four of which we reproduce, are still of striking excellence: vigorously drawn and composed with that happy knack peculiar to the nation; in which every incident of the subject and the very title of the picture are put together like the elements of a pattern; and both in the

use of the line and the opposition of the flat black and
the full white, some of the charm of arabesque is added
to the significance of representative art. One of our
examples has been already described. The second,
which represents the clan mustering at the castle, tells
its own story with too much spirit to require a commentary. But the third and fourth are in a different
case. One of the Rônins of Ako was a certain Haie-
Rouge (I am now quoting the French book with its
distracting nomenclature), a very drunken dog, a disgrace to his family, and a sore concern to his brother,
the Chevalier Tourbière, who was a severe, respectable
Samurai. Haie-Rouge has been seen at his brother's
house, drunk as usual, the day before, and has been refused admittance. Early in the morning a great clamour
in the city awakens the Chevalier Tourbière, who comes
to his door, as in our third picture, and learns from his
eager servant, Premier-Compagnon, that the deed has
been done, that the clan of Ako has wiped out their
chieftain's shame, that they are now retreating from the
ruined mansion of their enemy amid the acclamations
of the mob. Instantly the question arises: Has poor
Haie-Rouge wiped out the errors of his life by a share
in this heroic deed, or has he been lying somewhere
drunk while his companions trod the path of duty?
Premier-Compagnon is sent to spy out the facts; he
must not ask; to ask, and to be answered in the negative, were an intolerable shame. Everywhere the mob
is up, pushing for a glimpse of the heroes, and Premier-
Compagnon has much ado, tramping in the snow, to
get a sight of them. At length he gets into the front
rank of the crowd, and beholds them, in three com-
panies, leaving the mansion of the Prince of Sendai,
where they have been entertained. The first company
passes; no Haie-Rouge. The second company passes;
it is led by Kuranosuke, and almost all the men are

wounded, some even carried in litters; and still no Haie-Rouge. Poor Premier-Compagnon, who is a loyal servant, and holds his master's glory for his own, begins to grow sick at heart; when lo! here comes the third company, and, marching at their head, acknowledged leader, Haie-Rouge, in his battle armour. The servant falls on his knees in the snow; the transformed drunkard pauses, speaks to him, sends messages to his family, and gives the pennon of his lance by way of relic. And then, as his companions are already some distance before him, he overtakes them by running, and disappears for ever from men's eyesight. " Look at him! look at him! " cried the servant to his neighbours in the crowd. " Honourable gentlemen, this is the Chevalier Haie-Rouge, the brother of my honourable master. He only belongs by adoption to the clan of Ako, and behold him to-day among the avengers! " And so he wanders on, until his hero is long out of sight and the bystanders tell him he has gone " mad with joy "; thence he speeds home, when the drunkard's hat and half-emptied saki-bottle are religiously laid aside in honour of his memory. Happy drunkard, who has thus realised the last and dearest of human illusions, and at one blow gloriously wiped out the stains and dishonours of a life! The two pictures seem to me both excellent: Premier-Compagnon quite a creation in a rough way, and his grinning excitement in the first scene admirably distinguished from his hysterical glee in the second. I need not call the attention of the reader to the composition of the fourth plate, it speaks for itself sufficiently; but I hope he will not fail to observe the droll white dog in number three.

From Mr. Dickins's translation we reproduce, by the publisher's permission, no complete picture, but two groups, the fifth and sixth of our illustrations. They are much worse designed and executed than those we have already studied, but they have a certain interest of their own. In the fifth, Kuranosuke, after having long deceived a treacherous clansman, Kudaiu, has at last broken forth on him with blows and curses. " This very night," he has said, " the very eve of our lord's death-day—ah! what evil things have I been forced to say about him with my lips; but at least in my heart I heaped reverence upon reverence for his memory—this very night was it thou chosest to offer me flesh. I said nor yea nor nay, as I took it; but, oh! with what shame, with what anguish did I, whose family for three generations have served the house of Hanguwau, find myself forced to let food pass my lips on the eve of my lord's death-day! I was beside myself with rage and grief, every limb in my body trembled, and my forty-four bones quaked as though they would shiver to pieces." And then, having unpacked his heart with words, he orders the traitor out to die. The cut does not agree in details with the text; it has little merit, and that little seems to have evaporated from our reproduction; but there an effort after the heroic may be observed in Kuranosuke's attitude as he stands leaning on his sword, above the rest. In our sixth picture the final onslaught is shown with a certain grim intensity which can scarcely be paralleled in either of the volumes under study. Justice is rarely done either to passion or action. The assault, in the French book, is a piece of jumbled folly, and the conflict with the coolies almost undistinguishable. As for the midnight murder in the English book, it is melodramatic if you please, but sadly laughable.

That violent action should be thus inefficiently treated is, of course, exceptional in the vigorous and fantastic art of Japan; but that emotion, so much dwelt upon by the writer, should be thus slurred by the draughtsman, seems not only a characteristic, but probably a commendable feature. The eye of the Japanese is as quick to single out, as his hand is dexterous to reproduce, the truly pictorial features of a landscape, or an incident. But with these features he appears to rest content. The mass of incidental information which goes to the making of modern European landscape— the difference of planes, the intricacy of outline, the patient effort after a combination of local and general colour—contrasts strikingly with the few learned touches by which a Japanese will represent a mountain or a city. The Oriental addresses himself singly to the eye, seeking at the same time the maximum of effect and the minimum of detail. It may be an open question whether we should attribute the purely pictorial and unemotional character of the bulk of these illustrations to the same artistic singleness of purpose or to a mere defect of skill. Whatever is the cause, I should say the lesson to be learnt is the same, and it is one which the art of Japan is particularly fitted to enforce. Pictorial art in the West is still following false gods, literary gods; it strains after passion, which is beyond its purpose and beyond its capacity to communicate; it too often addresses itself to other faculties besides the eye, or, if to the eye, then without simplicity of means; and, in common with all our arts, it labours under the desire of the artist to represent, before all things, his own ability and knowledge.

XII

COLLEGE FOR MEN AND WOMEN

An inaugural meeting of this institution will be held at eight o'clock next Monday evening, at St. George's Hall, Langham Place, under the presidency of Mr. Thomas Hughes. For ten years it has been known to many good friends as the College for Working Women, 29 Queen's Square, and, under this designation, it performed a small, but not unimportant, educational function. Here came mothers, that they might be able to teach their children in the course of time. Here came certain brave girls out of a love of knowledge that was stronger than the love of pleasure or the natural weariness that follows a laborious day. And how constant and unflagging this love of knowledge was! Year after year found the same students following up one course of study after another. It would have been a pity, certainly, had there been a want of opportunity for this fine devotion. For a long time, however, it has been the desire of the managers to realise the idea of the late Professor Maurice and so enlarge the scope of their institution as to throw open classes, library, and conversation room to men as well as to women; and this after long deliberation, and after having assured themselves of the sympathy and co-operation of their old students, they have at last resolved to do.

We are all familiar with the current arguments against mixed classes. Similar classes, however, are already successfully carried on in many institutions alike in London and this country; and there are many special reasons why they should be employed under the circumstances. The council remind their friends generally " of the many evils which arise from the separation of men and women in the worlds of learning and thought, and of the ennobling influence which each sex has upon the other, when both are united in a common work with serious purpose and endeavour." But out of the special circumstances, as I say, there arise special reasons in favour of the scheme now adopted. The number of students with the old system was necessarily so limited that there was a certain waste of power, especially in the higher subjects which will, it is hoped, be now no longer the case. Again, wives and sisters will be free to come to the college under the new conditions, bringing husband or brother along with them; and the prosecution of some worthy subject will no longer entail upon them the discomfort and actual danger of another daily separation, besides that already entailed upon them by their necessary work. Men and women, besides, will be thus brought together by common devotion to culture instead of the usual haphazard juxtaposition and perpetual " handy-dandy " of the world. And once brought together, they will associate in an atmosphere not otherwise attainable for them; their intercourse will take on something of refinement from the example of those among whom they move; and so culture will be begun in them, not only of a deeper kind, but in a manner more intimate and effectual.

Besides increased supervision, and the care which the Council has taken to leaven the life of the college by the presence of those well qualified to do so, the programme will remain as before. The classes will include, as before, those on Mathematics, Literature, Languages, Physical Science, History, Law, and Art. The Saturday evening lectures will be given, for the present, by Professor Morley, Mr. Furnivall, and Mr. Newton, of the British Museum. To all who have the higher culture of the working-classes truly at heart, this announcement cannot fail to be of interest; and the interest will become more serious and hopeful, I believe, as the facts are more carefully weighed.

XIII

REVIEWS OF *SHAMROCK AND ROSE* by ERNTE
ARIEL WOLFE; *KILCORRAN* by THE HON. MRS.
FETHERSTONHAUGH; *MOTTISCLIFFE* by JAMES
WALTER FERRIER; *AGAINST HER WILL* by
ANNIE L. WALKER

SHAMROCK AND ROSE

It is only with a measure of delicacy that one can refer
to a work like *Shamrock and Rose*. Nice young ladies
and nice young officers comport themselves on its
pages in a most creditable manner; master and servant,
mistress and maid, are upon terms of intimacy that
would seem exaggerated in the Golden Age; a sound
of marriage-bells and scent of orange-flowers pervades
the little book from quite an early period; and it appropriately concludes with a double wedding, a reception
by loyal tenantry, a hired band and a tasteful display
of fireworks. There are many amusing signs of youth
about the style. Thus, in a great scene at the battle of the
Alma, on which no expense has been spared, the reader
will not be surprised that death " was present in many
a terrible form," that " no thought of his own danger
crossed the faithful fellow's mind," and that he waited
" with almost more than woman's tenderness " for
" the first gleam of returning consciousness which
should illumine those pallid features." I suppose this
is what you would call writing in good set terms.
There are four phrases at least which have a familiar,
not to say a classical, ring about them. Few who have
had early aspirations after authorship can declare with
truth that not one of them has ever escaped their fervid
pen: but the author of *Shamrock and Rose* may claim a
measure of originality in that she has used all four in
the same sentence. One more quotation, for the prettiness of the thing, and we have done. Some animation

is displayed all through about the marriage-service, about jewels, and generally about raiment for the perishable body. At one thrilling moment, " a plain band of dull gold with a Maltese cross in pearls " is produced from a blue leather case. " The three ladies exclaimed admiringly. It was simple, and yet so chaste and pretty." As a sort of literary baby-talk, I confess I have a warm heart to *Shamrock and Rose*.

KILCORRAN

The Hon. Mrs. Fetherstonhaugh figures with nineteen mottoes from Mr. Swinburne's *Poems and Ballads*, as against three from Keats, two from Murger's *Scènes de la Vie de Bohème*, and one apiece from Tennyson and Major Whyte Melville. Such an intolerable proportion of Swinburne in the intellectual diet seems to promise the very worst; but the reader may reassure himself—*Kilcorran* is neither eloquent nor wicked. I am not quite sure that the authoress would agree with either of these commendations. She has decided aspirations for the passionate, untutored business; but her high-mettled barbs and Ukrane steeds of the desert content themselves with inoffensive passagings in the stable. Her characters have " wild miserable moments," but they politely refrain from acting on them. Dark, romantic Neal Trench, coming upon us, as if out of a thunderstorm, from a career of nameless revelry in the past, proves but a niminy-piminy personage on close inspection, with little to distinguish him except a bold moustache. There is a dashing Irish mare—a lineal descendant of Bugaboo, let us say—which promises great things and leads us on to look for moving accidents in the field at every second page. To the inexpressible irritation of the reader, the Irish mare kills nobody but herself. And this irritation is felt all the more keenly as there is good reason to hope that she may kill the heroine. For the heroine is the only really bad thing about *Kilcorran;* a vulgar, flippant minx, neither more nor less, she shows herself to be; and if the Hon. Mrs. Fetherstonhaugh will glance at the top of page 63, volume ii., she will perhaps, on reconsideration, come to agree in this opinion.

MOTTISCLIFFE

AN AUTUMN STORY

Mottiscliffe, patently a first book, has many engaging qualities. There is no story to speak of. The characters are mostly very slight sketches. Sir Valentine Ormathwaite, indeed, makes a capital mouthpiece for the author's own vein of reflection, which is whimsical, humorous, and man-of-the-worldly, in an odd but highly palatable mixture. But the delight of the book lies in a sort of hazy, Epicurean atmosphere, which wooingly pervades the reader as he advances from page to page. The lines have fallen to him in pleasant places, and everyone around him is content. The rector dozes away the warm afternoon on manifold cushions; Sir Valentine smokes interminable cigars; the girls are playing croquet or bathing; thirsty souls have an eye to an afternoon drink; and you may be sure that there is some mild junketing on hand for the evening or the next day. Is there nothing happening? Well, perhaps not; unless you count it something to make the acquaintance of a most good-natured *cicerone*. For Mr. Ferrier himself has many meritorious points about him; and, above all, he can display a " greatness of gusto." He writes with a smack of enjoyment. It may be said that he smokes with Sir Valentine, eats with Cope, and dozes with Dr. Wilbraham. He holds up the long tumbler, and listens luxuriously to the clinking of the ice in a hock and seltzer. He cannot mention deer without viewing them " in connection with red-currant jelly and Burgundy." Here, for instance, is a couple of sentences on the ideal " court," which seems to be written in the true spirit of the " rural voluptuary ":

" There is summoned to my fancy a vision of a stately house, possibly in some manner surrounded by a cloister, mossy lawns, and umbrageous cedars, the long shadows of which a westering sun casts darkly over the fish-pool, where, from under the broad lily-leaves, obese but cunning carp eye the passer to see if he carry with him ever a crumb of comfort. If I might so far interfere in human affairs, I would people all ' courts ' with Roman Catholics; sleek priests should linger over folios in the library, and his Eminence should occasionally allow a glimpse of his brilliant stockings to be seen in the yew walks."

Mr. Ferrier, with this enviable quality on his side, among others, has only to try for more compression and solidity, and make his next book as good as the best parts of *Mottiscliffe*, to produce something worthy of himself.

AGAINST HER WILL

Against her Will, in its tame, transparent way, is really quite a readable book. It is too long, but that is the fault of the times and the publishers, and the long-eared vegetative public. The story moves on in a peaceable enough fashion, but still it moves. It is the story of a young lady with a singular inclination to marry anybody who asks her, and tells how she conducted herself in poverty and riches, and with her various suitors, in a plain, unpretentious, and perfectly capable manner. The heroine, principally from her remarkable matrimonial behaviour, becomes strangely, even unpleasantly, interesting to the male reader, and fills him with thoughts of La Trappe and a modest conventual existence in the future. None of the scenes are brilliantly executed; but some of them are so well conceived that they fix the reader's attention in spite of himself. In this, Miss Walker reaps the advantage of having something like a story to tell, and her book, from this circumstance, has a marked advantage over the other three with which we have been dealing. One of these scenes—that in which the High Church clergyman is accepted by the heroine, and then, finding some manhood in his heart, practically rejects her on such terms as she has to offer—is really original and just: two qualities not usually found together.

XIV

THE BALLADS AND SONGS OF SCOTLAND*

A REVIEW

This book with the tempting title is a prize essay reprinted for some occult reason. Probably there never
was published anything with less result, anything that
left the reader more entirely where he was. The tempting title which we have already conceded to it, is its
first merit and its last. It is only by the comparative
method that such a subject could be treated with
success; and yet Dr. Murray either knows nothing
about any other ballad literature, or, if he does, adroitly
conceals his learning from the reader. It is not by a
few sporadic references to Tom Thumb or Thor's
hammer, but by a systematic exhibition of identities
and differences that we should hope for any elucidation
of the dark and attractive subject. And again, to write
such a book even passably well, a man should have
some notion of elementary æsthetics. It would require
of him a way of thinking on such subjects a little more
accurate, a use of language a little more definite, than
Dr. Clarke Murray's. For example, our author defines
the object of the ballad as the " perfect imitation of
nature." It certainly should not be possible for anyone
to emit such a definition who had ever thought for two
consecutive minutes about the matter. Not even the
name of Addison (from whom Dr. Clarke Murray
imitates his phrase, as from a great critical authority)
can render tolerable so primitive a confusion of ideas.
The ballad is a means of expression quite at the other
end of the scale from any of the realistic arts; it is in-

* The Ballads and Songs of Scotland, in view of their Influence on
the Character of the People. By J. Clarke Murray, LL.D., Professor
of Mental and Moral Philosophy in McGill College, Montreal.
(London : Macmillan & Co., 1874.)

tensely abstract and subjective. This is to be learned in
the infant school of art criticism. Whatever may be Dr.
Murray's attainments in his own subject, it is obvious
that his views of æsthetics are neither precise nor interesting. He is not the man to stand up and instruct his
fellows. The root of the matter is not in him.

And accordingly, we turn over his leaves in a vain
search for the solution, even for the treatment of the
most pressing question. Making all allowances for his
ignorance of other popular literatures there is yet much
that he could have illustrated and cleared up for us.
One would have wished to know, for instance, whether
the proud, self-reliant, democratic sentiment, so strong
in Burns, is to be traced in any of the earlier songs of
Scotland. One would have wished to hear something
of the relations between the measure of the verses and
the music to which they were sung. One would have
hoped for some reference to a peculiar taking rhythm
that recurs in all Scottish versifiers down to Scott or
even Mr. Robert Buchanan. But of all this there is no
word. Dr. Clarke Murray goes on towards his own
end, and passes these minor questions blandly and
unconsciously by.

His own end, then, or rather that of the St. Andrew's
Society, of Glasgow, how is that accomplished? Well,
this is the strangest part of the whole affair. We hear
nothing whatever about the influence of this literature
upon the people, save in passing and guarded allusions.
Whether the Scottish are drunken because they have
good drinking songs or *vice versa*, the Doctor professes
himself unable to decide. Whether certain indecorous
verses, to which he alludes with a modesty highly becoming in a Professor of Moral Philosophy, may not
have something to do with the number of illegitimate
births in country districts, he is not altogether sure.
In short, Dr. Clarke Murray refuses, with singular

discretion, to commit himself to any definite opinion on the subject; he is restrained, by a pleasing diffidence, from deciding for us whether their ballads and songs have had a great influence, or no influence at all, upon the people of his native land; he had rather, it appears, leave the matter open for the better judgment of the reader. Now, modesty is a good thing in itself; but the same modesty which withholds a man from resolving a question, should certainly keep him back from publishing the fact of his indecision to the world in more than two hundred pages of type. Indeed, the psychological problem thus presented is not without interest. Having set before him a certain task, and having failed to accomplish it—having striven, honestly and strenuously no doubt, to set a certain question at rest, and having utterly failed to bring forth the least figment of an answer—having, in a word, miscarried of the whole purport of his book—we ask ourselves in wonder, what possible reason could have induced this unsuccessful enquirer to record, at such great length, the story of his failure?

PROTEST ON BEHALF OF BOER
INDEPENDENCE

1881

I was a Jingo when Jingoism was in season, and I own
I pall myself still of like passions with the Jingo. But,
sir, it may be possible for you to understand that a man
may be a Jingo and yet a man; that he may have been
a Jingo from a sense, perhaps mistaken, of the obligations, the greatness, and the danger of his native land,
and not from any brutal greed of aggrandisement or
cheap love of drums and regimental columns. A man
may love these also, and be honest. But there often
comes a time and the changes of circumstances, when
a man is pleased to have held certain opinions in the
past, that he may denounce them with the more
authority in the present. I was not ashamed to be the
countryman of Jingoes; but I am beginning to grow
ashamed of being the kin of those who are now fighting
—I should rather say, who are now sending brave men
to fight—in this unmanly Transvaal war. It is neither
easy nor needful to justify these changes of opinion.
We all awake somewhat late to a sense of what is just;
and it is ordinarily by something merely circumstantial
that the sense is awakened. A man may have been right
or wrong before, but it adds some weight to his intense
conviction if his former thoughts were of a different
and even contrary spirit. Now, sir, I am at the present
hour—in company, I am sure, with all the most
honourable and considerate of my countrymen—liter-
ally grilling in my own blood about this wicked business. It is no affair of ours if the Boers are capable of
self-government or not; we have made it sufficiently
plain to Europe of late days that we ourselves are not
as a whole the most harmonious nation upon earth.
That Colley and all his brave fellows are gone for ever,
that we have been beaten, and fairly beaten, by the

stalwart little state are not, to my mind, arguments for any prolongation of the war, but for an instant, honourable submission. We are in the wrong, or all that we profess is false; blood has been shed, glory lost, and, I fear, honour also. But if any honour yet remains or any chivalry, that is certainly the only chivalrous or honourable course, for the strong to accept his buffet and do justice, already tardy, to the weak whom he has misused and who has so crushingly retorted. Another Majuba Hill, with the result reversed, and we shall treat, I hear; but that may be long of coming; and in the meanwhile, many of our poor soldiers—many of them true patriots—must fall. There may come a time in the history of England—for that is not yet concluded—when she also shall come to be oppressed by some big neighbour; and if I may not say there is a God in heaven, I may say at least there is a justice in the chain of causes that shall make England drain a bucket of her best blood for every drop she now exacts from the Transvaal. As if, sir, there were any prestige like the prestige of being just; or any generosity like that of owning and repairing an injustice; as if in this troubled time, and with all our fair (?) and plucky history, there were any course left to this nation but to hold back the sword of vengeance and bare the head to that state, possibly enough misguided, whom we have tried ineffectually to brutalise!

The Mayflower Press, Plymouth. William Brendon & Son, Ltd.
20.725.